ONE TO ONE

ONE TO ONE
The Story of the Big Brothers/ Big Sisters Movement in America

By
George L. Beiswinger

With a Foreword by Gerald R. Ford

Big Brothers/Big Sisters of America/Publisher
Philadelphia

Designed by Jane Klein

Printed by the Winchell Company, Philadelphia

First Edition

Library of Congress Cataloging in Publication Data

Beiswinger, George L., 1924–
One to one.

Includes index.
1. Big Brothers/Big Sisters of America—
History. 2. Big Brothers of America—History. 3.
Children of single parents—Services for—United
States—History. 4. Children and adults—United
States—History. 5. Childhood friendship. I. Title.
II. Title: Big Sisters movement in America.
HV881.B42   1985   362.7'95   84-20399
ISBN 0-9613820-0-7

CONTENTS

PART ONE

PART TWO

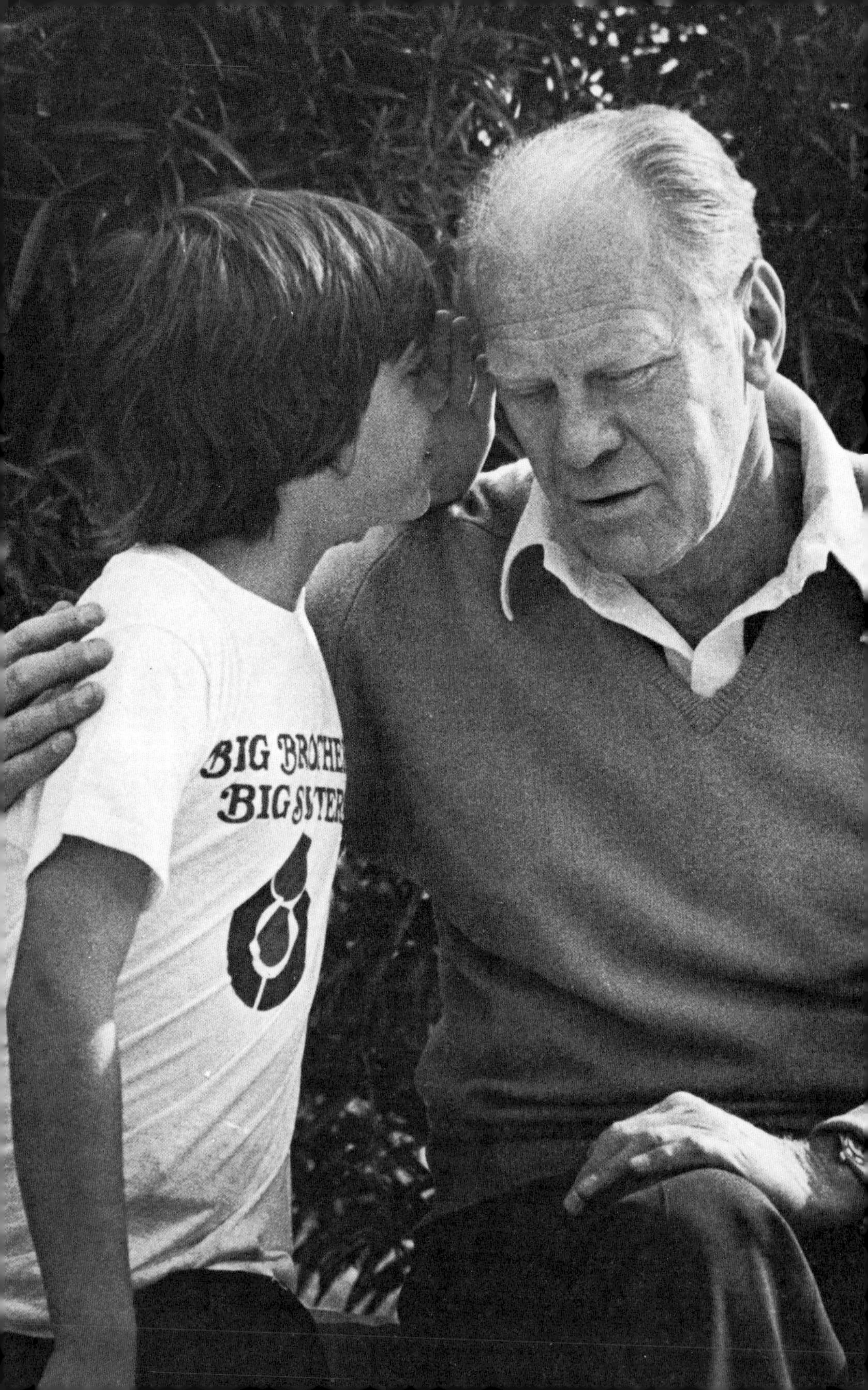
BIG BROTHE
BIG SISTER

Foreword

One of every five children under the age of eighteen now lives with only one parent, according to the Census Bureau; the projection within the decade is one of every four. About 12.6 million children are presently affected. This striking social phenomenon is blamed largely on a fast-accelerating divorce rate.

Because of undue economic or emotional pressures, a lone parent often lacks the time and resources to provide the love, understanding, and guidance that a child needs to become a mature, productive, emotionally healthy adult. As many as 9 million of these children can draw needed support from an extended family member, such as a grandparent, uncle, aunt, or older brother or sister.

But the remaining children — more than 3 million — have no such resources. Nearly 100,000 of these children are now receiving support through the affiliated agencies of Big Brothers/Big Sisters of America. This Movement has been helping children for more than eighty years. Its success is based on an exceedingly effective, yet surprisingly simple concept: one-to-one friendship between a mature, caring adult volunteer and a child who can benefit from that friendship. A professional support staff supervises the match.

The number of children being served by Big Brothers and Big Sisters is small compared to the large number who could be helped. Services are limited by the organization's resources. It urgently needs more operating funds and more volunteers.

It has been my privilege to serve as honorary chairman of Big Brothers/Big Sisters of America for the past eight years. It has been an extremely gratifying and fulfilling experience. I think that you will enjoy this story of the Big Brothers/Big Sisters Movement. After you have read it — if you are not already serving as a Big Brother or Big Sister — I urge you to contact your local BB/BS agency, to learn more about its work and about how you can help a child to develop the courage, self-esteem, and self-confidence that are vital to his or her emotional development.

Gerald R. Ford

Preface

This book chronicles a unique, successful, volunteer effort to remedy a common, yet devastating, social ill—loneliness and emotional insecurity in children; it is the story of the Big Brothers and Big Sisters Movement.

For many years the work of Big Brothers and Big Sisters has been an important part of the American social-service scene. Big Brothers and Big Sisters programs sprang up throughout the country during the early part of this century, as the nation sought solutions to the fast-growing problem of juvenile delinquency.

The programs caught on and grew because of their simple, yet effective approach. What can have more appeal than the one-to-one friendship and compassion of a mature, well-adjusted volunteer adult for a lonely, insecure, sometimes erring child who lacks direction and emotional support?

The Big Brothers/Big Sisters Movement is sometimes characterized as a service that utilizes volunteers to perform functions that are handled by social workers in other organizations. This is not true. The Big Brother and Big Sister never endeavor to replace trained professionals. Rather, they function as a tool of the professional; they apply the therapy of friendship, under the supervision of a trained social worker or caseworker. As someone once aptly put it, the psychiatrist, psychologist, social worker, or caseworker provides treatment. The Big Brother (or Sister) is the treatment.

Big Brothers and Big Sisters have helped thousands of lonely children, enabling them to develop into normal, emotionally secure adults. Many other professional casework organizations have long admired and respected the Movement's effectiveness; social scientists and writers have frequently described its activities in studies and articles. Major philanthropies have underwritten its work.

The Movement is highly visible. A recent survey by an independent opinion research organization found that Big Brothers/Big Sisters enjoyed a superior level of public recognition among organizations that work with children and adolescents, and was surpassed only by the Scouts and the YMCA/YWCA. The Movement's press coverage has always been excellent. It has been the subject of motion pictures, and celebrities often volunteer to endorse its programs.

The Movement has been supported or acknowledged by every U.S. president since Theodore Roosevelt. Big Brothers/Big Sisters of America, a federation of more than 460 Big Brothers and Big Sisters agencies, operates under a congressional charter.

I have tried to present a comprehensive, fully documented record of the Movement's major activities during more than eight decades. No history can ever be called complete. History is a record of activities, and is revealed through observation and research. Undoubtedly, many significant happenings were never recorded, especially in an endeavor as broad and as varied as the Big Brothers and Big Sisters Movement. Some information may not have been accessible. I would be grateful for any data from readers that would clarify, modify, or in any way supplement, and make more meaningful, the information in this book. Such information will be included when the book is revised.

I deeply appreciate the assistance of everyone who helped make this book possible. Special thanks go to David Klaassen, curator, and Kristi L. R. Kiesling, assistant to the curator, of the Social Welfare History Archives, University of Minnesota; to Barbara Dunlap, chief of Archives & Special Collections, The City College of The City University of New York; the Big Brother Movement of New York; and Big Sisters of New York for their assistance in locating early files of the Movement. I am grateful to David W. Bahlmann, president, and Betty Larkin, director of communications, BB/BSA, for their support and assistance in making available Movement records and other resources, and to members of the BB/BSA History Committee for reviewing the manuscript and offering helpful suggestions. Members of this committee include Maurice Schwarz, Joyce Black, Hilda Patricia Curran, Victor Gelb, Charles "Bud" Holloway, Jack Holtman, and Mildred Montague.

Deeply appreciated is the assistance of Carol M. Sutton, who word processed the manuscript, Jean Barth Toll, who did the editing, Suzanne Hilton, who handled the indexing, and Deborah Hirsh and Dick Booth of the Winchell Company, who provided technical direction.

Gratefully acknowledged are the gifts of Corina Robertson, William R. Deeley, John R. Park, and Acme Markets, Inc., which aided in the research and other development work for this book.

Publication of ONE TO ONE was made possible by a major grant from the J. M. Foundation, New York, for which BB/BSA expresses its deepest thanks and appreciation.

Funds recovered from book sales will be used to establish an information resource center at BB/BSA headquarters in Philadelphia.

*To the thousands of Big Brothers and
Big Sisters, whose unselfish and
largely unheralded volunteer efforts
on behalf of children from single-parent
families have made our nation a better
place in which to live.*

PART ONE

1

The Beginnings
(1902–1917)

F ew great rivers, such as the Mississippi, Amazon, or Nile, begin as single, well-defined streams. Their headwaters, in most cases, include several distinct and unrelated tributaries — smaller rivers and brooks — whose combined effluent creates and gives definition and identity to the larger, well-known channels. The Big Brothers/Big Sisters Movement in America evolved from such beginnings.

Big Sisters activity occurred as early as 1902, when a group of women in New York City began befriending girls who came before the New York Children's Court. Known then as the Ladies of Charity, the group later became Catholic Big Sisters of New York.

A story in the *New York Times* on December 28, 1902, told of an announcement made the previous day by Judge Julius M. Mayer, of the New York Children's Court. He had recently visited the New York Educational Alliance and secured from ninety influential men present promises that each one would befriend one boy who had been before his court. Judge Mayer reported that thus far twenty boys had been aided. He did not use the term *Big Brothers* in referring to these early relationships and, in all probability, he did not do so in retrospect later when he became associated with the Jewish Big Brothers of New York City. But the philosophy on which the Movement is based — that of a responsible adult helping a child through one-to-one friendship — was certainly present. Judge Mayer's activity could have influenced a member of his court, Clerk Ernest K. Coulter, who is credited with founding the organized Movement in 1904.

Big Brothers/Big Sisters of America (BB/BSA), the modern federation of more than 460 affiliated Big Brothers/Big Sisters agencies, officially traces the roots of the Movement to an act of kindness by a twenty-three-year-old Cincinnati businessman, Irvin F. Westheimer, which reportedly took place on July 4, 1903. According to later accounts by Westheimer, he had gone to his office on that holiday morning to catch up on some work. While sitting at his roll-top desk, he had glanced out the window to the alley below, where he saw a ragged boy and a mongrel dog scavenging through a garbage can for food.

A member of a closely knit, charity-minded Jewish community, Westheimer was deeply touched by what he saw. Reportedly, he ran down to the alley and introduced himself. He learned that the boy was one of five children from a poverty-stricken, fatherless home. Westheimer took him to a restaurant for a good meal, and met his impoverished family. Later, he took the boy to a ball game and provided him with simple gifts and treats, but mostly he gave him companionship, understanding, and a sympathetic ear for his troubles.[1]

Sensing that his young friend's plight was indicative of a much broader social malady which might be remedied by the friendship of mature adults, Westheimer urged his friends and business associates to befriend other troubled and disadvantaged youths. A number of them reportedly accepted the challenge, and when a boy referred to one of these men as "my big brother," according to Westheimer, the practice in the Cincinnati area had a name.[2]

Westheimer claimed that it was the finding and befriending of the hungry boy that first sparked his interest in the idea of having men aid troubled boys on an individual basis, an activity that led to the organization of a Big Brothers agency in Cincinnati in 1910. As already noted, other organized activity had occurred before that time. Later Big Brothers of America (which became BB/BSA) accepted the 1903 incident involving Westheimer as the Movement's official beginning, paying tribute to what was reportedly the origin of a concept, but recognized that Westheimer was not involved in the nation's first formal or organized activity.

Early Work in Cincinnati

Big Brothers work in Cincinnati, especially after 1910, did have a significant impact on the Movement. Among those who participated with Westheimer in Big Brothers activities, according to an article in the *American Jewish Historical Quarterly*, were Dr. Louis Grossman, then rabbi of Cincinnati's now historical Plum Street Temple, and Benjamin Mielziner, Sidney Rauh, Lawrence Marks, William Ornstein, and Samuel Trounstine, whose occupations were not identified.[3]

The fledgling, unorganized program reportedly flourished in the neighborhood of the city's Jewish Settlement House on Clinton Street, an affiliate of the United Jewish Charities (now the Jewish Federation of Cincinnati). It would seem a logical area to pursue such activity, since almost all Jewish charitable and philanthropic as well as social pursuits centered on the settlement house. While in London on his honeymoon in 1910, Westheimer reported that he learned of an English organization called *Elder Brothers*, which apparently aided youths who had been convicted of crimes. This model caused him to think about creating a more formal Big Brothers structure in Cincinnati.

After returning home, he conferred with Dr. Boris D. Bogen, then head of United Jewish Charities, about organizing such a group. Dr. Bogen, who later became internationally known for his work on behalf of Jewish charitable activities, is probably best remembered for his interesting and thought-provoking autobiography, *Born a Jew,* in which he reports that "Cincinnati Jewry . . . developed a technique of social service which years later was to be accepted universally and be known as the community chest [forerunner of today's United Way]."[4]

Westheimer and Bogen, together with several other area leaders, held a preliminary meeting in December 1910 to form the Big Brothers Association of Cincinnati.[5] A formal organizational meeting took place on Thursday evening, February 23, 1911, when thirty-five men met at the Rockdale Temple and elected Westheimer president and Robert Senior as secretary and treasurer.[6]

Irvin F. Westheimer about 1910 when he founded the Big Brothers Association of Cincinnati.

In an article in the *Cincinnati Times-Star* after the meeting, West-heimer disclosed several interesting facts about the boy he had befriended in 1903. He said that he had been in reform school twice before he found him but that today, eight years later, he was not only supporting his family but devoting both his time and money to charity. He had, in Westheimer's words, "developed into a first-class citizen."

Westheimer described Big Brothers as "big-hearted men" who devote a "minimized expenditure of time and money and a maximum of inter-est." The *Times-Star* article quoted the organization's creed: "The Big Brother movement is founded on the hypothesis that all men are not born free and equal. A great many are handicapped by heredity and are slaves of their environment."

The article said that the new organization picks up boys who are living with the submerged half of society, watches them to uncover their good traits, cultivates these by personal precept and example, and gets them either employment or an education, or both, until they are reformed.

Westheimer said that the policy of Big Brothers was to differentiate and individualize each case, rather than attempt any uniform or blanket procedure. "Individual human interest concentrated in a specific Little Brother is called for," he said. "By becoming a Big Brother you signify your desire to improve the condition of some poor unfortunate little fellow who needs your interest and sympathetic advice."[7]

The Cincinnati Big Brothers Association grew quickly, reportedly having a membership of four hundred volunteers in 1911. A field secretary was appointed, and the association brought Big and Little Brothers together in various ways, such as sports, camping, banquets, and an employment service. It is not known how many Little Brothers Westheimer had. An article in the *Cincinnati Commercial Tribune* for March 5, 1914, told of his match at that time — an eight-year-old boy named Jakie Spivak.

The association's 1917 annual report indicated a membership of 415, of which 181 were active. The report noted that 203 Little Brothers had been handled during the previous year. They had come to the attention of the association for various reasons. By far the greatest number — presumably predelinquency cases — had been referred for general supervision. Three were adjudged in need of help because of truancy, eleven were considered incorrigible, five could not hold jobs, three had run away from home, twelve had been referred for stealing, one because he sold newspapers late at night, and one because he sold newspapers in saloons. Only fifteen of the total cases handled during the period had come to the association's attention through the Juvenile Court, indicating the increasing emphasis being placed on preventive work.

Little Brothers at a Cincinnati Big Brothers Association-sponsored camp about 1918.

Baseball was a favorite activity of the Cincinnati Little Brothers, according to the report. The group organized an Association League, consisting of four teams of older boys and four teams of boys under the age of fifteen. More than one hundred boys participated in this activity. And, when America entered World War I, the boys put away their balls, bats, and gloves and cultivated vegetable gardens on fifty-foot-square plots to aid the nation's defense efforts.

According to the 1917 report, Irvin Westheimer had established an annual award to recognize outstanding achievement by a Little Brother. The 1917 award went to one who, forced to quit school at age fourteen, had advanced on his job, helped support his family, and imbued with a desire to obtain an education had completed a four-year night school course in three years.

In the association's annual report for 1918, Westheimer spoke of a publication, *The Freelance,* which was "edited, published, and financed by the Little Brothers themselves."

Early annual reports issued by the Cincinnati Big Brothers Association.

The Cincinnati association served only boys from Jewish homes, and consequently Protestant and Catholic Big Brothers groups were later established in that city.

Westheimer served as president of the association until 1915, but remained active in Big Brothers work, both locally and on a national basis, for the rest of his life.[8] His greatest contributions to the national Movement were probably during the late 1960s and 1970s, when his early efforts were widely recognized and publicized throughout the Big Brothers national organization (and later the Big Brothers and Big Sisters combined organizations) and resulted in a sharply increased public awareness of the Movement's work. Westheimer died on December 31, 1980, at the age of 101.

Some accounts credit Westheimer with being the founder of the organized Movement. As already indicated, this is not true. Nor was Westheimer the founder of Big Brothers of America (BBA) or Big Brothers/Big Sisters of America (BB/BSA), as is sometimes reported. These organizations did not evolve until after World War II.

New York Big Brothers

A separate and totally unrelated tributary became a major part of the Movement's mainstream. Before the organization of juvenile courts in America, even very young children, accused of minor offenses, came before the same tribunals that considered hardened adult offenders.

The first jurisdiction to establish a separate court for children was Cook County, Illinois, in 1900.[9] In September 1902, Ernest K. Coulter, a native of Ohio, and a former reporter for the old *New York Sun*, helped organize the first Children's Court in New York City. However, it was not a totally separate court, but rather a special section of the Court of Special Sessions for the trying of juvenile cases.

As clerk of that court, Coulter was appalled by the suffering, misery, and apathy he witnessed each day. The thousands of children who passed through the court were dealt with in accordance with the law, but little concern was shown for their personal problems or circumstances. Many went back to the streets only to return, again and again, to the court. Coulter felt that society should have some way to deal with these children on an individual basis, especially after they left the court.

Then, on the evening of December 3, 1904, he addressed the Men's Club of the Central Presbyterian Church of New York. As he looked at his audience, which included many of the area's business, professional, and community leaders, he had an idea. He told the men about a little boy who had just been brought into the Children's Court for an offense that would, upon conviction, send him to a non-rehabilitating reformatory for eighteen months.

"There is only one possible way to save that youngster," Coulter said, "and that is to have some earnest, true man volunteer to be his big brother, to look after him, help him to do right, make the little chap feel that there is at least one human being in this great city who takes a personal interest in him; who cares whether he lives or dies. I call for a volunteer."

Hardly had Coulter finished speaking when almost every person in the room volunteered. He had a Big Brother for the boy he had just described, and the names of thirty-nine other men who wanted to befriend troubled youths; the Big Brother Movement in New York was underway. Coulter may have been influenced by the earlier activity of Judge Julius M. Mayer, since both men worked for the same court. As far as is known, Coulter was the first person to use the term *Big Brother* in connection with the Movement.

Whereas a Cincinnati man claims to have given birth to the Big Brother idea, Ernest K. Coulter can take credit for forming the nation's first organized group, and thus the founding of the organized Movement in America.

The idea was popular and growth was rapid. As the Movement spread in New York City, Big Brothers worked closely with the city's YMCA branches, as well as with various church groups. The minister of the Central Presbyterian Church, the Rev. Dr. Wilton Merle-Smith, persistently put before his congregation the need for more men and money to carry on the work. He also spoke to other congregations, inviting men of all religious denominations to take part, and he himself set an example by becoming a Big Brother.[10]

Early Organization

Organized activities, begun in 1904, continued to expand. By 1907, a more formal organization was formed. Two years later, as more children were referred to the program and more volunteers were recruited, the need to incorporate, find permanent quarters, and obtain a larger administrative staff became matters of top priority.

On November 26, 1909, application was made to the New York Supreme Court for a state charter; Coulter and the Rev. Wilton Merle-

Ernest K. Coulter, founder of the organized Big Brother Movement in America .

Smith were two of the petitioners. At that time, it was estimated that one thousand Little Brothers who at one time or another had been before the Children's Court were participating in the program.[11]

Its papers of incorporation state that the organization was formed "to organize and direct a body of men of good will whose purpose shall be to interest themselves individually in the welfare and improvement of children who have been arraigned before the Children's Court of the City of New York and similar courts throughout the United States."

That the founders of the New York Big Brothers Movement intended it to be international in scope is clearly indicated by another section: "that the territory in which the operations of said corporation are to be principally conducted is the city of New York, comprising all the boroughs thereof, and also throughout the states and territories and possessions of the United States and any foreign countries."[12]

Although branches were soon formed in other city boroughs, there is little evidence that any planned, organized program existed for founding agencies in other states. Rather, the role of the nation's first agency appeared to be that of answering queries and supplying information, in person or by mail, to those who were interested in organizing similar units.

According to a letter in the Big Brothers archives of Temple University, the New York Movement's General Secretary R. C. Sheldon visited Philadelphia on December 11, 1915, to help organize an agency for that city, but his role seemed to be only that of an adviser. Sheldon may have acted in a similar capacity in other communities. But as far as can be determined, New York never assumed the role of a national Movement coordinator.

Early Methods

The early methods and procedures governing New York – area Big Brothers–Little Brothers relationships were largely formulated by Coulter as a result of his Children's Court experiences. These rules and instructions, modified and improved by several years of trial and error, were reported in a popular magazine of that era.

> *Be interested in the boy's interests. Invite him to your office and to your home, take him to the ball game, a concert, or a good, clean show, get him interested in one of the boy's gymnasiums, and if you find your Little Brother has a bent in any particular direction give him a chance to exercise it. Get him interested in church or Sunday school. Above all things, do not patronize. Just be a brother and a companion to your boy. Give the boy his individual chance to be honest and to grow up into a useful citizen.*[13]

The initial efforts of the first Big Brothers under Coulter's tutorage must have required considerable courage. These volunteers were not trained social-service workers who might have known what to expect. Rather, they were well-established business and professional people; many of them were leaders in their particular fields. Furthermore, they were separated from those whom they wished to befriend by the broad, formidable, social-economic-cultural gulf that always divides the comfortably affluent from the extremely poor.

The very first Little Brother to be befriended by the organized Movement was reportedly Michael Aloysius Hennessy, who had been arrested for throwing a brick through a window. Both of Michael's parents were dead and his brother was in Sing Sing. It is not known if this was the same boy Coulter referred to in his speech to the Men's Club. But Coulter later told of Michael's rehabilitation, saying that he had become a promising young businessman.

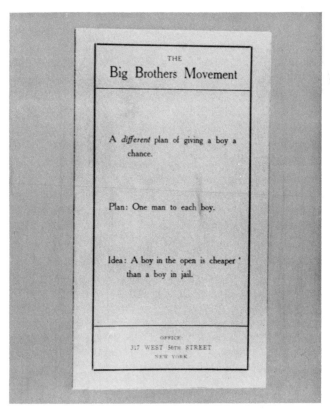

Early recruiting and information brochure issued by the New York Big Brother Movement.

One Big Brother from Central Presbyterian Church, when attempting to visit his Little Brother, was greeted by a frumpish, extremely distrustful woman, apparently the boy's mother, who brandished a large, rusty pistol. Another would-be benefactor was threatened with a pan of sudsy dishwater until the mother of the prospective Little Brother determined the true nature of his mission. In most cases, the new Big Brothers found only misery and suffering, resulting from neglect and poverty, and any kind of help was welcomed.

A Big Brother was assigned to a boy from the city's Hell's Kitchen section, who had been in court because of truancy. He discovered that the father was dead, and that the boy had been staying out of school to nurse his mother, who was dying of tuberculosis. The Big Brother arranged to have the family moved to brighter, cleaner quarters; to obtain work for an older brother; and to place the smaller boy back in school. Because of the interest and concern of the Big Brother, the boy developed his artistic ability and, later, secured an important position in the design department of a large retailer.

In seeking his Little Brother in an East Seventy-fifth Street tenement late at night, a Big Brother discovered five of the family's ten children out on the street because it was not "their turn in bed." The family had to sleep in shifts, so tight were their quarters.

Thousands of distraught, poverty-stricken children passed through the Children's Court. In one case, the judge was so moved by the plea of a young boy for the release of his younger sister — who had stolen a few potatoes from a peddler's wagon — that he himself became the boy's Big Brother. These children were orphans and the boy alone was supporting his sister on an income of $4.50 per week. The judge was Franklin C. Hoyt, who later became president of the Big Brother Movement of New York.[14]

Although limited monetary assistance as a first-aid measure and as a prerequisite for effective rehabilitation was clearly indicated in some cases, Coulter warned the early Big Brothers that their primary function was not that of providing material gifts. "A large percentage of boys out on probation don't have a decent friend in the world to help them. What the boys want is [sic] friends, not charity," said Coulter, in a 1909 article in *Good Housekeeping* magazine.[15]

The Big Brothers believed that every child has an inherent capacity for goodness, just waiting to be tapped by human concern. The *Good Housekeeping* article summed up this philosophy graphically: "The most beautiful flower that ever bloomed, if rooted in dry, thin and sterile soil, is only a stunted thing that withers before its time, while the same plant under a skillful gardener's care might fill the air with its full-blossomed fragrance."

The article also recognized the fact that Big Brothers gain tremendous personal satisfaction and emotional fulfillment from Big Brother–Little Brother relationships, suggesting that "one cannot point the steep and thorny paths to heaven . . . without that self-conviction and self-arraignment which make for one's own betterment."[16]

Early Big Brothers work in New York was purposely kept as free from administrative detail and red tape as possible. News of Big Brothers activity spread largely by word of mouth. For example, an article in the *New York Times* for March 6, 1908, mentions that Bishop Potter [Episcopal bishop of New York] spoke on Big Brothers work and its benefits at a meeting that was attended by former First Lady Mrs. Grover Cleveland.[17] The Big Brothers apparently eschewed print-medium publicity about their activities, preferring instead to wait until their program proved successful before seeking the public eye. Success did come, and it was followed quickly by ever-increasing media coverage.

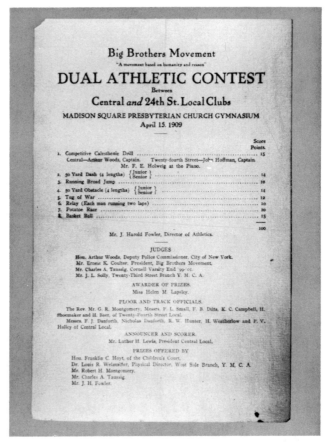

Group activities played a major role in the early Big Brother Movement and supplemented the One-to-One relationship.

Coulter, who had obtained a law degree in 1904, the year he founded the Movement, was elected president of the newly incorporated organization, and a headquarters was opened at 200 Park Avenue in Manhattan. The organization functioned largely by having a full-time representative in the Children's Court. The judge considered each case. If he thought that the influence of a Big Brother would be more beneficial than a jail term, the offender was turned over to the organization's court representative who, in turn, assigned him to a permanent Big Brother.

New York Big Brothers had to promise to see their Little Brothers at least twice a month and had to file periodic reports on their progress.[18] The one-to-one concept was emphasized from the beginning. But to an extent much greater than today, group activities were also provided. Rather than establish elaborate facilities or social structures for group programs, Big Brothers preferred, as much as possible, to utilize the existing facilities and programs of other groups. Thus, they often used the gymnasium facilities of the YMCA.

Summer camp was very much in vogue as a remedial tool. Much of the early casework material deals with removing children from their environments—preferably to a camp, farm, or other rural area. Although some children were assigned to work on privately owned farms, the New York agency, and subsequently organized agencies in other areas, operated their own camps or farms.

In 1911, two not publicly known donors deeded a 230-acre farm near Trenton, New Jersey, to the New York Big Brothers Movement, together with a gift of $4,000 for improvements. Part of the cash gift was used to establish manual training facilities at the location.[19] Sixty boys could be accommodated at the farm at any one time. That same year, the agency sent 309 boys to summer camps, and several prestigious private schools, such as Princeton University and Groton, made their summer camps available to Little Brothers.[20]

Banquets for Big and Little Brothers were a popular activity in New York. The report of one banquet in 1913 indicated that it was attended by 175 Little Brothers, all of whom were on probation from the Children's Court. They were accompanied by their Big Brothers, who included some city officials. The gathering, entertained by jugglers and magicians, heard several prominent speakers, including a judge from Denver, Colorado, who spoke of Big Brothers work in that city.[21]

Not everyone was in accord with the banquets and, presumably, other activities that might publicly identify juvenile offenders. After reading of the above described banquet, a member of the Manhattan School Board wrote a scathing letter to the *New York Times*, claiming that if a child is to be helped, no one except the court, his parents, and school officials should ever know that the child had been arrested, convicted, placed on probation, and assigned to a Big Brother—least of all the child's peers.[22]

The letter drew a quick and concise response from Rowland C. Sheldon, then general secretary of the New York Movement. Sheldon denied that Big Brothers were concerned with reforming criminals and said that the Movement did not look upon the Little Brothers as such. He indicated that there was no need for secrecy, since boys were encouraged to take pride in what they were and could become, rather than what they had been. He then invited the educator to become a Big Brother.[23]

Little Brothers in trouble were certainly not considered criminals by the New York Movement. They were simply victims of circumstances — at all times reclaimable, if only one exercised enough patience, courage, and one-to-one concern. That this philosophy was soundly embraced by the New York Big Brothers is demonstrated by the lengths to which some of them went to redeem their malfeasant Little Brothers.

The experience of one Big Brother, a prominent New York physician, in obtaining the release of his Little Brother, who had been arrested and jailed for fighting, provides a good example. The Little Brother was a delivery wagon driver for a department store. When ten boys on roller skates attached themselves to his wagon for a free ride, he attempted to dispatch them with his fists. Booked for assault, and finding himself in jail on a Sunday morning with bail set at $500, he called his Big Brother.

The doctor called Ernest Coulter for advice and was told to go the boy's bail. But he did not have enough cash, and personal checks were not accepted; he did not even have any real estate in the jurisdiction, which he could pledge as surety, and, of course, there were no card-actuated, computerized bank money machines in those days. So the Big Brother and Coulter set out on a Sabbath-day mission of mercy to raise funds needed for the Little Brother's bond.

They first obtained $200 from a third individual. Next they went to the Central Presbyterian Church in Manhattan, where a sympathetic sexton surrendered the contents of the collection plates in exchange for the doctor's personal check. With $300 now in hand, they visited a nearby funeral home, where an additional $75 was obtained in like manner. The remaining $125 came from the cash register of a restaurant, where the men were known. Tendering the required amount in small bills, the Big Brother obtained the release of his charge and returned him to his mother.

The detailed case of Coulter's own Little Brother, identified only as Latsky, provides another example of Big Brother perseverance.

Latsky had come to America from Russia, along with his father and younger sister, when he was only seven years old. He soon fell in with a street gang of pickpockets known as the "Fagins," after the infamous character in *Oliver Twist*. By the age of ten, he was considered to be one of the most agile young thieves on New York's East Side.

Latsky came to the attention of Coulter's court on a charge of snatching a purse in October 1902, at least two years before the New York Big Brothers came into being. He was placed on probation. In January 1903, he was again arrested and convicted in Children's Court, also for stealing a purse. He was sentenced to the New York Juvenile Asylum, only to escape. Free for more than a year, Latsky was again arrested in March 1904. Now thirteen years old, he was sentenced to the institution that received the worst cases — the House of Refuge on Randall's Island — until his twenty-first birthday. Sometime after this, Coulter decided that Latsky was ready for "big brothering."

Coulter could have befriended Latsky well before the much heralded meeting of the Central Presbyterian Church Men's Club. If so, he apparently never identified the relationship as the beginning of the Movement in New York.

He visited Latsky on Randall's Island, and kept in touch with him on a regular basis. Latsky was paroled in October 1906. He was fifteen and professed a desire to lead an honest life. Sent to a farm in Connecticut as part of a Big Brothers program, the boy found life there intolerable and asked to be returned to the House of Refuge. Coulter now arranged for another Big Brother, with a beautiful country estate on Long Island, to let Latsky live with him and go to school. Latsky did not like school, so his accommodating host arranged for him to work at a Long Island real estate firm. Again, losing interest in a few weeks, Latsky contacted Coulter and begged him to bring him back to New York.

Now, several Big Brothers volunteered to assist Coulter and be responsible for Latsky for several days each — a team effort, you might say — in order to introduce him to a side of the city that he had never known. By so doing, they thought Latsky might be better able to select a career path to pursue. He was entertained in some of the city's finest homes, restaurants, and hotels; he attended plays and visited business and professional offices.

Did Latsky "see the light" and decide that the pursuit of life on "this side of the tracks" was superior to his former lifestyle? Hardly. Within a few months, he was again arrested for pickpocketing, convicted, and returned to Randall's Island, where Coulter again assumed responsibility for his welfare and visited him on a regular basis. Paroled after two years, Latsky moved to the home of still another Big Brother in New Jersey. He was dissatisfied. Another Big Brother gave him a job. He did not like it. Just before his twenty-first birthday, Latsky disappeared, apparently for good. But the Big Brothers, according to the account, still stood ready to lend him a hand, when and if he ever surfaced again.[24]

Of course, Latsky's case is highly unusual. It is cited here only to portray the dedication and perseverance of these pioneering Big Brothers. The organization's success rate was in fact phenomenal.

At the New York Movement's annual meeting in 1911, Rufus D. Putney, its general secretary, reported that 2,195 boys had been cared for during the past year, most of whom had been referred by the Children's Court. Of that number, only 90, or less than 4 percent, were charged with offenses that resulted in a second court visit. Big Brothers also provided an employment and counseling service, and Secretary Putney reported that 1,202 boys had applied at the Movement's headquarters for advice or to seek employment.[25]

Not all Little Brothers were referred by courts. Some came from schools, churches, or other social-service organizations. Sometimes the prospective Little Brother himself came to the Big Brothers headquarters and asked for a Big Brother. One such youngster, identified only as George, came in and proclaimed, "I want a Big Brother. I guess I oughter have one. I know a feller as has one, and I need one as much as that feller ever did."

George was right. Subsequent investigation revealed that he was a ringleader in one of the city's most notorious gangs — the Car Barn Gang. He was described as the kind of boy who would be a natural leader — "a freckled-faced, snub-nosed kind of a boy with a daring twinkle in his eyes, and an alertness and ingenuity that made him the originator and the executor of all sorts of daring schemes." George got his Big Brother, left the gang, and began making excellent progress in school.[26]

As New York's Big Brothers Movement grew and expanded its services, increasingly less emphasis was placed on reclaiming juvenile court cases, and more and more activity was directed toward keeping children out of trouble.

Big Brothers, then as now, were warned not to expect quick results. One Big Brother reported working with his Little Brother for years without visible change. The boy was described as "sneaky, suave, and apparently unappreciative." He evidently maintained this attitude until the match was dissolved, and the Big Brother lost track of him. Then, one day after the boy had become a man, he returned to the Big Brother and asked for help for a member of his own family, his twelve-year-old brother, who had joined a gang.

𝔅𝔦𝔤 𝔅𝔯𝔬𝔱𝔥𝔢𝔯 𝔚𝔬𝔯𝔨

NEW YORK CITY

VOL. I   MAY, 1912   NO. 2

BIG BROTHER WORK is issued quarterly by THE BIG BROTHER MOVEMENT of New York City for the purpose of arousing broader interest in the work of the Movement. Offices; 200 Fifth Avenue, New York City. Telephone, 1204 Gram.

Subscription price, 50 cents per annum.

We are dealing daily with boys who have been the victims of bad environment, many boys who, save for this work, would have little chance to develop into useful citizens. If we good from it as the boys. It makes them bigger, broader, better citizens. We are hearing more of the brotherhood of man to-day than ever before, and here is a tangible, practical line of service in the brotherhood.

It is Ruskin who says: "All evil springs from unused (misused) good."

In every soul there is the divine spark sometimes hidden as the sun is hidden from us by clouds, but always existing, always there if the clouds are driven away.

A LITTLE BROTHER BASKET BALL TEAM

are going to help these boys we must understand them, and the motives for their actions. We must find their viewpoint, then, perhaps, we shall discover there are deficiencies on our side as well as on theirs.

All of these boys can be helped if we make the right approach, do not patronize and ever keep in mind the boy's definition of a friend: "A feller what knows all about ye and likes ye jest the same." The chief success of the Big Brother work lies in the personal relationship it establishes. The men get quite as much

Froebel says: "A suppressed or perverted good quality, a good tendency, only repressed, misunderstood or misguided, lies originally at the bottom of every shortcoming in man."

The smallest things in childhood are the principles of manhood. For instance: Destructiveness in little children is merely the active thirst to know how things are made. Rightly trained this activity is creative and preservative; perverted it becomes one of the most prevalent of petty crimes.

The instinct to eat and drink is natural

Newsletter published by the New York Big Brother Movement in 1912; former President Theodore Roosevelt praised the Movement in an article in this issue.

"I never realized how much you did for me till I began to see how that kid [his own brother] was going, and what it would mean to him to have a friend like you," said the formerly apparently ungrateful Little Brother. The Big Brother had waited a long time to hear those words — the first indication that his work had not been in vain. They made all the years of discouragement now seem worthwhile.[27]

Ernest K. Coulter, who resigned from his Children's Court post in 1912 to enter private law practice, remained active in Big Brothers work for many years. In fact, he embarked on a nationwide lecture tour on behalf of Big Brothers in 1914. He was an organizer of the Boy Scouts of America (National Council). He was also active in various child protective movements, including the New York Society for the Prevention of Cruelty to Children, Federated Boys Clubs, and other cultural, political, and social welfare organizations. Before World War I, according to articles in several New York newspapers, Coulter launched a campaign against drug abuse. During the war, Coulter served in the AEF, attaining the rank of lieutenant colonel.[28] He died in 1952, and is buried in Arlington National Cemetery.

By the beginning of the First World War, when Judge Franklin Chase Hoyt had assumed its presidency, the Big Brothers Movement of New York was a highly organized, efficient, well-accepted, and respected part of the city's social welfare structure. In fact, so dependent had the Children's Court become on Big Brother activity that Judge Hoyt told the New York Times, "there is no doubt that the lack of the facilities which are furnished by the Big Brothers would greatly hamper the court in its efforts to use the probation system efficiently."[29]

Big Sisters

Another important tributary is that of the Big Sisters. According to a story published in 1910, Coulter was often asked why there was not also a Big Sisters Movement. His reply was that the need for such an organization was not so pressing. Of the 11,494 children who passed through the Children's Court of New York in 1909, only 893 were reported to be girls, and this number included 611 cases of improper guardianship. The 10,601 boys who were arraigned included only 1,396 cases of improper guardianship. The rest were charged with various offenses.[30]

But when Coulter made the above statement, he undoubtedly was speaking only about the lack of a Protestant group of Big Sisters. It is difficult to understand how he could have been unaware of a group of Catholic women, mentioned at the beginning of this chapter, who had been helping girls in his court since shortly after it opened in September 1902. These women belonged to the Ladies of Charity. The group changed its name to Catholic Big Sisters (of the Ladies of Charity), according to one report, after Coulter's organization began referring to its volunteers as Big Brothers. Catholic Big Sisters is still functioning; by early 1985 it had operated continuously for nearly eighty-three years.

Catholic Big Sisters work was begun by a Mrs. John G. O'Keefe, who has been called the first Big Sister.[31] Also active in early Catholic Big Sisters work in New York were America-born Lady Armstrong, wife of the then British consul in New York, H. Gloster Armstrong, and Mrs. W. K. Vanderbilt, Jr. Both women played major roles in the organization's development. Jewish Big Sisters work, in connection with the New York Children's Court, was reportedly underway by 1908, although it could have begun much earlier.

It was once claimed that Milwaukee had the first Big Sisters agency.[32] Although evidence now indicates that this city has to defer to the Catholic Big Sisters of New York, and perhaps even the New York Jewish Big Sisters, Milwaukee had a viable Big Sisters organization as early as 1909. It may well have been the best organized and supported group and, during the early part of the century, one of the fastest-growing Big Sisters organizations. By 1924, it was caring for six hundred girls.[33]

The early group that received the most publicity and consequently became the best known was Big Sisters of New York, also known as the Protestant Big Sisters. Some accounts erroneously credit the Protestant Big Sisters of New York with being the first to engage in Big Sisters activity, possibly because of the extensive press coverage they later received.

This organization, still in existence as an independent agency, traces its beginning to 1908, when a Mrs. Willard Parker, Jr., director of a black orphans home (then called an orphans asylum) in New York City, went to the Children's Court to find out just how parentless children came to be committed to her institution. She discovered Catholic and Jewish Big Sisters, but found that no one was befriending Protestant girls. Mrs. Parker, a Protestant, decided to fill that role. She, too, has been referred to as the first Big Sister. More properly, she can be said to be the first Protestant Big Sister, at least in New York.

It is not known what Mrs. Parker did as a Big Sister during the first few years. It is known that she aided Coulter and the Big Brothers Movement. In a 1911 report Coulter expressed the Movement's gratitude to Mrs. Parker and her friends for obtaining funds from Episcopalian sources to support the Big Brothers court investigator.

In early 1910, Mrs. Parker was joined by a wealthy New York socialite, Mrs. William K. Vanderbilt, Sr., and the nucleus of a definite organization began to take shape.[34] Mrs. Vanderbilt was also a Protestant. She should not be confused with the wife of her stepson, Mrs.

William K. Vanderbilt, Jr., mentioned earlier in connection with the Catholic Big Sisters.

Mrs. William K. Vanderbilt, Sr., founder along with Mrs. Willard Parker, Jr., of the Big Sisters of New York.

How or why Mrs. Vanderbilt first became interested in the Big Sisters concept is unclear. She visited the New York Children's Court around January 14, 1910, reportedly staying for an hour and a half, and listened to the cases brought before the judge. Before leaving she questioned the judge about the court, the children who were brought there, and the status of their parents. She returned to the court on January 24, and the two visits sparked rumors that she was planning to fund a hospital for mentally defective children. She refused to confirm or deny the rumor when questioned by the press.

But Mrs. Vanderbilt's true interest in court activities was revealed when, in 1911, she took the initial steps formally to organize and charter a Big Sisters program. She joined in an active campaign for funds, contributed liberally herself, supported a membership drive, and took an active role in handling individual cases.[35]

The early Protestant Big Sisters followed the same procedures as the Big Brothers. That is, a representative attended Children's Court sessions, listened to the cases, and determined — along with the judge and court officials — which children might benefit from Big Sisters assistance. The judge was then asked to place these children in the care of the Big Sisters court representative who, in turn, would secure a permanent match for each of them.

The Protestant Big Sisters received a charter from the New York Supreme Court on June 7, 1912.[36] By that time, the organization reportedly had one hundred members, had a full-time secretary, Mrs. Madeline Evans, and an assistant secretary, and shared quarters with the Big Brothers Movement at 200 Fifth Avenue.

Mrs. Vanderbilt was the first president, and she and her own sisters, Mrs. F. C. Havemeyer and Mrs. Stephen H. Olin, and several friends were primarily responsible for the organization's creation, structure, and operating methods. Mrs. Willard Parker was among the incorporators, and Coulter of Big Brothers acted as the group's attorney.[37]

Mrs. Charles Dana Gibson, the former Irene Langhorne and sister of Lady Nancy Astor, was also active in early Protestant Big Sisters work. American painter and illustrator Charles Dana Gibson, using his wife as model, created the famous "Gibson Girl," who came to symbolize the modern girl near the turn of the century. In 1908, Gibson created a symbol for Big Sisters of New York — a sketch of a little girl in a patched dress holding a doll. Shortly before his death in 1944, he contributed a new sketch which became the organization's symbol.

Mrs. Vanderbilt established a home near her estate at Deepdale for delinquent girls who had been rescued from the Children's Court by the Big Sisters. When that home burned, she provided another residence for the girls. On the front page of the *New York Times* appeared a rumor that Mrs. Vanderbilt would soon endow the Big Sisters with a gift of $500,000, in addition to supplying $150,000 for the new girl's home.[38] Two days later, the heiress herself flatly denied the story.

Mrs. Vanderbilt and other Big Sisters did lease a farm near White Plains, New York, as an "experimental home . . . to see how much can be accomplished in improving the morals and character of the 'little sisters' who will be taught housework and sewing." The quarters were expected to accommodate more than thirty girls.[39]

Although not the first to engage in Big Sisters activity, the New York Protestant Big Sisters may be able to claim at least one first — that of the first cross-gender matches. Even today, the practice is considered experimental by many Big Brothers/Big Sisters agencies. Mrs. Vanderbilt and her associates were matching Big Sisters with Little Brothers, under the age of ten, at least as far back as the early 1920s.[40] The Catholic Big Sisters of Brooklyn (chapter 2) were also making cross-gender matches at about this time.

Other Activities

In the three to five years before America's involvement in World War I, scores of small tributaries, located below the headwaters, began contributing to the flow of Big Brothers and Big Sisters activities. Pinning down their numbers, locations, and exact dates of origin is difficult.

Most available figures support a continuing—rapid at times—pattern of growth. The 1909 article in *Good Housekeeping,* referred to earlier, stated that "the influence of the Big Brother movement has spread to hundreds of other cities."[41] A feature in *Hampton's Magazine,* the following year, stated that twenty cities with juvenile courts had Big Brothers organizations. On June 9, 1912, the *New York Times* reported that Big Brothers could be found in twenty-six cities. *Everybody's Magazine,* in 1913, noted Big Brothers in forty cities in the United States, Australia, and Canada—one of the earliest indications that the Movement had become international.

In early 1916, Coulter announced that there was activity in ninety-six cities. *Good Housekeeping* reported in 1917 that "there are now [Big Brothers] branch organizations in ninety-eight cities in the United States." The magazine stated that "the idea has also been taken up abroad, and one of the most flourishing societies is in Tokyo."[42]

Librarians in thirty-six eastern, midwestern, and southern cities were recently asked to check local telephone directories for the years between 1909 and 1916 for Big Brothers and Big Sisters listings. They found few. Probably most Big Brothers and Big Sisters activities then were sponsored by, and thus shared the identity of, other organizations, such as churches and church-related agencies, social-service agencies, and fraternal groups.

The term *Big Brother* was sometimes used in connection with activities that had no connection, and differed considerably, from those generally associated with the Movement. For example, in 1914, several golf clubs in the Chicago area organized a Big Brothers program to develop better caddies. In a number of cities, men who belonged to business or civic organizations sometimes referred to themselves as Big Brothers, although they did nothing more than deliver baskets to the needy at Christmas.

One effort that flourished for a brief period before World War I under the Big Brothers banner possessed many of the characteristics of the mainstream Movement as well as several sharply divergent attributes. Involved was an organization known variously as the National Big Brothers Association, the National Big Brothers League, and even the Big Brothers Movement. It was headed by a Chicagoan, Jack Robbins, headquartered in Chicago, and reportedly supported by a group of famous writers of that era — Upton Sinclair, Robert Hunter, and Jack London — as well as a noted labor crusader, Mary "Mother" Jones. These people had strong socialist ties, but Sinclair, famed as a leading muckraker and reformer, and London, are remembered mainly for their literary contributions.

Robbins's organization claimed to have established Big Brothers groups in various cities in which each member would befriend one boy who was in trouble. These were called Big Brother Clubs or Last Chance Boys Clubs. At one time thirty-two local units were reported. In 1913 Robbins launched a special campaign that garnered considerable publicity. He began a search to locate the worst boy in each of twelve midwestern and eastern states. After finding them, he planned to send them to a ranch north of Reno, Nevada, dubbed the Last Chance Boys Ranch, where presumably they would be turned into first-class citizens.

To identify this nefarious dozen, Robbins investigated thousands of candidates, reportedly some of the most abject delinquents known to local authorities in the cities where he visited. As part of his investigation, Robbins administered a thirty-question test to determine a subject's truthfulness. Points were accumulated for each known lie. A boy's final score, together with other qualified data based on his background, determined his "percentage of badness."[43]

In due time, the twelve boys were selected. A boy in Racine, Wisconsin, came away with "top honors," when he was determined to be 91 percent bad and only 9 percent good. The boy had a record of seventeen arrests and convictions for larceny. A boy from Sioux City, Iowa, came in second, with a rating of 90.5 percent bad, and a young malfeasant from Detroit ranked third. In a move that is hard to understand today, the names of all twelve boys, together with their cities of origin and their percentages of badness, were published in the *Chicago Journal* on January 13, 1914. The article also reported that the boys, with Upton Sinclair in charge, had already arrived at the Nevada ranch.[44]

Robbins continued to pursue his bad boy search for some time. He even visited prison officials in several states in an effort to get youthful convicts released to his custody. Those he sought to befriend included a fourteen-year-old who was serving a life sentence at Joliet Prison in Illinois for a triple murder and a seventeen-year-old murderer who was serving a life sentence in Michigan. Robbins and his group, possibly because of the questionable validity of their approach and perhaps because of their socialist leanings, often received a less than enthusiastic welcome in the cities they visited. The chief probation officer in Cleveland refused to help him find the worst boy in that city because of the embarrassment that such a tag would cause his family. Community and civic leaders in Indianapolis remained cool toward the program, even after Robbins rounded up three "street urchins" and took them before the mayor in an effort to gain the city's endorsement.

The fact that the organization received massive press coverage was undoubtedly because of the elements of sensationalism that it engendered, as well as its association with the several well-known writers and social reformers. In fact, word of its activities became so widespread, and Robbins's identification with the Big Brothers Movement became so great, that Coulter's organization in New York, which wanted nothing to do with the maverick program, found it necessary to distribute a press release denying any involvement.

It is not known what happened to the Last Chance Boys Ranch. Perhaps, in the annals of some obscure journal, the outcome of the experiment has been recorded. An official of the Nevada Historical Society, aware that the ranch had existed, said that it was located in Verdi, Nevada, near the California state line, and had been known as the Jack London Last Chance Boys Ranch.

A traditional Big Brothers agency in Chicago was established by 1917, and a number of other early Big Brothers and Big Sisters efforts existed before the end of World War I. There was Big Brothers activity in Fort Worth, Texas, by 1908, and in Pittsburgh and New Orleans by 1909.

A Jewish Big Brothers group was in existence in New York by 1910, according to an article in the *New York Times* for February 17, 1912, which tells of its second annual report. There is evidence of Big Brothers activity in both Denver and Toronto by 1913, although the Denver group did not incorporate until much later. The Jewish Big Sisters, known to be operating by 1908, were well established in New York City by 1915, as were the Catholic Big Brothers. The work of the former group probably began much earlier, possibly as early as 1902.

Big Brothers work was underway in St. Paul, Minnesota, in 1913, as indicated by a listing in the St. Paul *Directory of Charitable and Benevolent Organizations* for that year. This listing gave the address of the New York Big Brothers Movement, but indicated that locally Big Brothers activity was endorsed by the St. Paul members of the Grand Lodge of the Benevolent and Protective Order of Elks (BPOE), who were ready to cooperate in the work. The listing is an indication that Big Brothers in other states may have looked upon the New York Movement as a kind of "parent organization."

The Elks (BPOE) strongly supported the Philadelphia Big Brother Association, organized in 1915. Note titles on billboards in lower photo, made around 1922.

The Elks

For several years before and during World War I, the Elks were exceptionally active in Big Brothers work throughout their organization, according to early BPOE records. Rather than establish separate Big Brothers agencies, they promoted the work within their local lodges. The scope of their activity is deserving of special mention.

In July 1911, at the fraternal order's national convention in Atlantic City, Grand Exalted Ruler August Herrmann made an eloquent plea to the delegates on behalf of the Big Brothers Movement:

> I know of no subject which has appealed so strongly to me, nor any that will appeal more strongly to you, my brothers, than The Big Brother Movement. . . . The movement is simple in its operations. It is bound neither by rule nor by lines. Its fundamental provision is kindness, which, when exercised by the Big Brother, brings the Little Brother in touch with the fact that he is not an outcast and that the world is not so harsh as his previous experiences may have led him to believe . . . . Who is there who does not know one or more boys of the street in whom he recognizes capability that could be employed to the advantage of the boy, and of society if means were taken to elevate him in his own estimation and inculcate in him the knowledge that there is a better future before him . . . . Let each Elk take some Little Brother by the hand and with words of encouragement and of companionship lead him to the plane . . . of self-respect and of confidence in and love for his fellow man. [45]

Sometime after that, the Hammond (Indiana) Elk Lodge began a Big Brothers program. At the Elks National Convention in Rochester, New York, in 1913, John F. Reilly, past Exalted Ruler of the Hammond Lodge, reported that twenty Elks in his Lodge were looking after twenty Little Brothers, who had been referred by the Juvenile Court. Mr. Reilly recommended that a committee on the Big Brothers Movement be appointed, whose duty it would be to present the Hammond Program to other lodges. [46] The committee was named, with Reilly as its chairman. Within a year, the group reported that it had sent out more than 7,000 communications on the Big Brothers Movement to local lodges, as well as 20,000 booklets on the Hammond Program. [47]

Their efforts were eminently successful; the Big Brothers idea spread like grass fire. At the 1914 Elks convention, the Committee on the Big Brother Movement reported that 5,000 boys were being looked after by Big Brother Elks in 901 lodges. By 1915, 1,011 lodges were participating in Big Brothers work, and by 1917, Committee Chairman Reilly reported that Elks were looking after approximately 30,000 Little Brothers. Chairman Reilly continued:

The past year has been one of expectancy and fruitful accomplishment, and we believe that our efforts to extend the work of the Big Brother Movement have not been in vain. This Movement in Elkdom has passed the experimental period and has assumed such proportions as to command the attention of all persons interested in the proper development of the little brothers. It is an unselfish work and one that appeals particularly to the members of our great Order. Let every Elk, then, take upon himself the duty of looking after some unfortunate little brother.

By the 1918 Elks convention, 1,152 lodges were participating in Big Brothers work, but the program was soon to receive less emphasis. At the 1919 meeting, the Committee on the Big Brothers Movement was merged into a new group known as the Social and Community Welfare Committee, which was to be concerned with "the broader field of endeavor for the uplift of humanity." The new committee continued to support the Big Brothers Movement but, perhaps because it also espoused other social welfare programs, the interest of local lodges in Big Brothers activity soon began to wane.[48]

Other Organizations

Other Big Brothers and Big Sisters groups — both independent and sponsored by various organizations — continued to be formed across the country. By 1914, there were Big Brothers groups in Grand Rapids, Michigan; Portland, Oregon; Jacksonville, Florida; Seattle, Washington; and in Canton, Columbus, Dayton, and Cleveland, Ohio, in addition to Cincinnati, mentioned earlier. There were also a Big Sisters agency in Columbus, Ohio, and a Big Brothers/Big Sisters organization in Washington, D.C.

A Big Brothers Movement began in St. Louis in 1914. In Kansas City, a Big Sisters program started in 1915, and reportedly could boast five hundred members two years later. The prime objective of the Kansas City group seemed to have been to befriend naive girls from small towns who came to the city to work.[49] On the West Coast, also in 1915, a group of young business and professional men founded the Jewish Big Brother Association of Los Angeles. Its first president was Paul Lowenthal, a juvenile court judge.

Other agencies or groups that were in operation or had their beginnings in 1915 include the Big Brother Association of Philadelphia, although there is evidence of less formal Big Brothers activity in that city as early as 1909, and the Big Sisters of Evansville, Indiana. Big Brothers organizers in Philadelphia included Judge Raymond Mac-Neille, District Attorney Samuel P. Rotan, and Charles Edwin Fox, a lawyer, who was the agency's first president and a longtime supporter of the Movement in that city.

In Evansville, the Big Sisters early distinguished themselves with their work in the local juvenile court. Said the court's presiding judge, Elmer Q. Lockyear:

> The Big Sisters are among those who help me most. They are represented in court by one of their number every Saturday, and they are as their name implies "big sisters" to the girls who have got a bad start in life. There are a great many women of high character who wouldn't associate with the girls that these women help. But the Big Sisters will. And they do great things for their community in reclaiming girls sometimes apparently lost.[50]

The Jewish Big Brother Bureau of Baltimore officially organized on January 30, 1916, following a preliminary meeting on December 15, 1915. However, the organization's roots go back to October 1914, when Louis Levin, secretary of the Federated Jewish Charities of Baltimore, organized an informal group under the same name to deal with the problems of delinquency among young people. Levin took this action after discussions with William A. Schwab, a local businessman, who had begun a practice of visiting Jewish inmates at the Maryland penitentiary.

Both men wanted to do something about the problems of crime. However, Levin preferred a preventative approach, whereas Schwab still favored remedial action. Schwab persuaded several friends to visit the prisoners with him. This activity continued for several months — the men even referred to themselves as "big brothers" to the inmates. However, Schwab soon became convinced of the need to deal with young people before they became involved with the law. He joined Levin as one of the original incorporators of the Baltimore organization.[51] Within a short time, the name of the organization was changed to the Jewish Big Brother League.

A charter was granted to a Big Sisters group in Pittsburgh on February 20, 1916.[52] It was known officially as the Big Sisters Organization of Pennsylvania. Although the group may have been responsible for starting several other nearby agencies, there is no evidence that it functioned as a state organization. But it was extremely active in the Pittsburgh area. Its members quickly became involved in many aspects of social-service work.

In less than a year the group established a hospital visitation program, set up an emergency fund, opened a community center, appointed a war relief committee to assist the National Red Cross, and campaigned for "penny lunches" in the Pittsburgh schools. They even became involved in social issues, adopting a resolution "That the Big Sisters Organization urge the government to adopt national prohibition as a war measure and that a copy of this resolution be forwarded to the President."[53]

Reasons for Growth

Did the beginnings of these Big Brothers and Big Sisters organizations, and possibly scores of others, result from any kind of centralized effort or force, or did they occur spontaneously? There were outside influences in some cases, to be sure; many interested communities contacted the early New York organizations for information. Westheimer claims to have espoused the cause in his business travels, and successes in one community were bound to be an influence in nearby towns and cities. But spontaneity, triggered by local, almost universally shared social and economic conditions, appears to be a more plausible explanation.

Sometimes in a bed of yeasty, decaying leaf or wood mulch near an old tree stump, when conditions of soil, climate, nutrients and moisture are just right, unique, variegated mushroom-like plants spring into being almost overnight. What were the climatic conditions, and other elements of growth, that brought so many Big Brothers and Big Sisters organizations into being in such a relatively short time?

During the first decade and a half of this century, millions of Americans lived in abject poverty—many barely avoiding starvation. Unskilled laborers for the factories, mills, and mines were plentiful—their ranks distended by millions of newly arrived immigrants. Wages, in most cases, were unconscionably low, the hours long, and working conditions often unbearable.

Sixty-to-eighty-plus-hour work weeks were common. Unskilled laborers in many industries received no more than eight to ten cents per hour, and others received as little as seventy-five cents for a ten-hour day. Coal miners shared an even harder lot. They were paid by the ton and never knew from day to day whether there would be work. Since they generally worked in remote areas, with few opportunities for other kinds of employment during mine layoffs, they often "owed their souls to the company store" for most of their lives.

Child labor and its attendant abuses were to be found everywhere. When Irvin Westheimer reportedly befriended the boy who was digging through a garbage can in 1903, there were 1.5 million child laborers in America under the age of sixteen, many as young as eight. They often worked grueling thirteen-hour days for a few pennies.

Tuberculosis and other debilitating diseases ran high among children and adults alike. Crowded city tenements bred crime and despair. In 1906, an economist indicated that as many as 50 million Americans, out of a population of 76 million, could be classified as poor.[54] For them, the American dream never existed.

Crowded tenements were breeding grounds for delinquency

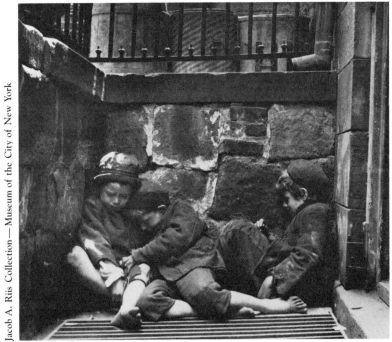

Some children had no place to sleep but the streets

At the other end of the socioeconomic spectrum were the extremely wealthy, who wielded tremendous economic power. Among their number were such names as Carnegie, Rockefeller, Morgan, and Vanderbilt, as well as Harriman, Hill, Weyerhaeuser, Armour, Widener, Frick, and Hanna. These were the industrialists and financiers who controlled the mines, oil wells, basic processing industries, manufacturing plants, railroads, utilities, large banks and financial institutions. They generally answered to no one except themselves—least of all the state and federal governments.

Then, there was another important group of citizens whose name came from the position its members occupied somewhere between the two classes—the middle class. Its people were traditionally characterized by conservative, moderate views on most political issues, a strong belief in competitive free enterprise (as opposed to a monopolistically controlled economy), and an empathy with those less fortunate.

The middle class included small merchants, small bankers, farmers, and professional people, such as lawyers, judges, doctors, clergymen, teachers, and small manufacturers, as well as many skilled tradespersons. They were, for the most part, community-minded, family people who embraced traditional values. The middle class included the Westheimers and the Coulters and others like them.

Increasingly, middle-class citizens began taking a more militant stance on many issues. They resented the unfettered economic power of the very rich, and the control these powerful interests had over their lives and means of livelihood. They saw the misery and human wreckage in the wake of an unregulated industrial economy.

Looking in the opposite direction, the middle classes were also becoming alarmed by the large voting blocs being formed by immigrants and other disadvantaged people, who were being exploited and manipulated by machine politicians. Many middle-class citizens felt that it was time to correct these injustices and inequities. The vehicle they chose for reform was the Progressive movement.

The middle classes had many allies—many peripheral special interest groups—in their crusade to correct society's ills. They were joined by early women's rights proponents, by university professors, social scientists, and even the prohibitionists, such as the Big Sisters in Pittsburgh.

The wives and daughters of many of the wealthy industrialists, such as Mrs. W. K. Vanderbilt, Sr., also subscribed to certain tenets of progressivism, perhaps because they were distressed by the many abuses wrought by the huge industrial empires that their husbands and fathers had created. Or perhaps they thought that it was wrong for a few to be so comfortable and so many others to be so wretchedly poor. Professional politicians jumped on the bandwagon and many social-service organizations joined the parade—a parade led by Theodore Roosevelt and such prophets of the new cause as Robert M. La Follette of Wisconsin.

Progressivism provided the elements of growth — the seedbed, climate, and nutrients—which quickly spawned the efforts to correct the abhorrent conditions. And it also gave rise to the tools, means, methods, and organizations — such as the Big Brothers and Big Sisters Movement—that were required to make these efforts effective.

It is significant that many religious bodies, heretofore concerned only with the salvation of souls, now joined the Progressive movement and began spreading the social gospel as well. Many, perhaps most, early Big Brothers and Big Sisters organizations were either started, affiliated, or associated in some way with churches or religious groups.

The interest of religious groups in progressivism (and the Big Brothers and Big Sisters Movement) embraced almost all creeds and faiths. The Federal Council of the Churches of Christ in America began an effort to unite the Protestants under the Progressive banner in 1905. The Rev. Endicott Peabody taught his students at Groton that wealth brought with it a responsibility for social service. Among his students was young Franklin D. Roosevelt. A prominent Catholic priest campaigned for labor's right to a living wage, calling attention to the social injunctions of the papal encyclical *Rerum novarum*.

American Jews, under the leadership of several prominent rabbis, reinterpreted the "Messianic hope for the establishment of the Kingdom of truth, justice and peace among all men" as a mandate to solve the social problems of the day.[55] As Boris Bogen, mentioned earlier, so effectively put it in speaking of charitable activity in his area, "Social service was [not only] par excellence the medium of religion in the Reform Jewry of Cincinnati; it was religion."[56]

Progressivism, then, was the real founder of Big Brothers and Big Sisters work in America. If the Westheimers, Coulters, Vanderbilts, and others were responsible for the Movement's rivers and streams, progressivism would have to be called its watershed. Progressivism provided the topography, which directed the Movement's various streams of activity.

A Single Spirit

Before World War I, the Big Brothers and Big Sisters Movement was characterized by many forms of organization, under a variety of sponsors, utilizing a number of approaches. But all of the efforts were united under a single spirit—the spirit born of a desire to help children, generally from one-parent homes, whose moral, mental, and physical development was endangered by their environments and backgrounds.

This spirit was certainly present at a mass rally at the Casino Theatre in New York on the evening of April 30, 1916, when two thousand persons, white and black, and from all major religious bodies, joined hands in an unprecedented show of support for the one-to-one concept in dealing with the problems of growing up.

Said Father Thomas J. Lynch, speaking for Cardinal Farley:

> *There is too much moral vivisection in the present treatment of the bad boy. This is an epoch-making night in the history of New York City, for New York needs some great care for its boys and girls, and the Big Brothers and Big Sisters give that care. The Catholics have not been foremost in such work, but the day has come . . . when [we] must come forward and, man for man and woman for woman, get into this work for the children.*

Rabbi J. L. Magnes, in an eloquent appeal, declared:

> *What can be more noble than to hold in your care the soul of a growing human being? It is as though you held a tender plant which to touch wrongly is to blight. In this day of cold efficiency—efficiency in business, efficiency in charity—it is a miserable small justice our great organized charities do. The personal touch is absent. It can't be put into a scientific system. It is not Gentile, not Jewish—it is human. Being a Big Brother or a Big Sister is doing some little good for some little person.*

Episcopal Bishop David H. Greer, representing the Protestants, told the huge gathering that New York was a great storage battery of kindness.

> *Thousands are ready to do good if they have the opportunity, and this great, happy, growing movement gives them the opportunity. I like this thing [Big Brothers and Big Sisters Movement] because it is the natural human way of doing good. Then it is the economical way, for the city could save millions it spends for the care of children in institutions if there were more Big Brothers and Big Sisters. Not by social machinery are bad boys to be made good boys, but by the warm, personal touch in life.*

As the rally came to a rousing close, in what might be described as almost revival-like fervor, nearly every one of the two thousand participants "signed a card joining the Big Brothers and Big Sisters Movement and pledging personal interest in at least one boy or girl who needed help."[57]

. . . .

This movement is based on humanity and reason. There is no more practical form of helpfulness than that which sets the feet of child victims of environment and neglect on the road that leads to useful citizenship. The condition of the tenement child is not of his own making. Whether he is to become a friend and helper or an enemy of the State rests largely with his neighbor. He is in a formative state, mentally and physically, and easily molded.

MEETING EXTRAORDINARY

UNDER THE AUSPICES OF THE

" 2 - 3 - 2 "

TO BE HELD IN THE CHURCH PARLORS

HANSON PLACE METHODIST EPISCOPAL CHURCH

Thursday Evening, Feby. 6, 1908

To discuss the "Big Brothers" Movement—a movement organized to aid the Juvenile Court in preventing crime by saving juvenile offenders.

GUESTS OF THE EVENING:

HON. ROBERT J. WILKIN

President Brooklyn Juvenile Probation Association and Justice Juvenile Court

"The Juvenile Court—Its Work and Needs"

MR. C. HENRY HOLBROOK

Executive Secretary "Big Brothers" Movement of New York

"The Big Brothers Movement—Its Inception and Work"

. . . ALL MEN WELCOME . . .

If you believe that a boy in the open is better than a boy in jail, you are in sympathy with the Big Brothers. If you believe that a boy unaided cannot always overcome the tendency of unfortunate environment, or be happy and good without any of the things which make for happiness and goodness, you concur in the Big Brother platform. If you are willing to do something yourself to help a boy you may at once become a Big Brother, and we can supply the very boy who needs you to brother him a little, to give him some fun, to show him how to be manly, to take some of life's handicap off his undersized body and undeveloped mind.

H. Earle Shull, Jr.

Notes to Chapter 1

1. Westheimer himself provided this account in several recorded interviews on file at BB/BSA headquarters, Philadelphia. No record could be found of Big Brothers work in Cincinnati between 1903 and 1910. It is possible that this activity was viewed as part of other neighborhood settlement house programs and, thus, was not otherwise identified.
2. "Big Brothers Association of Cincinnati Serves through the Years," *The American Israelite*, September 19, 1968, 32.
3. Simon Cohen, "Jewish Pioneers in the Big Brothers Movement," *American Jewish Historical Quarterly* 61, no. 3 (1972):226.
4. Boris D. Bogen, *Born a Jew* (New York: MacMillan Co., 1930), p. 74.
5. Cohen, "Jewish Pioneers," p. 227.
6. "Big Brothers," *Cincinnati Times-Star*, February 24, 1911.
7. Ibid.
8. Cohen, "Jewish Pioneers," p. 229.
9. Rheta Childe Dorr, "The Child's Day in Court," *Hampton's Magazine* 25, no. 5 (1910):636.
10. Henry Rood, "Big Brothers and Little," *Everybody's Magazine* (August 1913):249.
11. "Incorporate 'Big Brothers,'" *New York Times*, November 27, 1909, 2:7.
12. Papers of incorporation filed with the New York Supreme Court.
13. "The Little Father of the 'Big Brothers,'" *Hampton's Magazine* (July 1910):121.
14. Ernest K. Coulter, *The Children in the Shadow* (New York: McBride, Nast & Co., 1913).
15. "Big Brothers," *Good Housekeeping* (May 1909):600.
16. Ibid.
17. "Choate Urges Aid for East Side House," *New York Times*, March 6, 1908, 7:5.
18. Clara Savage, "Wanted — Big Brothers!" *Good Housekeeping* (August 1917):58.
19. "Fine Farm a Gift for Big Brothers," *New York Times*, October 4, 1911, 5:3.
20. Ibid.
21. "Big Brothers Dine Little Brothers," *New York Times*, April 29, 1913, 18:2.
22. William I. Sirovich, Letter to the Editor, *New York Times*, May 3, 1913, 10:7.
23. R. C. Sheldon, Letter to the Editor, *New York Times*, May 5, 1913, 8:5.
24. Frank Marshall White, "How a Boy Was Made a Thief and the Fight to Reclaim Him," *World's Work* (September 1911).
25. "Fine Farm a Gift," see note 19 above.
26. Savage, "Wanted — Big Brothers!" p. 58.
27. Ibid.
28. *Who's Who in America*, vol. 26, 1950–51.
29. Interview with Judge Franklin Chase Hoyt by a *New York Times* reporter, *New York Times Magazine*, October 17, 1915, 20.
30. "The Little Father," p. 122.
31. Radio Address by Lady Armstrong over WNYC, New York, October 3, 1940.
32. Agenda for the first Big Brothers and Sisters Conference, Grand Rapids, Mich., May 28–29, 1917.

33. R. R. Kelley, "Milwaukee Enters upon Nineteenth Year of Service," *The Ounce*, Big Brother and Big Sister Federation (BB/BSF), January 1926, 13, Archives and Special Collections, The City College, City University of New York (CUNY).
34. Alissa Franc Keir, "A Big Sister Wanted in Every Town in the World," *Success Magazine* (June 1925):130.
35. Ibid.
36. "Big Sisters Get a Charter," *New York Times*, June 8, 1912, 6:2.
37. "To Be 'Big Sisters' for Little Girls," *New York Times*, June 9, 1912, 10:3.
38. "Hear of Vanderbilt Gift," *New York Times*, December 2, 1912, 1:2.
39. "Home for 'Little Sisters,'" *New York Times*, May 11, 1913, 2:2.
40. Keir, "A Big Sister Wanted," p. 52.
41. "Big Brothers," *Good Housekeeping*, p. 600.
42. Savage, "Wanted—Big Brothers!" p. 125.
43. "Is State's Bad Boy in City?" *Rochester Herald*, December 18, 1913.
44. "Chicago Has the Best Boys, Toledo Worst," *Chicago Journal*, January 13, 1914.
45. Proceedings, Grand Lodge of the BPOE, Atlantic City, N.J., July 11–13, 1911, 36–38.
46. Proceedings, Grand Lodge of the BPOE, Rochester, N.Y., July 8–10, 1913, 197–199.
47. James R. Nicholson et al., *History of the Order of Elks, 1868–1979*, revised edition (Chicago: Grand Secretary's Office, BPOE), p. 233.
48. Ibid.
49. "'Big Sisters' of Kansas City," *World's Work* (June 1917):137.
50. "Lockyear Believes in Reforming Children," *Evansville Journal*, October 3, 1915.
51. Joseph F. Hecht, *The History of the Jewish Big Brother League, Inc.* (Baltimore: King Brothers, 1973), pp. 48–57.
52. "Big Sisters Granted Charter," *Pittsburgh Gazette Times*, February 20, 1916.
53. Ibid.
54. Ernest R. May, *The Life History of the United States, The Progressive Era*, (New York: Time-Life Books, 1964), p. 33.
55. Oscar Handlin, *The Americans* (Boston: Little, Brown & Co., 1963), p. 342.
56. Bogen, *Born a Jew*, p. 80.
57. "Big Brother's Help the Bad Boy's Hope," *New York Times*, May 1, 1916, 4:1.

FIRST ANNUAL BIG BROTHER FARM DAY AT STOCKTON, N.J. SATURDAY, OCTOBER 19, 1912

A CORDIAL INVITATION is extended to all Big Brothers of New York City and elsewhere, friends of the Big Brother Movement and others interested in boys who have not had a fair chance in life, to visit the Big Brother Farm at Stockton, New Jersey, on Saturday, October 19, 1912. There will be an opportunity to make a tour of the Farm. A brief program has been arranged which will present the work of the Big Brother Movement including the story of the Farm; the little brothers of the Farm family participating. Luncheon will be served by the ladies of Stockton.

Train leaves Pennsylvania Station 8.08 A. M., Hudson Terminal 8.00 A. M. Returning trains leave Stockton at 2.30 P. M., arriving Pennsylvania Station at 5.19, and at 4.24 arriving at 7.23.

If 25 go we can have a special car. It may be an advantage therefore if you will write us that you are expecting to be there. Go any way if you can, whether or not you have notified us.

The fare for a round trip ticket is $3.58.

We will have conveyances at the Station for those who may prefer to ride. The farm is about a mile from the station.

The Farm containing 230 acres is beautifully situated on the banks of the Delaware River at Stockton, New Jersey, 20 miles north of Trenton. Here street boys away from the criminal influences of the gang, may have a home under Christian influences and receive wholesome training to make them useful men.

The Farm Committee hopes for a large attendance. The invitation includes their neighbors at Stockton as well as friends in Trenton, Lambertville and nearby villages.

Sincerely,

CHARLES L. INSLEE
JOHN H. PRALL
FRANK W. PEARSALL
Farm Committee

ROY F. PARSONS
*Acting General Secretary
Big Brother Movement*
EDWARD C. MacDONALD
Superintendent Big Brother Farm

Kindly address correspondence about Big Brother Farm Day to Frank W. Pearsall, 215 West 23rd Street, New York City

H. Earle Shull, Jr.

39

2

Between the Wars:
A Potpourri of Activity
(1918–1944)

The Big Brothers/Big Sisters Movement grew from a common need at the beginning of the Progressive period in America politics —the need in local communities to deal with the fast-emerging problems of American youth that were the result, both directly and indirectly, of a largely uncontrolled national economy. Local conditions and local priorities determined the focal points and programs of each group that undertook Big Brothers/Big Sisters work.

Local groups shared the name *Big Brothers* or *Big Sisters* (and in a few cases, both). Almost all Big Brothers/Big Sisters activity involved the one-to-one approach to problem solving, as opposed to group action. It was this characteristic that set Big Brothers and Big Sisters work apart from other social welfare activity. It was probably this common element, together with a desire of the disparate groups to develop more uniform administrative techniques and operating standards, that led to the formation of the Big Brother and Big Sister Federation in 1917 (discussed in chapter 3).

Throughout the country, during the two decades before the Second World War, programs were locally oriented and diverse. Although some of the agencies described are still in operation, coverage of their activities in this chapter, for the most part, deals with 1918–1944.

Jewish Big Brother League of Baltimore

The beginnings of the Jewish Big Brother League of Baltimore were mentioned briefly in chapter 1. Almost as soon as a constitution had been adopted, the league launched an elaborate, multifaceted social-service program, to be implemented by specialized committees.

A Committee on Penal Institutions and Parole was charged with the responsibility for looking after the interests of Jewish inmates at penal institutions, including providing the means for inmates to observe Jewish holidays. This committee also supervised parole cases, and recommended parole in warranted situations.

The Committee on Education and Recreation was responsible for seeing that retarded youth in the community satisfied the minimum educational requirements for obtaining work permits. This committee also explored and developed vocational training for those with the necessary aptitude and arranged annual outings.

A Committee on Employment and Sheltering helped boys obtain both full-time and after-school work, and provided temporary shelter for runaways. The Civic Affairs and Legislation Committee studied social problems and recommended appropriate agencies. There was also a Public Relations Committee.

Perhaps one of the most important committees, as its name implied, was the Committee of Experts. It was the responsibility of this group to train all new Big Brothers before they were entrusted with their charges, and a detailed, graduated program was developed for this purpose.

The beginning Big Brother or "novice," after preliminary training, was designated as eligible for "Class A" work and could be trusted with a Little Brother who might be guilty of no greater offense than truancy. If he handled such an assignment successfully, he might — after additional training — be advanced to "Class B" and become eligible to handle someone who had been judged a delinquent. Success there led to a "Class C" assignment with a "reformatory graduate," and so on until the Big Brother became eligible to handle a hardened ex-convict or narcotic addict. In addition to a close relationship with the Little Brother, the Big Brother was also expected to act as an adviser and counselor to the boy's parents when necessary.[1]

In May 1919, Abraham Caplan, the league's executive secretary, attended the convention of the Big Brother and Big Sister Federation (discussed in chapter 3) in Cincinnati, and reported back to his board that groups in other parts of the country did not work with men in penal institutions and that, furthermore, they "do not interest themselves in the various large problems, such as the drug situation." Caplan's report was the basis for many discussions, and consideration was given to aligning the league's interests more closely with those of other Big Brothers groups. However, the final decision was to retain current policies and practices.[2]

The league continued its broad spectrum of activities, which ranged from providing magazines, Hebrew instruction, and courses in religious ceremonials for inmates of the Maryland Training School, and direct intervention on behalf of defendants in juvenile court cases, to actions related to the enforcement of child labor laws and the control of street gangs. But, increasingly, especially as the socioeconomic effects of the Great Depression began to be felt, more and more attention was devoted to the development of one-to-one relationships between Big Brothers and predelinquent boys.

From time to time, the influence of an individual man or woman on the development and growth of an organization is so great that the name of the organization and that of the individual become almost synonymous. Such is the situation involving the Jewish Big Brother League of Baltimore and its late executive director, Meyer D. Levin. Levin, who died in 1972, became executive director of the league in 1923, shortly after receiving a degree in engineering from Johns Hopkins University, and served in that capacity for a phenomenal forty-three years.

It is not within the scope of this chapter to relate all of his accomplishments before his retirement in 1966, but current league officials and board members agree that Levin's knowledge and unique ability to inspire others, coupled with his wisdom and capacity for compassion and understanding, accounted for the league's many successes.

Levin had wanted to be an engineer. However, during his student days, he had become a Big Brother and had become very much interested in the work. When Executive Director Caplan resigned, Levin applied for the position and was hired. He quickly became interested in the legal aspects of social welfare and soon developed a close liaison with local, state, and federal court officials, who often consulted him and sought his advice and counsel. In 1928, by attending night school, Levin added a law degree to his credentials.

A somewhat amusing yet thought-provoking anecdote effectively illustrates Levin's close ties with the courts, as well as his pragmatic approach to problem solving. Levin learned that four Jewish boys from a poor Baltimore neighborhood were involved in a series of petty thefts. Levin pleaded with the parents of the four families, asking them to take the children out of their current environment. All were fairly prosperous, all could afford housing in better areas. The parents flatly refused, contending that what was good enough for them was good enough for their children. This attitude and lack of concern for their children's welfare and futures infuriated Levin. When the boys were arrested and brought before a court, he recommended to the judge that they be sent to reform school *until* their parents bought homes in better neighborhoods. The judge accepted Levin's suggestion and acted accordingly.

When Levin reported this scenario to the league's board, some of its members thought that he had gone too far in pursuing Big Brothers activity. But his judgment was soon vindicated. All four families moved to better neighborhoods and, as the judge had promised, the boys were allowed to go to their new homes. None of the boys was ever involved with the law again.[3]

Although the league's programs and activities were widely varied, its prime targets during the time reviewed were the juvenile delinquent and both the youth and adult prisoner.

The league was interested in assisting Protestant, Catholic, and other groups in sponsoring Big Brothers programs. On May 3, 1922, as part of Big Brother Day activities, a mass rally was held at the Baltimore Armory to generate interest in the work by non-Jewish organizations. Ernest K. Coulter addressed the gathering.[4]

In July 1923, the Catholic Big Brother Association of Baltimore was organized under the sponsorship of the Holy Name Society, which sponsored other Big Brothers groups throughout the country during the 1920s. It was not until 1953 that a nonsectarian group — Big Brothers of Baltimore — was founded.

Big Sisters of Kansas City

As indicated in chapter 1, the Big Sisters of Kansas City felt that their greatest opportunity for service was in helping young women, generally from rural areas, to adjust to city life. Their technique was based on what today might be termed "networking." Members of the Kansas City Big Sisters Association, all working women or former working women themselves, maintained contact with auxiliary associations in surrounding small towns. When a young woman from one of these towns decided to go to Kansas City to seek employment, the KC group was notified and a Big Sister was assigned to meet the woman's train, welcome her to the city, help her locate suitable lodging, and assist her in every way possible to adjust to her new surroundings.

Not much is known about the leadership of the association other than it was headed by a Miss Nettie Huff near the end of World War I. But its presence in Kansas City appeared to be quite pervasive from accounts of its activities and projects. It was reported that most of the factories and large offices had Big Sisters representatives, and that a committee of Big Sisters was assigned to each floor of every department store, where many young women from small towns worked.

Their job was to be on the lookout for the young woman who appeared to be lonely, distressed, or in danger. Big Sisters also searched for those in need of aid in such places as cheap boardinghouses, low-priced restaurants, and on streetcars. When they found someone who appeared to need help, they were required to ask themselves, "Suppose she were my little sister," and then act accordingly. Aid was extended in the form of limited financial aid, assistance in locating suitable housing, employment referral, and help in obtaining job training. Big Sisters also arranged social functions and planned recreational activities.

Sometimes the assistance of a Big Sister went beyond the bounds of what might typically be considered "big sisterly" concern. A Big Sister saw a young woman looking longingly at a display of wristwatches in a jeweler's window. A man joined the woman and the Big Sister overheard him say, "If you'll come with me, I'll show you some watches much prettier than these." The man and young woman then walked off together and the Big Sister followed. When the three had reached a neighborhood of cheap rooming houses, the Big Sister approached the young woman, put a hand on her shoulder, and said, "I hope I'm not making a mistake, but I thought perhaps you were a stranger to the city. Have you seen this man before? Do you know where you are going?" The man, according to the source, made a hasty retreat, as the young woman expressed her profound gratitude for being rescued.[5]

After a Little Sister became established and self-supporting, she was expected to become a Big Sister and assist newcomers. The organization held monthly dinner meetings which were attended by both Big and Little Sisters. The Big Sister office served as a referral center for persons offering assistance as well as for those seeking aid.

Catholic Big Brothers of Los Angeles

A unique feature of the Catholic Big Brothers, Inc., of Los Angeles, during the 1930s and early 1940s, was the operation of referral homes for boys who would otherwise have been committed to reform schools.

Representing a coalition of Catholic organizations, the Los Angeles agency was organized on February 4, 1926. The Holy Name Society of the Diocese of Los Angeles and San Diego had conducted preliminary organizational work the previous year.[6] Joseph Scott was selected as chairman of the Governing Board, and Dr. Peter J. Barone was named executive secretary of the new organization. The agency received a state charter in May 1929.

During its early years of operation, it encountered considerable difficulty in sustaining a viable volunteer program, but the situation improved during the early 1930s. Agency personnel had felt frustrated by not being able to offer alternate plans when Catholic boys requiring institutional care were sentenced to state institutions. In November 1933, the agency rented a facility in Redondo Beach, California, to house boys referred by the county probation department. The home, which cared for as many as thirty-three boys, became the Los Angeles Catholic Big Brothers' major interest. In 1936, the agency's wards were moved to a new home, which it had constructed in the San Fernando

Valley. Called Rancho San Antonio, the facility was operated by the agency until January 1944, when operations could no longer be sustained because of wartime staff shortages. The home was then deeded to the Archbishop of Los Angeles, and Big Brothers responsibility for its operation ceased. After the war, the agency returned to the one-man one-boy approach that it had utilized during its early years, and never resumed an institutional-care program.[7]

New York Big Sisters

Prior to World War II, it was not unusual for there to be several Big Brothers or Big Sisters agencies in the same city, each sponsored by or affiliated with a different religious body or denomination. Cooperation among such agencies ranged from only benign acknowledgment of the other's activities to joint participation in mutually advantageous projects. But probably nowhere, and at no time, did cooperation among such groups attain the level achieved by the three Big Sisters agencies — Protestant, Catholic, and Jewish — in New York City during the 1920s.

So close was their relationship that they almost functioned as a single organization with three departments. Just before the beginning of the decade, the three agencies — all founded several years apart earlier in the century — faced common problems that could be solved better and more quickly through a combined effort. A Cooperative Committee, with representatives from each organization, was formed to determine joint policies and practices and plan group activities.

"Truly an extraordinary friendship of three creeds working harmoniously, constructively, cooperatively . . . without jealousy or bickering — in spite of every prophecy to the contrary," wrote Alissa Keir in *Success Magazine*.[8] Said Bird S. Coler, then New York commissioner of Public Welfare, in a letter to the editor of the *New York Times*:

> *This committee [the Cooperative Committee of the three agencies] is a convincing refutation of a quite commonly held assumption that Protestant, Catholic and Jew cannot work together and at the same time retain their spiritual independence. Nowhere within my observation is the spirit of cooperation and understanding among the three great faiths so well exemplified as in the work of this body.*[9]

At the time the agencies joined forces, Mrs. William K. Vanderbilt, Sr., and Mrs. Willard Parker, Jr., were heads of the Protestant Big Sisters, Lady Armstrong was president of the Catholic agency, and Mrs. Sidney C. Borg was in charge of the Jewish organization. The three organizations not only exchanged ideas and techniques, but also conducted joint fund drives and benefits, and maintained a common treasury for field work.

Lady Armstrong, *left*, head of Catholic Big Sisters of New York, and
Mrs. Sidney C. Borg, head of the city's Jewish Big Sisters .

Some of the fund-raising affairs were quite elaborate. Guests at a
committee-sponsored ball at the Ritz-Carlton Hotel on Monday evening, May 5, 1919, were entertained by such popular luminaries of the
day as Fanny Brice, Clifton Webb, and sixty beauties from the Ziegfeld
Follies. For the ball's guest of honor, a World War I general, Irving
Berlin even composed a special song, which he sang to the guests.[10]

The committee often sponsored teas or forums to exchange ideas,
plan activities, or hear prominent speakers. Famed aviatrix Amelia
Earhart was a speaker at one of these meetings.[11] That some of the
New York Big Sisters might have had a rather broad view of their
responsibilities is indicated by a statement made by Mrs. Willard Parker,
Jr., during an interview:

> *The elimination of discord between father and mother — the bringing
> home of the runaway in a different frame of mind — smoothing the
> school problem — finding congenial jobs — coping with drunkenness
> and immorality — sickness and death in the homes — placing some
> little old lady in a convent — arranging for a group of tired mothers
> and babies to go to the beach on a hot summer's day — the giving of
> a monster Christmas party for thousands of little kiddies whose lives
> would otherwise be bare and lacking true Christmas joy — all these
> things are within the active scope of Big Sister work.*[12]

Sisters' Dance

AT THE RITZ-CARLTON HOTEL
MONDAY EVENING, MAY FIFTH
AT TEN-THIRTY O'CLOCK

FOR THE BENEFIT OF

THE BIG SISTERS
ORGANIZATIONS
(Catholic—Protestant—Jewish)

Tickets of Admission, $5.00   Boxes, $100.00
Supper, $3.00   Table Reservations, $10.00

Tickets may be obtained from MRS. CHARLES DANA GIBSON, *Treasurer,*
681 Fifth Avenue, telephone Plaza 7536,
And at the Ritz-Carlton and Vanderbilt Hotels.
Number of tickets limited

Advertisement for fund-raiser sponsored by the Cooperative Committee of the three Big Sisters' organizations in New York City.

However, most Big Sisters work involved one-to-one relationships with girls referred by juvenile courts or parents — activity that was taken very seriously. Big Sisters had to undergo thorough training, and modern evaluative techniques were used to determine the needs of Little Sisters. If a behavior problem was suspected, the child was examined and tested by a psychiatrist. The child's background was carefully reviewed to determine what corrective measures or environmental changes might be in order. Only then was a course of action prescribed.[13]

The three Big Sisters agencies and their Cooperative Committee received numerous commendations for their efforts from social welfare and law enforcement authorities, as well as from the general public. The activities of the committee seem to have diminished considerably

TENTH ANNUAL REPORT
OF
THE BIG SISTERS
1921

"HE WHO HELPS A CHILD HELPS HUMANITY"

Artist Charles Dana Gibson, creator of the "Gibson Girl,"
drew the little girl on the cover of the 1921 Annual Report
of the Big Sisters of New York. The organization used the
sketch as its symbol for many years. Gibson updated the
drawing shortly before his death in 1944.

with the onset of the Great Depression; however, it was still functioning
as late as 1938.

Of interest here—although not directly related to the Movement—
is the fact that Mrs. William K. Vanderbilt, Sr., Lady Armstrong, and
Mrs. Borg, together with Ernest K. Coulter of the Big Brothers Movement, were also active in the Society for the Prevention of Cruelty to
Children (SPCC). In November 1920, the three women resigned from
the society's Auxiliary Committee, after becoming embroiled in a bitter
policy dispute with Coulter, who had recently been appointed general
manager of the SPCC. It is not known what effect this dispute had on
the heretofore good relations between Coulter and the heads of the Big
Sisters groups.

Big Brothers of St. Louis

Membership in the Big Brother Organization of St. Louis from the time of its founding in 1914 by Juvenile Court Judge Thomas C. Hennings until about 1950 was limited to business and professional men. Weekly, one-to-one contact between Big and Little Brothers took place at the Big Brothers' offices or places of business.[14] Although the group had no formal relationship with the Rotary Club, it worked closely with that organization. During the 1930s and 1940s, the Big Brother Organization also maintained a close relationship with the Thomas Dunn Memorial, a St. Louis hotel for homeless working boys and students. The organization maintained its headquarters at the hotel.[15]

Robert M. Hyndman was the group's first executive secretary, a post he filled with distinction for more than twenty years. From its inception until 1927, the St. Louis organization worked with both delinquent and predelinquent boys. From 1927 on, it specialized exclusively in preventive work.[16]

St. Louis was probably one of the first Big Brothers agencies to participate in group fund raising. There is evidence that it participated in the St. Louis Community Fund as a charter member in 1921.[17] Before that time, it supported itself through various activities.

During a fund-raising and recruiting campaign in 1922, famed comedian Eddie Cantor spoke on the agency's behalf at a St. Louis Chamber of Commerce luncheon. Cantor told how he was left an orphan at age two, and how he roamed the streets of New York at age seven, associating with a variety of juvenile lawbreakers. At age twelve, he was given an opportunity to go to summer camp for two weeks. All he had to do was raise $1.50 for train fare, an amount he was able to steal within thirty minutes. The first night in camp he got into trouble for stealing blankets. Cantor said he expected a beating or harsh reprimand. Instead, the camp director talked to him "in a quiet, big brotherly way," and made him see the error of his ways. Cantor claimed that the incident marked a turning point in his life and that he owed his current success to the kindness and understanding of the camp director, who later became his lifelong friend and adviser. Cantor repeated the emotion-packed story the next evening to a local theater audience, where he was appearing, and made an eloquent plea for more Big Brother volunteers.[18]

The early St. Louis Big Brothers were communication-minded; and as far as can be determined, they were the first in the nation to use the medium of radio to tell the Big Brothers story. An officer of the agency, Martin J. Collins, talked about the Movement on the fledgling *St. Louis Post-Dispatch* station, KSD, during the first week of May 1922. Milton L. Daugherty, the agency's general secretary, gave a talk on Big

Brothers work later that month over a station operated by one of the city's department stores.[19]

In the late 1920s, the agency published two regular bulletins, *The Bulletin* and the *Junior Bulletin*. The latter was published exclusively for Little Brothers, and carried articles on such subjects as fair play, respect for the law, and the secrets and principles of success. A large sign on one of the city's busiest thoroughfares was used to attract new Big Brother recruits.[20] By 1933, 150 Big Brothers in St. Louis were providing counsel, guidance, and friendship for 410 Little Brothers. The agency also provided medical, dental, and optometrical services for many of the Little Brothers.[21]

Jewish Big Brothers of Cleveland

By 1928, the Jewish Big Brother Association of Cleveland, Ohio, founded in 1919, operated on the premise that the development of a young life was too important to be left to a haphazard arrangement. Consequently the association accepted Little Brothers for matching only after they had first been accepted, investigated, evaluated, and recommended by a recognized case-method agency, such as the Jewish Social Service Bureau, the Jewish Orphan Home, or the Welfare Association for Jewish Children. The association expected the referring agency to recommend a course of action for each referral, and once a match was made, the Big Brother was expected to work closely with the applicable agency's professional staff and other involved persons, such as a probation officer or school official, utilizing a team approach. The Big Brother scheduled periodic meetings with such specialists to discuss plans of action and evaluate results. He fully recognized the value of the specialized skills they had to offer, and they acknowledged the unique contribution that could be offered by the Big Brother one-to-one association and guidance.

The Big Brother, in most cases, became the implementing arm of the team. He might be asked to place his Little Brother in a Boy Scout troop, or seek employment for him or stimulate his interest in achieving an educational goal. The concept and methods employed by the Jewish Big Brother Association of Cleveland placed its work in the vanguard of progressive Big Brothers activity of that era.[22]

Big Brother Association of Philadelphia

The Big Brother Association of Philadelphia probably offered one of the most broad-based, comprehensive programs to be found anywhere during the period covered by this chapter. In addition to a traditional, one-to-one matching program, the nonsectarian association operated a

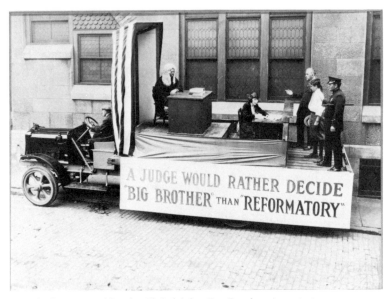

Parade float created by the Philadelphia Big Brother Association

Philadelphia Family Court

A Philadelphia Big Brother-Little Brother match. Photo may have been posed for publicity purposes. (Both photos probably 1920s.)

large boy's club, which included a gymnasium, swimming pool, and library. Besides supervised sports, the facility offered instruction in such skills as woodworking and printing, as well as in art and other subjects. The club, opened in 1919, was available to all Little Brothers, as well as boys from settlement houses, the Boy Scouts, and other organizations, who were between the ages of ten and a half and seventeen. In 1933, a club annex was opened for boys over seventeen and Big Brother boys club alumni.

The association also operated its own medical and dental clinics. The dental clinic opened in 1924. Volunteer dentists examined and treated Little Brothers and club members. A dental hygienist was provided. All boys who were associated with the facility could have thorough physical examinations at the medical clinic that opened in 1930. When required, boys were referred to their family physicians or to cooperating hospitals or dispensaries.

The Philadelphia agency also sponsored a summer camp program. In 1920, it acquired a camp facility near the city, which could accommodate about 450 boys each season. Much later, a large facility was acquired on the Delaware River near Stroudsburg, Pennsylvania.[23]

The Philadelphia Big Brother Association enjoyed strong financial support. Even at the height of the Great Depression, it could boast of an endowment fund of approximately $100,000, in addition to many other valuable assets.[24] The agency was founded on December 11, 1915, and incorporated in 1918. Charles Edwin Fox served as president until 1937, and was responsible for many of its advances during that period. Fox later served as the first president of the first national organization, the Big Brother and Big Sister Federation (chapter 3), and several Philadelphia association directors later played key roles in the formation of Big Brothers of America (chapter 4).

Jewish Big Brothers of Los Angeles

Professional, academically trained social workers have sometimes voiced a concern that Big Brothers and Big Sisters groups, with untrained lay volunteers, would attempt to undertake casework for which they were not qualified. The responses of Big Brothers and Big Sisters agencies have been to show a willingness to cooperate and work with professional social workers and social work agencies, to employ professionals as agency directors when possible, and to delineate carefully the duties of lay volunteers.

Soon after being organized in 1915, the Jewish Big Brothers Association of Los Angeles sought both to recognize and to define clearly the contributions of each area by establishing a social casework function and a one-to-one Big Brothers program within the same agency. This farsighted agency also pioneered in another area — that of using the camp experience as an observational and diagnostic tool in the treatment of troubled children, as well as a recreational activity. The groundwork for this program was laid in 1936 with the acquisition of Camp Max Straus near Glendale, California. Incidentally, after 1945, all agency professional staff vacancies had to be filled with persons with at least a master's degree in social work.[25]

Henry Straus was the first part-time executive secretary of the agency. He was succeeded in 1922 by Edna Shuster, who soon became a full-time executive and remained with the agency for twenty-three years. Years later, when recalling the organization's many successes in developing Little Brothers, Shuster noted that there had been at least one failure. She cited the case of notorious racketeer Mickey Cohen, whom the association had once matched with a Big Brother.[26]

Milton L. Goldberg joined the association as executive director in 1945. Like the late Meyer D. Levin of Baltimore, Goldberg has compiled one of the longest and most successful records of service in the Movement. Completing 40 years of service with the agency in 1985, Goldberg has been responsible for many notable advances in the field of child welfare. He holds a master's degree in social work from the University of California at Los Angeles and a master's degree in education from the University of Southern California. He has also been active in Scouting and has received several major awards for his work in that field.[27]

Catholic Big Sisters of Brooklyn

The Brooklyn (N.Y.) Catholic Big Sisters believed that their organization should serve as a central clearinghouse for the community's social needs, receiving and routing — to the appropriate dispensing agency — a wide variety of requests for services. As an aid in this endeavor, the Big Sisters developed and published a guide to community resources, which they used in directing Little Sisters to organizations that could supply specific needs, such as medical care, employment, or specialized education. The Brooklyn group did not do one-to-one matching. Rather, one Big Sister was expected to work with several Little Sisters, supplying individual counsel, guidance, and support only when particular difficulties were encountered.

A unique method was used to train the Big Sisters. Helen P. McCormick, founder of the Brooklyn group in 1918, and its first president, believed that Aristotle, and his "question and answer" method of teaching, represented one of the world's greatest advances in education. Accordingly, she held monthly meetings of all Big Sisters. Each was expected to speak to the group about her experiences since the previous meeting. Lively discussions ensued; questions and suggestions were freely solicited. The participants learned to question their own techniques, as well as profit from the experiences of others.

It was not surprising that McCormick initiated this approach. She was a lawyer and the first woman in America to serve as a district attorney. In addition, she was a teacher and trained social worker.

In the absence of a Big Brothers organization in Brooklyn at that time, the energetic Big Sisters accepted Little Brothers to age fourteen, at which time the boys were turned over to other social agencies.[28]

Big Brothers Association of Cincinnati

Much has already been said about the Jewish Big Brothers Association of Cincinnati, founded by Irvin F. Westheimer. During the period being reviewed, the agency pursued a program that was followed by many agencies. The Big Brothers first worked with boys who had come in contact with the courts, then gradually switched to a preventive program with nondelinquents. They enjoyed a higher degree of success with the latter group.

However, the high level of community support and enthusiasm for the association's activities was indeed unusual. According to one source, more than seven hundred persons were involved in various ways with the program by 1923.[29] Having observed its effectiveness, Cincinnati Jews were firmly committed to the Big Brothers concept, and their experience undoubtedly influenced other groups there to form agencies.

By the summer of 1928, there were five other such groups in the city. They were the Catholic Big Sisters, the Big Sister Club of the Federation of Churches, the Federation of Churches Big Brother Club, the Catholic Big Brothers League, and the Jewish Big Sisters Association.[30]

Big Sisters of Detroit

The path followed by the Big Sisters of Detroit was similar to the one taken by the three Big Sisters agencies in New York, described earlier. However, instead of a joint committee formed by representatives of three Big Sister groups, as was the case in New York, the Detroit Big Sisters created an Operating Committee which consisted of representatives from three service organizations with other areas of interest — the League of Catholic Women, the Council of Jewish Women, and the YWCA. A Big Sisters representative in each of the cooperating groups directed activities related to her own organization.

A Little Brother visits with his Big Brother at his office, about 1925.

The committee program was established in 1923. By February 1926, there were more Big Sisters volunteers than Little Sisters — approximately 325 of the former to about 250 of the latter.[31]

Milwaukee Agencies

Big Brothers activity began in Milwaukee in 1907. Two years later, as indicated in chapter 1, a Big Sisters group was formed, once purported to be the nation's first Big Sisters agency. Sometime before 1920, the two operations were combined to form Big Brothers and Big Sisters of Milwaukee — one of the first combination agencies in the nation, and the only one during this chapter's period for which significant data could be located. It was also one of the largest. By 1924, the agency was providing services to 750 boys and, as reported earlier, 600 girls. In 1919, Arthur J. Seher was named executive secretary of Big Brothers and Big Sisters of Milwaukee, and by 1926, he had eight paid assistants. His staff included, among others, a court representative, a health secretary, an employment and vocational guidance representative, and a housing secretary.[32]

Other Early Programs

Six other agencies that were founded before 1940 and their dates of incorporation were: the Catholic Big Brothers of New York, 1918 (although formed by 1915); Big Brothers of Dallas, 1927; Jewish Big Brothers Association of Boston, 1929; Big Brothers of Minneapolis, 1931; Big Brothers of Denver, 1938 (although formed many years before); and Big Brothers of Columbus, Ohio, 1939.

Founder of the Dallas agency was county Judge Fred H. Alexander.[33] He was assisted by Miss Jessie A. White, an officer of the Juvenile Court of Dallas.

The Boston group was organized in 1920 by the ten Federated Jewish Charities of that city. The agency's first executive director was Philip Slepian, a Harvard graduate with an extensive background in social work.[34] Like Levin of Baltimore and Goldberg of Los Angeles, Slepian was a notable Jewish pioneer in Big Brothers work. Over the years, he served as a consultant on juvenile problems to several Massachusetts governors. He was also a delegate to one of the White House conferences on youth. When he retired in 1961, he had completed forty-one years of service as the association's executive director.[35]

The Minneapolis Movement grew out of the Big Brother Committee of the Children's Protective Society of Minneapolis, which was formed in 1919 by Charles L. Burt, a social-service worker with the society.[36]

Many groups that organized between 1918 and 1944, under various auspices, later disbanded, and records of their formation and activities are not easily located; they exist perhaps only in the pages of old, unindexed local newspapers.

About 1933, representatives from twenty cities in Illinois formed a statewide Big Brothers Association. As far as can be determined, it was the first organization of its kind, although there are several state federations today. The objective of the Illinois organization was to accredit local groups that engaged in Big Brothers work. The association was sponsored by a division of the state Department of Public Welfare and governed by a board of directors, consisting of representatives from government, industry, labor, and the religious community.

The state was divided into six districts, and plans called for placing six professionally trained workers in each district. It was an ambitious undertaking, but evidently it was never entirely implemented. There is evidence that the association was still functioning as late as 1947, and that it was granting charters to both Big Brothers and Big Sisters groups at that time. Its ultimate fate could not be determined.

Activity among Blacks

Not much is known about early Big Brothers and Big Sisters activity among blacks. At a time in America when the armed services, churches, schools, and most social-service organizations and social clubs, as well

Dr. Randolph Taylor, first black Little Brother, later
became a Big Brother, board member and vice-
president of Big Brothers of America.

as most public facilities, were strictly segregated, it is unlikely that there
were many integrated agencies — units where both black and white
matches were made. Most work with black children appears to have
been carried out by all-black agencies.

However, the New York Big Brother Movement was accepting black
Big and Little Brothers by 1914. A report issued that year indicates
that the agency had seventy-seven black volunteers. The first black Big
Brother in that organization was Charlie Allison, a probation officer.
He was soon matched with Little Brother Randolph Taylor, a resident
of Harlem. Allison and Taylor are reported to be the nation's first black
Big Brother/Little Brother match—and what a successful match it was!

Allison kindled the fires of ambition in young Taylor and inspired
him to get a good education. After finishing high school in New York,
he entered Tufts University, where he received a bachelor of science
degree. He then completed both a master's degree and doctorate in
microbiology at Ohio State University. In the years that followed, he
coached football and taught biology, bacteriology, and microbiology at
several colleges and universities, including the School of Medicine of
Howard University.

Mrs. Edwin F. Horne and William Augustus Bell
were prominent black leaders in the Big Brothers/
Big Sisters Movement during the 1920s .

Wishing to repay his debt to the Movement, Dr. Taylor became a Big Brother in Washington, D.C., and his Little Brother later received a scholarship to the University of Notre Dame. In 1967, Dr. Taylor received the Big Brother of the Year Award from Big Brothers of the National Capitol Area. The presentation was made by famed columnist Drew Pearson, then president of that agency. Dr. Taylor was later named to the board of Big Brothers of America, and served as a vice-president of that organization. He died in 1972.[37]

Sometime after 1918, before the time it was incorporated, the Denver agency had an integrated operation, with about fifty black Big and Little Brother matches. However, after experiencing difficulty for several years in obtaining interested black Big Brothers, the agency discontinued the effort.[38]

Much of the all-black Big Brothers and Big Sisters work between the wars appears to have been sponsored by the Urban League. By 1923, a black Big Sisters Club in Brooklyn (N.Y.), sponsored by the Brooklyn Urban League, had approximately fifty Big Sisters.[39]

The chairperson of this group was Mrs. Edwin F. Horne, grandmother of world renowned singer and actress Lena Horne. An early feminist, as well as an activist in the NAACP, Mrs. Edwin F. Horne was also a member of the board of directors of the Big Brother and Big Sister Federation (chapter 3). Lena Horne's parents were divorced when she was quite young, and she was raised by her grandmother. Miss Horne later recalled that her grandmother gave her a piece of lasting advice. She told her to look people in the eye, speak distinctly, and never let anyone see her cry.

Another prominent black leader in the Movement during this period was William Augustus Bell of Atlanta, Georgia, who, according to one source, was president of the Tri-State Colored Big Brothers and Big Sisters Federation, which was evidently an organization of several black agencies in the Southeast. Mr. Bell was also a director of the Big Brother and Big Sister Federation. *Who's Who in Colored America*, vol. 1, 1927, indicates that Mr. Bell, a businessman and active in the Urban League, was a former college teacher and college president.

During the early 1920s, the Colored Big Sisters of the Louisville (Ky.) Urban League announced a campaign to separate delinquent reform school inmates from girls who were being housed there merely because of dependency.[40]

In 1923, the Colored Big Brothers Association of the Milwaukee Urban League was organized.[41] By 1928, there was an Urban League–sponsored Big Sisters program in Columbus, Ohio. Also by 1928, there were black Big Sisters organizations in Jersey City, New Jersey, and Toledo, Ohio, and a black Big Brothers and Big Sisters Movement in Memphis, Tennessee.[42]

Service Club Work

Many service clubs and fraternal groups engaged in Big Brothers/Big Sisters work during the period covered by this chapter, either within the framework of their own memberships, or as sponsors of associate groups. Included were such organizations as the Rotary, the Kiwanis, Lions, Knights of Columbus, Optimist, and B'nai B'rith. The extensive work of the Elks was covered in chapter 1.

The Rotary Club of Waterbury, Connecticut, was largely responsible for establishing the Big Brothers agency in that city—the first in that state—in 1922.[43]

At an annual meeting of the International Association of Lions Clubs, held during the early 1920s, a resolution, presented here in part, was adopted: "That every Lion should be a Big Brother to some handicapped boy or girl, and to the end that such work may be done systematically and the best results accomplished, we endorse . . . the Big Brother Movement." At that time, there were 685 Lions clubs in the United States and Canada, and they had a membership of 32,225 men.[44] A good example of work by this organization was the Big Brothers agency sponsored by the Lions Club of St. Paul, Minnesota, in 1925. The club underwrote the salaries of the agency's executive secretary and a stenographer.[45]

Local Kiwanis clubs created Big Brothers committees to coordinate Big Brothers work in their communities. In San Antonio, Texas, the Kiwanis Committee hired a public defender to investigate cases of juvenile offenders and make recommendations to the courts regarding their dispositions. Previously, youthful lawbreakers were sent to jail along with hardened criminals. As a result of the Kiwanis Program, many of these children were placed on probation, and reported to the public defender. The Big Brothers Committee helped them to find employment and in several other ways.[46] The Kiwanis Big Brothers Committee in Harrisburg, Illinois, asked the county judge to place juvenile cases involving boys under its supervision. The Harrisburg program called for a Big Brother to be appointed for each referral, whose duty "will be to make a companion of the boy, win his confidence, learn his ambitions and inspire him to become a useful citizen."[47]

Another example of Big Brothers activity by a service organization was the Big Brothers group in Sharon, Pennsylvania, sponsored by the Optimist Club. The group's first activity was to befriend the community's small newsboys.[48] In 1925, the Big Brothers Club of the Pittsburgh, Pennsylvania, Knights of Columbus reported a membership of five hundred men.[49] During the mid-twenties, many colleges and universities also sponsored Big Brothers and Big Sisters groups.

From time to time, the American Legion was mentioned in relation to Big Brothers activity, generally in connection with the Legion's

Americanism Commission. It is not known, however, if legionnaires ever became Big Brothers within the framework of their organization. In June 1924, Allan Waters of the Legion's Community and Civic Betterment Bureau, wrote to the Big Brother and Sister Federation (discussed in chapter 3) in New York and requested assistance in answering queries from Legion posts across the country. The federation's executive secretary, Rowland C. Sheldon, not only assured Waters of the federation's full cooperation, but also presented a rather comprehensive program for the Legion to consider.

Sheldon proposed that the Legion utilize its many local posts as information agents to help boys and girls from small towns who go to cities to seek employment. Parents of a boy or girl job seeker would contact a local Legion official and tell him where their son or daughter was going, and where he or she intended to live in the city. The local Legion official would then contact a counterpart in the city, who would call on the boy or girl and appoint a Big Brother from the city Legion post for the boy, or a Big Sister from the Legion Auxiliary for the girl. It would be the function of the Big Brother or Sister to report the young man's or young woman's activities to the Legion representative "back home" who, in turn, would report to the parents.[50] Although seemingly overpaternalistic, the suggested plan must be viewed in the context of the times, when rural young people seeking employment in large cities were neither so old nor so sophisticated as their modern counterparts. However, there is no evidence that Sheldon's suggestions were ever implemented. Perhaps, even then, the procedure appeared more to represent what today might be characterized as "Orwellian Big Brothering."[51]

Publicity

Any social-service Movement as popular and prolific as Big Brothers/Big Sisters was bound to attract the attention of the media. Activities of the Movement were of special interest to local newspapers. These publications reported organizational efforts, carried notices of meetings, listed special events, and presented feature material. In 1925, Arthur H. Seher, executive secretary of the Milwaukee Big Brothers Organization, conducted a newspaper support survey of twenty-two Big Brothers and Big Sisters agencies throughout the country. He found that, on the whole, the papers were giving the Movement strong support.[52]

There were marked differences of opinion, however, among agencies on the value of such support. To avoid any bad publicity, Big Brothers of Philadelphia stated that the agency would "rather keep away from the Newspapers" altogether.[53] Jewish Big Brothers of Pittsburgh expressed a similar feeling and gave their opinions for staying as far away as possible from the fourth estate: First, this Agency felt that the best qualified Big Brothers were not attracted by publicity. Second, it considered enthusiasm generated by publicity as short-lived. Furthermore, the agency thought that dramatization of the needs of Little Brothers should be avoided. Finally, the Jewish Big Brothers did not want to be identified as an agency that dealt with delinquent or maladjusted boys.

In sharp contrast, the Big Sisters of Rochester (N.Y.) stated that the agency was "always gratified by the number of interested people who come to offer their services as Big Sisters after newspaper publicity of any kind."[54] And, Big Brothers of Scranton (Pa.) stated that "a good deal of our work in Scranton is due to the publicity that we receive from local newspapers."[55]

Agencies also differed in their opinions of the type of newspaper coverage that was positive or acceptable. Some felt that it was all right to report notices of general meetings, social events, notices of classes for Big and Little Brothers, and financial reports, but that human interest stories should be avoided for fear of exploiting a child. Others felt that human interest features were acceptable and effective. Some of the agencies that frowned on human interest material in the public press themselves issued pamphlets that contained such material — the rationale apparently being their full editorial control.[56]

The *New York Times* provided excellent coverage of Big Brothers and Big Sisters activities in its area. It reported annual meetings and frequently included the remarks of Movement officials and other speakers in the articles. The *Times* also published interviews with Movement leaders. Whereas newspaper coverage of Big Brothers/Big Sisters work was good, feature presentations in national publications were rare during this period between the wars, perhaps because of the reluctance of agencies to furnish case material. An article on the Big Brothers Movement, which appeared in the *Rotarian*, the publication of Rotary International, was reprinted in the September 1936 issue of *Reader's Digest*. An article on Big Brothers and Big Sisters appeared in the September 22, 1937, issue of *Christian Science Monitor*. There are few other examples.

A popular novelist of the day, Rex Beach, wrote a short story that was titled simply "Big Brother." The story, based on a Big Brother and Little Brother relationship in a gang-infested neighborhood of New York, became the basis for a Paramount motion picture with the same title as the story. Released on December 23, 1923, for the Christmas theater trade, the picture starred actor Tom Moore and popular child star Mickey Bennett. The story was about a small boy, "Midge" Murray, whose older brother was killed in a gang fight. As a dying request, the brother asked a pal, Jimmy Donovan, to look out for Midge, who now had no one else to care for him. Jimmy did the best he could to replace Midge's brother. Then, one day he attended a church meeting and

Scenes from the Paramount Picture *Big
Brother*, released in 1923.

heard about the Big Brothers Movement for the first time. He quickly mended his ways and became a real Big Brother to Little Brother Midge.[57]

A reviewer, writing in *Life* magazine for January 24, 1924, had high praise for the film. The writer and director were complimented for making the story "realistic, depending on actual life instead of on the established tricks which are part of the equipment of every successful hokum vendor." Concluded the reviewer, "'Big Brother' contains a moral lesson, to wit: 'It takes a tough picture to put over a convincing moral lesson—and 'Big Brother' is just that.'" It is not known if copies of this silent movie still exist; several major motion picture archives were searched to no avail. But the Rex Beach story can still be found in some large city libraries.

The Movement enjoyed the public acknowledgment and support of Presidents Theodore Roosevelt, Warren G. Harding, Calvin Coolidge, Herbert Hoover, and Franklin D. Roosevelt. Said President Harding, "I believe in Big Brother work with all my heart. There is nothing finer in life than a kindly word or deed at the right moment. It often saves the young man and is sometimes the turning point in his life, inspiring him with renewed courage and a fresh hold in life."[58]

President Harding accepted an invitation to attend the annual boys' picnic, sponsored by the Seattle (Wash.) Elks' Big Brother Committee, on August 15, 1922. Every boy in the city had been invited, and the president was to administer the oath of allegiance to the thousands who were expected to attend.[59] Harding did not make it, but he did attend a similar event the following year, just before his death. Before accepting the latter invitation of the Elks, Harding, a Big Brother Elk himself, indicated that he would attend the picnic only if he could come as Big Brother Harding, not as the President of the United States.[60] A monument was erected on the spot where the president stood as he addressed the boys. The memorial was demolished several years ago to make room for an expansion project at the Seattle Zoo.

Big Brother Movement of New York

A discussion of the activities of the Big Brother Movement of New York between 1918 and 1944 has been left to last, not only because this agency and its founder, Ernest K. Coulter, were principally responsible for inspiring the organized Movement in America, but also because the officials of this "flagship" agency played a major role in the creation of the first national federation — the Big Brother and Big Sister Federation, Inc.

In 1920, this agency's 600 Big Brothers served nearly 1,300 Little Brothers, 350 of whom were referred by the Children's Court. Only

Camping was an important part of the early New York Big Brother Movement's program; for many years, the Movement operated its own camp near Stillwater, New Jersey.

71 failures were recorded during the year.[61] At the organization's annual dinner in 1926, at which then heavyweight boxing champion Gene Tunney was the speaker, agency General Secretary Joseph H. McCoy reported that 1,390 Little Brothers had been cared for during the previous year. Of these, McCoy said, only 37 had been rearraigned by the court — the best annual record since the agency's founding.[62] By 1933, the number aided had grown to 1,984, with a rearraignment of only 68 cases.[63] The *New York Times* called the Movement one of the city's most important social-service agencies.

The New York Movement was fortunate in being able to attract many well-known people as volunteers. Among the agency's 966 Big Brothers volunteers in 1944 were such personages as Edward R. Stettinius, U.S. secretary of state; Orson D. Munn, then editor and publisher of *Scientific American*; Denys Wortman, a United Features syndicate cartoonist, and William S. Paley, head of CBS.[64] Comedian Eddie Cantor, mentioned earlier, spoke at both the twentieth and thirtieth anniversary celebrations of the New York Movement.

Noteworthy during the 1920s was the formation by the New York Movement of a little theater group, known as the Knickerbocker Boy Players. In 1923, the group presented a Big Brothers staff-written play, *Fingers*, to a summer camp circuit. So successful were their efforts that hundreds of requests were received from throughout the country for copies of the play. It subsequently was published by Samuel French, New York, and amateurs were permitted to perform the play without paying a royalty. *Fingers* told the story of a young pickpocket who, in escaping from the police, finds himself in a boys club, where he is befriended by a Big Brother. The boy ceases his delinquent behavior and becomes a useful citizen.[65]

The Big Brother Movement of New York probably enjoyed greater community support than almost any other agency in the nation. A favorite method of recruiting new volunteers in the mid-twenties was Movement-sponsored luncheons, to which men who had attained success in various fields were invited and told of the need for new Big Brothers. It was reported that several new volunteers joined the Movement after each luncheon. A speakers bureau, featuring Big Brothers, was another useful device for publicizing the work of the Movement.[66]

Rowland C. Sheldon, previously mentioned several times, served as general secretary of the Big Brother Movement of New York from 1912 until 1924, when he became executive secretary of the Big Brother and Big Sister Federation. Sheldon's background will be discussed in more detail in the next chapter. Joseph H. McCoy succeeded Sheldon, and served the agency until his retirement in 1956 (see chapter 7).

Big Brothers/Big Sisters work between the two World Wars took many forms and moved in many directions. As indicated at the beginning of the chapter, the omnifarious efforts shared a common need of dealing with the mushrooming problems of young people, a common name, and, in most cases, a strong belief in the remedy of one-to-one friendship. A major emphasis on service to children from single-parent homes had not yet occurred. Although the early literature, as well as the literature of this era, often spoke of situations where a parent was missing, aid to such children, as a major objective of the Movement, was not mentioned. This concept, as a tenet of the Movement, was not developed fully until after World War II.

There was one other cohesive force during this period that promoted a national effort and contributed an element of professionalism to the Movement's diverse activities — the Big Brother and Big Sister Federation (BB/BSF). It was not the purpose of the federation to establish uniform practices or standards during its early years. Rather, it sought to serve as a forum for the exchange of ideas on the handling of juvenile delinquency. It also aided in the development of new agencies and provided information and counsel to existing organizations. The next chapter focuses on the activities of the federation, which, during its twenty years of existence, had a profound effect on the Movement.

* * * *

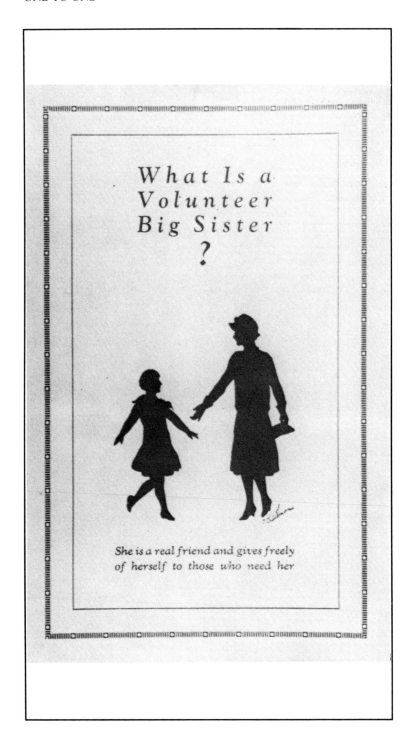

Notes to Chapter 2

1. Joseph F. Hecht, *The History of the Jewish Big Brother League, Inc.* (Baltimore: King Brothers, 1973), pp. 60–62, 65.
2. Ibid., pp. 87–88.
3. Ibid., pp. 11–12.
4. "I See by the Papers," *The Ounce*, Big Brother and Big Sister Federation (BB/BSF), May 1922, Archives and Special Collections (A&SC), The City College of The City University of New York (CUNY).
5. Alice Mary Kimball, "The 'Big Sisters' of the Lonely Girl," *World's Work* (July 1917):306–310.
6. "Progress in the Field," *The Ounce* (BB/BSF), September 1925, 16, A&SC, The City College, CUNY.
7. History of the Catholic Big Brothers, Inc. (Los Angeles), a manuscript on file with that agency.
8. Alissa Franc Keir, "A Big Sister Wanted in Every Town in the World," *Success Magazine* (June 1925):53.
9. "Aid Needed for Good Work," Letter to the Editor from Bird S. Coler, *New York Times*, May 3, 1928, 26:7.
10. "Bal Bleu a Fine Spectacle at Ritz," *New York Times*, May 6, 1919, 15:3.
11. "Big Sisters to Give Friendship Tea," *New York Times*, September 30, 1929, 20:5.
12. Kimball, "Big Sisters," p. 130.
13. "Big Sisters Work at New Problems," *New York Times*, February 19, 1928, sec. 9, 10:1.
14. Robert M. Hyndman, "Working with Boys," *The Pepper Box*, official publication of the Rotary Club of St. Louis, July 19, 1938.
15. History of the St. Louis Big Brother Organization, folder 67, Big Brothers of America (BBA) records, Social Welfare History Archives (SWHA), University of Minnesota.
16. Ibid.
17. Ibid.
18. "Big Brother Eddie Cantor," *The Ounce* (BB/BSF), March 1922, 4, A&SC, The City College, CUNY.
19. Letter to the Editor, *The Ounce* (BB/BSF), July 1922, 3, A&SC, The City College, CUNY.
20. "Little Brother in St. Louis," *The Ounce* (BB/BSF), August 1927, 6, A&SC, The City College, CUNY.
21. "410 School-Age Boys Had Counsel in 1932 of 150 Big Brothers," *St. Louis Globe Democrat*, January 22, 1933.
22. Samuel Sibulkin, "How We Do It in Cleveland," *The Ounce* (BB/BSF), Summer 1928, 5–6, A&SC, The City College, CUNY.
23. "Brief Chronological History of the Big Brother Association of Philadelphia," Big Brothers records, Paley Library Archives, Temple University.
24. Annual report, Big Brother Association of Philadelphia, 1936.
25. *Jewish Big Brothers Association and Camp Max Straus*, a pamphlet published by Jewish Big Brothers Association of Los Angeles, about 1980.
26. Telephone interview with Edna Shuster by author on January 12, 1983.
27. Biographical material on file with the Jewish Big Brothers Association of Los Angeles.
28. Grace Lawrence, "An Ideal (*sic*) That Works," *The Ounce* (BB/BSF), February 1926, 7, A&SC, The City College, CUNY.

29. "I See by the Papers," *The Ounce* (BB/BSF), July 1923, 8, A&SC, The City College, CUNY.
30. Membership list, Big Brother and Big Sister Federation, June 1, 1928, *The Ounce* (BB/BSF), Summer 1928, A&SC, The City College, CUNY.
31. Mrs. Kingsley MacGuffey, "The Work of the Big Sisters in Detroit," *The Ounce* (BB/BSF), February 1926, 12, 17, A&SC, The City College, CUNY.
32. R. R. Kelley, "Milwaukee Enters upon Nineteenth Year of Service," *The Ounce* (BB/BSF), January 1926, 13, 19, A&SC, The City College, CUNY.
33. Historical sketch, Dallas Big Brothers, folder 60-61, BBA records, SWHA.
34. Leo Shapiro, "Jewish Big Brothers Proud of Fine 25-Year Record," a reprint from the *Boston Sunday Globe*, January 21, 1945, folder 65, BBA records, SWHA.
35. Philip Slepian obituary, *Big Brothers Ambassador*, Summer 1972, 2.
36. History of Big Brothers, Inc., of Minneapolis, folder 66, BBA records, SWHA.
37. "First Negro Little Brother Receives D.C.'s Big Brother of the Year," *Big Brother Bulletin*, December 1967, 6.
38. History of the Big Brother Movement of Denver, folder 64, BBA records, SWHA.
39. Mrs. Edwin F. Horne, "The Problem of the Negro Girl," *The Ounce* (BB/BSF), February 1923, 3, 7, A&SC, The City College, CUNY.
40. "Urban League Plans Big Sister Work among Colored Girls," *The Ounce* (BB/BSF), April 1923, 7, A&SC, The City College, CUNY.
41. "Progress in the Field," *The Ounce* (BB/BSF), July 1925, 16, A&SC, The City College, CUNY.
42. Membership list, see note 30 above.
43. "What Rotary Clubs Are Doing for Boys," *The Ounce* (BB/BSF), June 1923, 4, A&SC, The City College, CUNY.
44. "Lions Become Big Brothers," *The Ounce* (BB/BSF), November 1923, 5, A&SC, The City College, CUNY.
45. "Lions Club Undertakes Big Brother Work," *The Ounce* (BB/BSF), August 1925, 6, A&SC, The City College, CUNY.
46. "The Kiwanis Club and the Under-Privileged Child," *The Ounce* (BB/BSF), March 1923, 2, A&SC, The City College, CUNY.
47. "Kiwanis Club Starts Big Brother Movement," *The Ounce* (BB/BSF), April 1923, 4, A&SC, The City College, CUNY.
48. "Sharon, Pa., Optimist Club Undertakes Big Brother Work," *The Ounce* (BB/BSF), September 1925, 16, A&SC, The City College, CUNY.
49. "Progress in the Field," *The Ounce* (BB/BSF), July 1925, 16.
50. Memorandum to Mr. Barton, a Legion official, from Allan Waters of the Legion's Community and Civic Better Bureau, November 20, 1925, on file at American Legion's National Headquarters, Indianapolis, Indiana.
51. George Orwell, *Nineteen Eighty-Four* (New York: Harcourt, Brace & World, 1949).
52. Arthur J. Seher, "Publicity Survey Brings Composite Opinion from Twenty-two Organizations," *The Ounce* (BB/BSF), July 1925, 7, A&SC, The City College, CUNY.
53. Ibid.
54. Ibid.
55. Ibid.
56. Ibid., pp. 7, 14.

57. "Big Brother," a Paramount Picture with Tom Moore, *The Ounce* (BB/BSF), November 1923, 7, A&SC, The City College, CUNY.

58. President Warren G. Harding quoted in *The Ounce* (BB/BSF), May 1923, 1, A&SC, The City College, CUNY.

59. "Harding to Attend Big Brother Picnic," *The Ounce* (BB/BSF), July 1922, 5, A&SC, The City College, CUNY.

60. "Big Brother Harding," *The Ounce* (BB/BSF), August 1923, 1, A&SC, The City College, CUNY.

61. "Big Brothers Save Boys on the Brink," *New York Times*, February 13, 1921, sec. 2, 4:1.

62. "Gene Tunney Extols the Big Brothers," *New York Times*, December 2, 1926, 16:2.

63. "Aided 1,984 Boys in Year," *New York Times*, February 16, 1933, 17:3.

64. Douglas Gilbert, "Big Brother," *New York World-Telegram*, December 1, 1944, 22; box 70, BBA records, SWHA.

65. " 'Fingers' Is Published," *The Ounce* (BB/BSF), January 1925, 7, A&SC, The City College, CUNY.

66. "Big Brother Movement of New York Campaigning for New Members," *The Ounce* (BB/BSF), November 1925, 20, A&SC, The City College, CUNY.

3

The First Federation:
Toward Greater Professionalism
(1917–1937)

Whenever anyone has a special interest or concern, he or she is apt to seek out others who are similarly motivated. When enough people share an area of involvement, an organization may be formed to promote mutual interest, effect improvements, share experiences, and exchange ideas. Local organizations, in turn, improve their effectiveness by forming national bodies, alliances, or federations.

Considering the rapid, spontaneous creation of local Big Brothers and Big Sisters organizations in every part of the country during the first two decades of this century, it is not surprising that local leaders soon sought the advantages of national unity.

The first formal national conference of local leaders took place in Grand Rapids, Michigan, on May 28 and 29, 1917, when delegates from Big Brothers and Big Sisters agencies in a dozen states, together with several delegates from Canada, gathered to discuss solutions to common problems dealing with delinquency, tell of local activities, and lay the groundwork for a concerted national effort. "C'mon Skinnay [sic] to the Big Brothers and Sisters Conference," proclaimed the cover of the conference brochure, in what was undoubtedly current idiom. In a novel depiction, the bold invitation appeared to be scrawled in cursive writing on the side of a roughly hewed child's fort or playhouse.

An article in the *Grand Rapids News* for May 6, 1914, three years before, had indicated that a national conference had long been planned and that the city would seek the first meeting.

Ernest K. Coulter, Alexander H. Kaminsky from Jewish Big Brothers of New York, and leaders of other New York area agencies appear to have played major roles in bringing the group together. However, Dr.

Apostles of the Big Brothers and Big Sisters Movement

Delegates to the first national conference of Big Brothers and Big Sisters, held in Grand Rapids, Michigan, in May 1917. Irvin F. Westheimer (*circled left*) and Ernest K. Coulter (*circled center*) were among those on the program. Others in photograph could not be identified.

Grand Rapids Herald

H. W. Dingman, then president of the Grand Rapids agency, was probably responsible for bringing the group to his city. The format and discussion groups were not unlike those of a similar conference today, but at least one thing has changed. The registration fee for the two-day meeting was only $1.50. An extra $1.50 fee was required if one wished to attend the concluding banquet. Excellent hotel accommodations were priced at $2.00 per day. Delegates were reminded that "kids dress informally and so shall we."

According to the program, delegates at the first general session on May 28 heard representatives from the Elks and B'nai B'rith describe Big Brothers work in their organizations. At dinner that evening, Ernest K. Coulter described the beginning of the organized Big Brother Movement of New York. At a Big Brothers section meeting on May 29, Irvin F. Westheimer discussed "The Problem of Boys over Sixteen." And at a Big Sisters section on that date, Frances Schneebeli, from one of the New York area agencies, spoke on "Correcting Delinquency in Older Girls."

Covered at a roundtable luncheon discussion on May 29, as indicated by the program, were such subjects as "Keeping Big Sisters Interested," "Big Brother Work and the Courts," "Juvenile Delinquency in Wartime," and "Kids and the Gang Trait." At a late-afternoon session, William A. Schwab, of the Jewish Big Brother League of Baltimore, spoke on the need for the Movement to cooperate with other welfare agencies.[1] At one of the general sessions Israel Cowen, of Chicago Big Brothers, suggested a Big Brothers plan for world peace after World War I, and received prominent coverage in a Grand Rapids newspaper. Cowen suggested that the scope of the Movement be enlarged to include large nations, which would become "Big Brothers" to the smaller countries after hostilities ended. "Why not make our idea fit in with the future so that the spirit of brotherhood will end world delinquency?" asked Cowen.[2]

Speaking at the final banquet, Mrs. Schneebeli asked the Big Brothers to urge their Little Brothers to be more considerate of little girls. Said Mrs. Schneebeli, "You Big Brothers find enjoyment in your work, but we Big Sisters find only tragedy, which is brought on largely by the Little Brothers who are needing attention. It is up to you Big Brothers to teach the boys respect for the girls," she concluded.[3]

At an organizational meeting, the delegates created an International Advisory Council (IAC) as the first step in forming what would later become the Big Brother and Big Sister Federation (BB/BSF). Ernest K. Coulter was elected president and Dr. H. W. Dingman became secretary-treasurer. Vice-presidents included Julius Rosenwald, Chicago; Judge William F. McCarthy, Kansas City; Judge Thomas F. Scully, Chicago; Jesse Lillenthaw, San Francisco; Judge Franklin C.

Hoyt, New York; Judge H. D. Jewell, Grand Rapids; Dr. Franklin Johnson, Toronto; Judge Thomas C. Hennings, St. Louis; Mrs. Willard Parker, New York; Judge Robert J. Wilkin, New York; August Herrmann, Cincinnati; Judge Julian Mack, Chicago; Mrs. Caroline B. Wilcox, Grand Rapids; and Judge Cornelius Collins, New York.

Among those named to the Executive Committee were Alexander Kaminsky, New York; Irvin Westheimer, Cincinnati; Lady Armstrong, New York; William A. Schwab, Baltimore; and Mrs. Frances Schneebeli, New York. The object of the IAC was "to assist in the formation of new organizations, spreading of propaganda and interesting various other organizations in the movement, and to arrange the details of future conferences."[4] In addition to soliciting membership from Big Brothers and Big Sisters organizations in the United States and Canada, IAC delegates decided to ask established Big Brothers groups in Japan, Australia, and other countries to join the new organization. With the exception of Canada and the Philippines, there is no indication that any foreign groups ever became members.

The Grand Rapids press reported that muckraker and journalist Upton Sinclair attended the conference, but no other reference to his presence could be found.[5] As indicated in chapter 1, Sinclair did have a deep interest in current social and political issues. Writer of more than eighty books, he is best known for *The Jungle*, an exposé of the meat-packing industry, which helped bring about many reforms.

Although an obscure reference to a conference in St. Louis the following year was noted, no other information on a federation meeting in 1918 could be located. That a meeting was held somewhere is indicated by the consecutive numbering system of later conferences. A conference was held in Cincinnati in 1919, but no information on the proceedings was found, nor could information be found on a conference in 1920.

Rowland C. Sheldon, mentioned several times previously in connection with the New York Movement, became part-time executive secretary of the IAC in 1920, officially devoting one-fifth of his time to its activities and the remaining four-fifths to New York. Sheldon had a reputation as an excellent administrator. After attending the U.S. Military Academy during the latter part of the last century, he joined the faculty of the Montclair (N.J.) Academy, where he taught military tactics and mathematics and later became commandant. After leaving the Academy in 1912, he joined the New York Movement as general secretary, remaining in that position until joining the national organization on a full-time basis in 1924. His name and that of the federation became almost synonymous.[6]

Rowland C. Sheldon, who became
full-time executive secretary of the Big
Brother and Big Sister Federation, Inc.
in 1924.

On November 2, 1921, the IAC was incorporated in the State of New York, becoming The Big Brother and Big Sister Federation, Inc. (BB/BSF). Officers of the federation were presidents of prominent Big Brothers and Big Sisters organizations. The Board of Directors, elected to staggered one-, two-, three-, and four-year terms, came from eleven states and Canada. The board functioned through an Executive Committee, whose eight members from the New York and Philadelphia areas met monthly and provided direction for the part-time executive secretary. The federation was supported by donations and affiliated agency fees. Each agency paid ten dollars per year.

President of the new federation was Charles Edwin Fox, who was also president of the Big Brother Association, Inc., of Philadelphia. Vice-presidents included George MacDonald, treasurer of the Catholic Big Brother League, Inc., New York; Israel Cowen, former president of the Jewish Big Brothers of Chicago; Lady Armstrong, president of Catholic Big Sisters of New York; Mrs. Sidney C. Borg, president of Jewish Big Sisters of New York; Mrs. G. V. R. Mechin, president, Big Sisters, Inc., St. Louis; Clarence W. Noble, former president of the Toronto Big Brother Movement, Inc.; and C. L. Burton, president of the Toronto Movement.

Named secretary was Mrs. Willard Parker, Jr., president of Big Sisters, Inc., New York, and a founder, along with Mrs. W. K. Vanderbilt, Sr., of the Protestant Big Sisters of New York. Chairman of the Executive Committee was C. Robert Langenbacher, a member of the Board of Directors of the Big Brother Movement, Inc., of New York. On October 5, 1921, a delegation of federation members had called on President Warren G. Harding at the White House, and both he and Mrs. Harding had agreed to become patrons of the soon to be incorporated organization.

Ernest K. Coulter became honorary president of BB/BSF. Twenty-seven youth and service club leaders, both inside and outside the Movement, were named honorary vice-presidents, including the president of the Girl Scouts, the Supreme Knight of the Knights of Columbus, president of the Kiwanis Club, International, president of the Boy Scouts of America, president of the General Federated Women's Clubs, and the executive secretary of the Boys' Club Federation.[7] A national conference was held in Toronto in 1921, but as in 1918, 1919, and 1920 no information on the proceedings is available. The federation shared office space with the New York Big Brother Movement at 200 Park Avenue.

Actually, the Big Brother and Big Sister Federation was not the first federation. In the fall of 1914, Big Brothers and Big Sisters agencies in the Greater New York area formed an area federation. It is not known if this organization continued to function after the formation of the national group. The founding date of a small black federation, the Tri-State Colored Big Brothers and Big Sisters Federation, mentioned in chapter 2, could not be determined.

Publicity

The new national federation early realized the value of good communications. As a major part of its program, and involving a major portion of its budget, it established a publication as a link among its staff, member agencies, and the general public. Named *The Ounce*, from "An ounce of prevention is worth a pound of cure," the well-designed and well-prepared little tabloid made its debut in February 1922, with an issue of five thousand copies. *The Ounce* was reproduced by letterpress, contained a considerable number of photographs, and, even by today's standards, was an excellent publication in its class.

Mailed to all Big Brothers and Big Sisters organizations, the publication also went to ten civic and religious groups, as well as to public libraries, college and high school libraries, public schools in larger cities, and many reformatories.[8] The May 1922 issue, for example, went to

5,338 recipients in every state and fourteen foreign countries, although there were only 112 paid subscribers by then. Fifty of the last number went to Big Brothers and Big Sisters agencies, as part of their federation membership dues. A subscription to *The Ounce* cost one dollar per year, with the masthead proudly proclaiming that you could get one ounce for a dime and twelve ounces for a dollar.

It is not known who produced the first issues. In later mastheads, the editor is listed as Martin Clary, who was responsible for the federation's publicity and public relations efforts. Listed as associate editor was Beatrice Black. By 1927, the editor was listed as Mary Childs Nearney. *The Ounce* appeared as a monthly until August 1927, when it became a quarterly. Publication apparently ceased after the Summer 1928 issue. No later issues could be located, and the Union List of Serials (a comprehensive list of regularly issued publications) does not record any later issues. An indication of the importance of *The Ounce* in Big Brothers and Big Sisters work is the fact that the federation earmarked more than one-third of its $15,490 annual budget for the publication in 1923.[9] With such a large circulation, a number of copies of *The Ounce* should still exist. Copies preserved by the Russell Sage Foundation, and later donated to the City College of New York, can be found in the college's archives.

Executive Secretary Sheldon, always extremely active with the New York Movement, continued his hectic pace on behalf of the federation. On one whirlwind tour, lasting 38 days, he visited 27 cities, made 17 speeches to a total of more than 1,500 persons, and had conferences with 126 persons. His objective was to contact local leaders who were capable of sparking community interest in Big Brothers and Big Sisters work, and convince them of the value of such activity. He hoped that they, in turn, would begin local campaigns that would result in the formation of new agencies. He must have achieved success. When Sheldon began his work with the federation, it had fifteen member agencies. At the end of his first year, fifty agencies had affiliated with the national organization.[10]

The federation's sixth annual conference was held in Minneapolis on June 6, 7, and 8, 1922. Local hosts were the Big Sister Committee of the Minneapolis Women's Cooperative Alliance, and the Big Brother Committee of the Children's Protective Society. A new word, "Brister," was coined for the conference — meaning both Big Brothers and Big Sisters. Each affiliated agency that had paid the ten-dollar annual membership fee was entitled to send three voting delegates.[11] Approximately fifteen member agencies sent delegates; eleven were represented by proxy.

The delegates adopted several significant resolutions. They resolved that December 3 be designated as Big Brother and Big Sister Day (this was the day that Ernest K. Coulter met with the Men's Club of New York's Central Presbyterian Church, and suggested that each member befriend a delinquent child), and that the President of the United States and the Governor-General of Canada be requested to issue proclamations to that effect. The group also empowered the Board of Directors to have the names *Big Brother* and *Big Sister* copyrighted.[12] There are no indications that these resolutions were implemented.

Early Federation Statistics

Statistics recorded at the convention in 1922 presented a good picture of agency work. Of 106 known Big Brothers and Big Sisters organizations in the United States and Canada, 50 were affiliated with the federation. Forty-four of the latter submitted data to the conference, which indicated that they represented a total agency membership of 5,289 volunteers, who were assisted by 99 paid workers—a ratio of one paid professional to 53 volunteers.

Agency representatives (volunteers and paid staff) assisted 16,110 children during the year (which is presumed to be the twelve months of 1921), 68 percent of whom had never been arraigned in any court. Sixty-two percent of these children were between the ages of ten and sixteen, 32 percent were over sixteen, and 6 percent were under the age of ten.

Of the more than 16,000 cases handled, over 11,000 were befriended for the first time. Less than half of the new cases were assigned to volunteers. The others were provided with short-term benefits by agency executives. Such benefits included the securing of more than 3,000 jobs for Little Brothers and Sisters; 698 children were placed in foster homes, 45 were maintained in boarding schools, 249 boys were assigned to farm work, and more than 1,000 children were sent to camps.

Volunteers saw their Little Brothers and Little Sisters an average of 3.6 times each month. Each agency spent an average of $10.66 per year on each child. The average agency budget was $7,089. Affiliates were financed by individual contributions and by their sponsoring organizations. Twenty-two of the fifty federation members were nonsectarian, whereas five served only Catholic children, eleven confined their work to Jewish referrals, four were for Protestants, and two served black children.[13]

Charles Edwin Fox was reelected president of the federation in 1922. First vice-president was Lady Armstrong. Other vice-presidents included the Honorable Franklin C. Hoyt, Mrs. Sidney C. Borg, Mrs. G. V. R. Mechin, Clarence W. Noble, C. L. Burton, and George Mac-Donald. Mrs. Willard Parker was reelected secretary. Honorary vice-presidents included John D. Rockefeller, Jr., of New York.[14]

A New Program

An innovative rehabilitation program was introduced at the conference by Milton L. Daugherty, secretary of the St. Louis agency, and
unanimously adopted by the delegates. Known informally as the "boy
exchange," it called for moving Little Brothers to homes in new areas,
when past deeds and reputations were likely to hamper reform programs
in their hometowns. Big Brothers in the new areas would help such
boys make fresh starts. The case of a St. Louis delinquent, who was
successfully relocated in Kansas City, was cited. Living in a city where
his past was not generally known, the boy was reported doing very well.

Daugherty cited three other cases that would likely result in transfers.
One involved a St. Louis boy who could not overcome a gang problem.
Another concerned a boy who could not study at home, where a family
of six lived in one room. A third boy could not refrain from stealing
because of peer pressure.

Each case was to be tailored to individual needs. Some miscreants
would do better if moved to smaller towns, whereas a move to a larger
city would benefit others. Accordingly, the New York Movement indicated that it planned to send a number of children to rural areas, and
the Grand Rapids agency reported that it would send a boy to New
York, because he had an interest in learning the shipping trade.

Under the program, the originating city would pay the boy's expenses
to the new area, where a representative from the local Big Brothers
agency would meet him. The boy would be assigned to a new Big
Brother, who would help him find a new home and suitable employment. Regular reports would be made to the hometown agency. Many
of the delegates said that they would try the technique, but no additional information relating to either participation or experience was
ever noted.[15]

Minimum Standards

A basic requirement of any successful federation or association is that
its affiliates or members subscribe to a set of standards. In fact, such
adherence is generally critical to the organization's existence. The
Board of Directors of BB/BSF evidently knew how important it was for
the federation's early standards to be accepted. However, it was also
keenly aware of the wide variety of practices discussed in chapters 1
and 2, the varied objectives, and the many local sponsoring groups
with their own rules and standards. The board's members knew that
rules and regulations that were too strict and too confining, too soon,
could easily abort the federation's efforts to achieve Movement unity.
Strict compliance, such as that required of today's agencies by Big
Brothers/Big Sisters of America, was avoided.

Instead, the early federation used a softer approach with phrases like "in determining the endorsement of any organization . . . the Federation will give careful consideration to compliance" and "the following standards . . . have been adopted by the Board of Directors as the minima to be desired."[16] The standards, published in 1922, are presented here in their entirety because of their role in helping to standardize activity at that early date and to enable today's volunteers and professionals to compare them with current requirements. The board required:

1. Individual and personal effort on the part of volunteers in behalf of the children (one-to-one concept)

2. Reasonable efficiency in the conduct of the work, and reasonable adequacy of equipment, both material and personal

3. Active and responsible governing body holding regular meetings or other satisfactory form of administrative control

4. No avoidable duplication of the work of another efficiently managed organization

5. Ethical methods of publicity, promotion, and solicitation of funds

6. Agreement to consult and cooperate with the proper social agencies in local community

7. Annual audited accounts prepared showing receipts and disbursements classified and itemized in detail. New organizations should submit a statement that such a financial system has been established as will make the required financial accounting possible.

8. Itemized and classified annual budget estimate

9. Complete annual statement of work accomplished in the form of answers to the questionnaire prepared by the federation.[17]

By the early 1930s, the standards had become more stringent, and contained terms like "must" and "shall render" and "is required" in setting forth the minimum requirements.

Visit with President

The federation's seventh annual conference was held in Washington, D.C., on May 15 – 16, 1923 — the two days preceding the National Conference of Social Work. Meetings were frequently held on dates adjacent to those of the social workers, to enable delegates to attend the meetings of both organizations. The Big Brothers and Big Sisters conference was attended by 120 delegates from 17 states, the District of Columbia, Canada, and New Zealand (one delegate).[18] It is not known if the New Zealand delegate was from a member agency.

A highlight of the meeting was a visit with President Harding. George MacDonald, active in the Catholic Big Brothers Organization

In October 1921, President Warren G. Harding received Big Brother and Big Sister Federation delegates at the White House. The president (*left circle*) and Mrs. Harding agreed to become patrons of the organization. Among the group, only Ernest K. Coulter (*center circle*) could be identified.

of New York, was elected federation president, succeeding Charles Edwin Fox of Philadelphia.

Elected treasurer was Theodore Roosevelt, Jr., son of the late president. Roosevelt was assistant secretary of the Navy at the time. He was an organizer of the American Legion and an unsuccessful candidate for governor of New York in 1924. He served as governor of Puerto Rico from 1929 to 1932 and as governor general of the Philippines from 1932 to 1933. As a brigadier general during World War II, Roosevelt served in North Africa, Italy, and France.[19] Roosevelt served the

Theodore Roosevelt, Jr., was elected treasurer of the Big Brother and Big Sister Federation in 1923.

federation as treasurer for many years, and was an enthusiastic supporter of the Movement. Of Big Brothers work he once said, "There is no question but that it is good for all concerned. I personally think it does as much good to the Big Brothers as anyone else."[20] When Roosevelt was succeeded as treasurer, around 1927, by Harold L. Bache, a partner of the investment firm Bache & Company (now Prudential-Bache Securities), he became a federation vice-president. Roosevelt died in 1944, while serving in the Army.

Secretary Sheldon reported to the Washington conference that, of the federation's $15,611 budget for the current year, $6,622 had been raised in New York City alone. Sheldon indicated that the national organization hoped to avoid the local criticism that its chief interest was raising money for the national budget by working in any new area for six months before asking for financial support.[21]

Chairman of the Executive Committee C. Robert Langenbacher told the delegates that of 214 known Big Brothers and Big Sisters organizations throughout the world only 54 were then affiliated with the federation. He decried the fact that 69 other independent organizations (not underwritten by another organization) had not joined. Of these, 34 were Big Brothers agencies, 31 served only Big Sisters, and 4 were combination organizations.

Of 76 dependent Big Brothers groups, 33 were sponsored by Rotary clubs, 21 by Elks, 7 by the YMCA, 6 by Kiwanis groups, 3 by the Knights of Columbus, 2 each by the Holy Name Society and B'nai B'rith, and one each by the Lions Club and the Council of Catholic Men. Dependent Big Sisters groups included two each sponsored by church organizations, the Urban League, and high schools, and one each by the Epworth League, Queen's Daughters, and the YMCA. Although the first obligation of sponsored groups was to their parent organizations, many of them did affiliate with the federation.[22] Information on several groups was apparently not reported.

Mrs. Edwin F. Horne (chapter 2), an Urban League leader and grandmother of singer Lena Horne, was a director of the Big Brother and Big Sister Federation in 1923. She was an authority on the special problems encountered in black Big Sisters work, which was just getting underway during the early 1920s. Mrs. Horne died around 1930.

No record of a federation meeting of any kind could be found for 1924. By December of that year, the federation had moved from its offices at 200 Park Avenue, New York, to quarters at 1775 Broadway. The eighth annual meeting began on January 13, 1925, when more than four hundred delegates gathered at the Hotel Commodore in New York and heard Lady Armstrong report that it had been estimated that over one million children in the United States were in need of the type of assistance offered by Big Brothers and Big Sisters. Mrs. Armstrong reported that the Movement had provided aid for more than 131,000 children during the previous year. Stressing the preventive approach, Mrs. Armstrong said that 67 percent of the children aided had never been arraigned in any court.[23]

Other speakers, from inside and outside the Movement, included a popular and well-known rabbi, Stephen S. Wise; Mrs. Sidney C. Borg, a federation vice-president and chairwoman of the Jewish Big Sisters of New York; Theodore Roosevelt, Jr., federation treasurer; and Angelo Patri, a well-known educator and writer. A disciple of educator John Dewey, Patri was already the author of four books and was to write at least four more, in addition to becoming a syndicated columnist. He brought an inspirational note to the meeting by urging the delegates to emulate St. Francis in their work. Patri noted that no place else in the world could match America for its enthusiasm for the welfare of its children.

Mrs. Borg, recognizing that local needs and practices differed, noted that the underlying principle of Big Brothers and Big Sisters work is personal service (one to one). Theodore Roosevelt, Jr., told the delegates:

> The last fifty years [has seen] a terrific material expansion. Everybody has been thinking in terms of electric lights and rapid transmission, automobiles, comforts of every sort. Things of the body are important, material comforts, but things of the body are not nearly as important as things of the soul, and it is to the things of the soul that all of you devote much of your attention and things of the soul in the the real meaning of things of the soul, that is without regard to creed in any shape or manner, which is the only way good Americans should behave.

Helping Hands

Four of the delegates to the federation's eighth annual meeting in New York caught the eye of a caricaturist. They are, *left to right,* Lady Armstrong, of the New York Catholic Big Sisters, Mrs. Willard Parker, Jr., of Big Sisters of New York (Protestant), Mrs. Sidney C. Borg, Jewish Big Sisters of New York, and Troy Kaichen, representing the Big Brother Association of Cincinnati. Depiction appeared in the old New York *American* for January 14, 1925.

Rabbi Wise noted that there was a need for organization in social-service work, but cautioned that there was a possibility of over-organization, which could be a deterrent to human considerations. He indicated that Big Brothers and Big Sisters were applying the spirit of brotherhood where it was most needed and most effectively redeeming.

On hand to lend a lighter note to the proceedings was famed humorist Will Rogers. Rogers told the group, in his well-known, low-key manner, that he was often called upon to speak before separate Jewish, Catholic, and Protestant organizations, and he tried to please them all since they all go to the theater, but that it was a wonderful pleasure to find one organization "where you are all together in one."[24]

George MacDonald was reelected as federation president. President Calvin Coolidge was chosen as patron of the group and, after being informed of this action by Theodore Roosevelt, Jr., the President promptly accepted, becoming the second U.S. chief executive to serve in that capacity. Shortly before the conference, according to an article in the *New York Times*, the federation announced a rule that forbade the publication of names or photographs identifying Little Brothers and Little Sisters, stating that such publication would be unethical.[25]

First Agency Executive Conference

On June 8 and 9, 1925, in Denver, Colorado, the federation held its first conference exclusively for agency executives. More than fifty delegates attended and discussed such topics as how agencies can be of more assistance to volunteers, the value of committees within Big Brothers and Big Sisters organizations, the value of the Movement to communities, and working with other organizations.

Rowland C. Sheldon proposed that two committees be formed in each state — one to represent Big Brothers and the other Big Sisters. Such committees, he believed, would bring unity to the national effort, while allowing for local flexibility. Although the executives reportedly were enthusiastic about this plan, there is no evidence that it was ever implemented. George W. Casey, for many years in charge of the Big Brothers agency in Philadelphia, was elected chairman of the conference.[26]

The federation represented agencies in nineteen states and the District of Columbia in 1925. In addition, there were member agencies in Canada and the Philippines. Heading the list was New York, with sixteen groups. Next came Ohio with eight, five of which were in Cincinnati, and California with six. Minnesota and Pennsylvania each had four. A complete list of these and other member groups that year can be found in appendix 1.

Charles Brandon Booth

In spring 1925, possibly one of the most colorful and visible personalities ever to be associated with the Movement joined the federation. He was Charles Brandon Booth. Although employed as a field secretary, Booth was mainly a lecturer on behalf of the federation. He was an accomplished, spellbinding speaker.

Booth displayed an evangelistic enthusiasm for Big Brothers and Big Sisters work, as he crisscrossed the country, urging local communities to adopt the one-to-one technique in dealing with the problems of youth. Perhaps his fervency is not hard to understand when his background is considered. Booth was the grandson of General William Booth, founder of the Salvation Army in Britain, and the son of Ballington and Maud Booth, who established the Salvation Army in America, and who later broke with the organization and founded the Volunteers of America (VOA).[27]

Field Secretary Charles Brandon Booth, the federation's silver-tongued orator, about 1925.

Charles Brandon Booth attended Montclair (N.J.) Military Academy and the Hill School in Pottstown, Pennsylvania. His first job was with the Volunteers of America, where he assisted with the VOA's prisoner rehabilitation program. In 1915, he joined the staff of St. George's Church, New York, where he served as clerk of the vestry, secretary of the corporation, and assistant treasurer. He later became an independent lecturer, before joining the federation.[28]

Booth's speaking activities are credited with a surge of interest in Big Brothers and Big Sisters activities. Shortly after joining the federation, he made speeches in nine cities in a fifteen-day period, where he addressed 1,145 adults and 3,385 high school students.[29] By August 1925, he had delivered a total of 119 addresses and had planned an extensive tour covering eight states.[30]

Said the *Owego* (N.Y.) *Gazette* of Booth's podium mastery: "Versed in eloquence as few men are and using a power of description exceptional in its beauty and clearness, this speaker drives home his points with a realistic force that astounds his hearers and leaves his message firmly and happily embedded in their memories."[31]

Booth's influence and popularity must be viewed in the context of a time when lectures were both a major art form and a well-accepted method of community enlightenment. Lecturers developed a stock of speeches involving an area of expertise. Then, honing their presentations through constant repetition, they delivered the same talks for months or even years. Today's speakers may, to some extent, do that in practice, but the impression is given that the remarks have been prepared especially for each audience. Not so in the heyday of the professional lecturer, when speakers became identified with specific lectures.

Booth's well-known lectures for Big Brothers and Big Sisters included "The Child That No One Understands," which was presented to parents or other adult audiences; "Where Brother Meets Brother," designed for men's service clubs; "The Little Sisters' Big Sister," prepared especially for women's service clubs; "The Greatest Miracle," a presentation prepared for churches; and "You and Company," an inspirational talk for high school assemblies. The last lecture was presented to half a million high school students.[32]

Charles Brandon Booth remained with the federation until 1929, when he left to return to the Volunteers of America. He subsequently rose to commander-in-chief of that organization. He maintained a lifelong interest in the Big Brothers and Big Sisters Movement. Booth died on March 27, 1975, at the age of eighty-seven.

Dr. Herbert D. Williams

Another important contributor to the federation during the second half of the 1920s was Dr. Herbert D. Williams. Williams joined the federation in 1927 as regional director, with responsibility for activities in Illinois, Indiana, Ohio, Michigan, and Wisconsin. He was based in Chicago. His specialty was child psychology. For two years prior to joining the federation, while a referee in the Juvenile Court of Toledo and Lucas County, Ohio, he studied the cases of two thousand delinquent children. The research was the basis of his "Study of Problem School Children in Ten Midwest Cities." Later, after coming to the federation, the study was extended to cover twenty-six cities and towns in New York State.

A graduate of the University of Georgia, with a doctorate from Iowa State, Williams had taught psychology and education at Brenau College, Gainesville, Georgia; the University of Iowa; Tulane; Northwestern; Ohio State; and New York University. From all indications, Williams was the first person within the Movement to utilize scientific methods in the study of child behavior. He left the federation in 1932 to join the Children's Village in Dobbs Ferry, New York, as director of social work. He was later named superintendent of the New York State Training School for Boys at Warwick. Before retirement, he served for ten years as head of the St. Petersburg (Fla.) Juvenile Welfare Board. Williams died in 1960. [33]

What Charles Brandon Booth sought to do from behind the podium, Herbert D. Williams approached with the tools of psychology and the written word. He authored many monographs and wrote papers on Big Brothers and Big Sisters service. These bore such titles as "Philosophy of Big Brother and Big Sister Service," "Causes of Social Maladjustment in Children," and "Conflicting Authorities in the Life of the Child." Other articles or papers, which were distributed by the federation, covered such subjects as the use of the analytical interview, the necessity for diagnosis and a definite program in the handling of delinquents, and vocational guidance. [34]

New Approaches

The relationship of Big Brothers and Big Sisters to the parents of Little Brothers and Sisters was the keynote of the federation's ninth annual meeting, held at Chicago on January 19 and 20, 1926. George MacDonald was retained as president. The leaders felt that much had been said about the inability of many parents to deal with the problems of their difficult children. It was now time for the organization, whose work was accomplished almost entirely within the home, to address this critical situation. Delegates heard a number of prominent jurists, theologians, and others.

Among the speakers was comedian Eddie Cantor, who frequently addressed Movement audiences. Said Cantor, "Love is the greatest religion in the world and this boy [referring to himself] tells you right from this table in all seriousness, right from the depth of his heart, that it is the greatest Movement in America — this Big Brother and Big Sister Movement." [35]

The tenth annual meeting took place in Cleveland on January 25, 26, and 27, 1927. An important aspect of this meeting was the presentation to the Board of Directors of a recommended plan for evaluating agencies. Designed for self-appraisal, the plan was intended not as a means of standardizing agency service, but rather as a checklist for improving operations, and as an aid in preparing inquiries that might be made by representatives of community chests and other organizations.

The program called for assigning all participating groups to one of six categories, which indicated the breadth of service at that time. The categories were:

1. Agencies rendering personal, individual service to children, with a board of directors and a full-time executive
2. Committees of various organizations, such as the Lions Club or Elks, which rendered personal and individual service
3. Big Brothers and Big Sisters groups made up of college and university students
4. Those groups maintaining a home or shelter for children
5. Church Bible classes offering service
6. Radio stations that maintained Big Brother clubs.

No explanation of the last category (radio stations) was given. The plan presented a yardstick of desired characteristics of a good agency: Was it administered by an executive secretary or director who was a graduate of a school of social work? Was a field assistant employed for each fifty volunteers in excess of fifty? Were the agency's finances audited by a professional? Was an annual report published? Did predelinquent cases (preventive work) constitute at least 60 percent of intake? Did each Big Brother or Big Sister maintain an average of four volunteer-child contacts per month?

Other questions pertained to desirable practices: Did volunteers submit monthly reports? Did the agency publish a regular bulletin or other periodical? Were public addresses made to publicize the work? Were newspaper accounts of the work obtained? Was vocational counseling provided? Were summer camp opportunities afforded? Did number of volunteers for a particular period exceed the number for the previous year? These and some fifteen other questions concerning such things as budgeting, training of volunteers, employment for Little Brothers and Little Sisters, and the providing of medical and dental care indicate what the Movement considered important in 1927. They also provide an index of the level of professionalism reached by that time.[36]

In addition to serving its members through conferences, the distribution of professional papers, publication of *The Ounce*, agency visits, speaking engagements, and advice and counsel when requested, the federation also produced and distributed suggested agency guidelines, which covered such areas as service delivery and volunteer training. A two-page memorandum on a new method for selecting Big Brothers and Big Sisters was issued over the signature of Executive Director Sheldon.

Sheldon stated that "it is no longer wise, nor even necessary" to depend on volunteers who come to the agency to offer their services.

He claimed that the acceptance of such volunteers was often counter-productive. Rather, agency personnel should handpick candidates from among men and women in the community who possessed the desired characteristics for Big Brothers and Big Sisters service. Among prerequisites were patience, persistence, sympathy, and good health.

Sheldon further indicated that successful parents were the people most likely to possess such attributes — parents whose children had received good home training, achieved academic excellence, and demonstrated physical fitness and emotional stability. He suggested a search of the records of public, parochial, and private secondary schools, as well as churches and Sunday schools, to locate such children. Then, their parents would be contacted and persuaded to befriend delinquent or predelinquent children. Sheldon claimed that the idea was successfully implemented in several communities, but no mention of the approach was ever noted again. [37]

A more pragmatic, and therefore more useful, guideline contained excellent suggestions for publicizing the Movement. In fact, this ten-page memorandum contained material that would be considered highly useful today, even though the field of public relations was still in its infancy during the 1920s and 1930s. Agencies were urged to utilize newspaper editorial, news, and feature columns. Ideas were included for obtaining each type of coverage. Suggestions were also offered on using folders and pamphlets, establishing a speaker's bureau, holding contests, preparing exhibits and displays, including street banners, streetcar and truck posters, and billboards. The guide suggested ways to use motion picture theaters, and mentioned two Movement films, which had not been noted in previous research. The films were titled *Big Brother* and *Boy O' Mine*. It is not known if the former was the Paramount picture mentioned in chapter 2.

The use of radio was urged, although the first commercial station had gone on the air only a few years before. Suggestions were made that milk bottle caps be used for publicity (cardboard milk cartons are used in this manner by modern agencies), that utility companies be asked to enclose Movement fliers with monthly bills, that stores be asked to place Movement stickers on customers' packages, that advertisers be asked to place a small Movement appeal in their newspaper advertising, and that information booths be obtained at conventions. Suggested newspaper editorials were included, as was a suggested sermon, a sample paid advertisement (ready for the sponsor's name), and finally a sample proclamation for a Big Brother Week (this is the first time that mention of such a week was noted. In the modern Movement, Big Brothers/Big Sisters Week is generally observed in February). [38]

During the early 1920s, the federation apparently encouraged the use of the names *Big Brothers* and *Big Sisters* by almost any group that

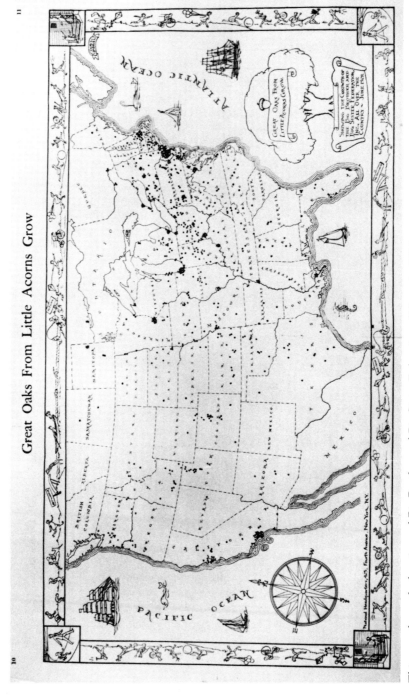

Great Oaks From Little Acorns Grow

This map shows the locations of Big Brother and Big Sister Federation affiliates in 1928.

appeared to offer BB/BS–type services. However, as the degree of professionalism increased and standards were formulated, the federation became increasingly concerned about use of the names by organizations that did not meet certain requirements that the federation had developed.

Thus, beginning around 1927, letters of protest were sent to high school, college, church, and other groups that used the names, but did not subscribe to federation-approved practices. A few newspapers and radio stations were among the violators, the former in connection with Christmas funds sponsored by the newspapers.[39]

No information is available on a 1928 annual meeting, which is believed to have been held in Memphis. By 1929, the federation had moved its headquarters to 425 Fourth Avenue, New York. All subsequent meetings were apparently held in that city. In the absence of *The Ounce*, the federation's former publication, only random information from newspaper accounts is available. A meeting, although not billed as an annual meeting, was held at the Hotel Biltmore on March 8, 1930, according to an article in the *New York Times*. The newspaper account indicated that six hundred delegates from throughout the United States and Canada attended and heard several experts speak on crime prevention, including New York Police Commissioner Grover A. Whalen. Whalen was later named to the federation's board.

The meeting is of incidental interest to the modern Movement because of a statement made by federation President George Mac-Donald. For many years, extending to the present time, the Movement has used the slogan, "No Man Stands So Tall As When He Stoops to Help a Boy." Many people have inquired about its origin, but no one seems to know when it was first used. The statement may have grown out of a remark made by MacDonald at the end of a talk at this meeting when he said, ". . . he or she who stoops above the fallen stands erect." His full statement to the delegates was, "I want to say to you and to all who are engaged in social service that it is a great practical spiritual work. The desire to aid our fellow men ennobles ourselves, and he or she who stoops above the fallen stands erect."[40]

From available information, the annual meeting on November 17, 1931, was considerably less elaborate than many of those in the past, perhaps reflecting the ever-tightening economic grip of the Great Depression.[41] However, minutes of a meeting of the federation's Executive Committee, for September 9, 1931, indicated that the organization was still striving to improve its professional image. The committee approved a new set of minimum standards for federation membership.[42] These standards were not too unlike those which must be met today by member agencies of Big Brothers/Big Sisters of America.

In 1932, an attempt was made to obtain a federal charter for the federation. Congressman John J. O'Connor, New York, introduced a bill calling for such action on February 5, 1932, and on February 23, a companion bill was introduced in the Senate by Senator David A. Reed of Pennsylvania. The legislation was never enacted, the bills apparently dying in committee.[43]

A series of meetings, covering a variety of topics related to service delivery, was held in Philadelphia in May 1932. The meetings, which took place over a period of five days, were scheduled in connection with the National Conference on Social Work. No information was located on an annual meeting that year or during the two following years.

Minutes of an Executive Committee meeting, dated December 28, 1933, indicate that staff salaries had been cut, then partially restored, and a budget reduction implemented — further indication of the economic difficulties of that period. Of interest was a notation that President and Mrs. Franklin D. Roosevelt had accepted an invitation to become patrons of the Movement.[44] President Hoover had served in that capacity during his term of office.

At the annual meeting in New York in April 1935, famed criminologist Sheldon Glueck was elected president. He replaced longtime President George MacDonald. During his long and successful career, Glueck served as Roscoe Pound Professor of Law at the Harvard Law School, as well as the school's Director of Research in Juvenile Delinquency and Criminology. He authored many books in the field and served as an adviser at the Nuremberg Trials after World War II. In a speech to the delegates at the 1935 meeting of the federation, Glueck blamed economic strife for much of the nation's lawlessness.

Said Glueck, "Reliable researches have demonstrated that there is an increase in certain offenses, particularly property crimes and vagrancy, during periods of economic stress. This shows that the individual's power of resistance has been overbalanced by the strength of other circumstances." Glueck advocated raising the level of economic security as a means of strengthening the resistance capacity of many individuals. He felt that this could be done by suppressing what he called "economic cannibalism" or greed among businessmen and through the adoption by business of "a set of ethical principles in harmony with the poignant cry for social justice."[45]

The Year 1936

An annual report issued on April 15, 1936, contained considerable information on the state of both the federation and the Movement at that time. The report stated that there were then 342 groups of Big Brothers and Big Sisters and combination groups in the United States,

Canada, and other foreign countries. Of these, 311 were in the United States, 24 in Canada, and 7 in other countries; there were 196 Big Brothers groups, 108 Big Sisters units, and 38 combined organizations.

The federation had further divided these groups into three major categories. Fifty-eight of the units were, for purposes of this division, termed "Organizations," and listed as having a board of directors, elected officers, and a paid professional staff. Thirty-nine of the groups were called "Departments" because they were part of a parent body, such as the Elks, Lions, Rotary, or a religious body. Such groups had professional caseworkers, who were paid by their sponsors. The third category, termed "Committees," numbered 245, and its members were composed entirely of lay personnel. "Committees" differed from "Departments" only in that the former had no paid professionals. Also, according to the report, "Organizations" and "Departments" were generally located in population areas of 150,000 or more.

Except for the classifications reported in the above paragraph, the terms *organization, department, and committee* are used in a generic sense throughout this book, unless a reference is made to a specific group.

The 1936 annual report indicated that 71.4 percent of the total units were nonsectarian, 13.9 percent were Catholic, 7.9 percent were Jewish, and 6.6 percent were Protestant (it is noted that these figures do not total 100%). Black groups accounted for 5 percent. By states, there were 55 groups in New York, 50 in Illinois, 29 in Ohio, 26 in California, 18 in New Jersey, 16 in Michigan, and 16 in Pennsylvania. The report noted that there were from 1 to 15 groups in every state with the exceptions of Idaho, Mississippi, Nevada, New Hampshire, Oregon, and Utah. Sadly, only 50 units — 25 Big Brothers, 19 Big Sisters, and 6 Big Brothers/Big Sisters agencies — were dues-paying members of the federation in 1936.[46]

The entire Movement was shocked and saddened by the tragic death of Rowland C. Sheldon on December 5, 1936. Sheldon jumped from the window of his eleventh-story apartment in New York.[47]

According to the newspaper account of his suicide, he was in ill health, but this may have been only one factor. Sheldon was a precise, highly motivated, results-oriented administrator, who liked to formulate elaborate plans and programs, work hard to implement them, then observe the planned results. In the Depression year 1936, a lot of things were not going as planned in the federation.

The Federation Disbands

The federation's board chose not to replace Sheldon. Within a few months, the organization would close its doors forever. Sheldon's death was apparently not the entire reason for this action, but it was certainly the precipitating factor. Information in the Social Work Yearbook for 1937 indicates that federation membership had dropped to an all-time low for the decade.[48] Severe financial difficulties were undoubtedly being encountered.

However, Joseph H. McCoy, general secretary of the New York Big Brother Movement, felt that the federation failed because it simply was not feasible for one organization to represent both Big Brothers and Big Sisters. This philosophy would be refuted some forty years later with the merger of Big Sisters International (BSI) and Big Brothers of America (BBA), to form Big Brothers/Big Sisters of America (BB/BSA) (chapter 6).

From 1937 until 1946 for Big Brothers and until 1971 for Big Sisters there was no central coordinating body for the Movement. There was no body to organize new agencies, formulate and maintain standards, sponsor seminars and conferences, conduct studies, and publish educational materials. There was no national voice. Once again, as before 1917, scattered agencies were on their own.

To come were efforts to create a new federation, and the formation of Big Brothers of America.

* * * *

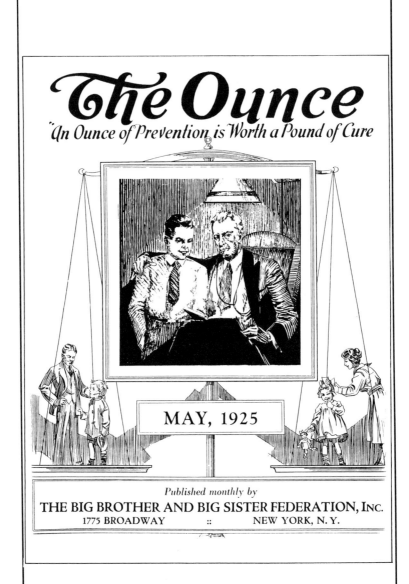

The Ounce

"An Ounce of Prevention is Worth a Pound of Cure

MAY, 1925

Published monthly by

THE BIG BROTHER AND BIG SISTER FEDERATION, Inc.

1775 BROADWAY   ::   NEW YORK, N.Y.

Notes to Chapter 3

1. Brochure from the first Big Brothers and Big Sisters Conference at Grand Rapids, Michigan, May 28 – 29, 1917, on file at BB/BSA Headquarters, Philadelphia.
2. "Sees Urgent Need for Big Brothers in War of World," *Grand Rapids Herald*, May 29, 1917, 1, 4.
3. "Big Brothers and Big Sisters Form First Organization," *Grand Rapids Herald*, May 30, 1917.
4. Ibid.
5. "Big Brothers and Sisters Are Here," *Grand Rapids Press*, May 28, 1917.
6. *Who Was Who in America*, vol. 1, 1897 – 1942, p. 1114.
7. "The Big Brother and Big Sister Federation, Inc.," *The Ounce*, Big Brother and Big Sister Federation (BB/BSF), February 1922, 1, 4 – 5, Archives and Special Collections (A&SC), The City College of the City University of New York (CUNY).
8. Ibid., p. 6.
9. "Action Taken by the Executive Committee," *The Ounce* (BB/BSF), July 1923, 4, A&SC, The City College, CUNY.
10. "The Editor Interviews the Executive Secretary," *The Ounce* (BB/BSF), May 1922, 4, A&SC, The City College, CUNY.
11. "The Minneapolis Conference," *The Ounce* (BB/BSF), May 1922, 4, A&SC, The City College, CUNY.
12. "Minutes of Annual Meeting of the Big Brother and Big Sister Federation, Inc.," Held at Minneapolis, Minn., June 6, 7, and 8, 1922, *The Ounce* (BB/BSF), July 1922, 2, A&SC, The City College, CUNY.
13. Ibid., p. 5.
14. Ibid., p. 2.
15. "Big Brothers Start Boy Exchange," *The Ounce* (BB/BSF), September 1922, 8, A&SC, The City College, CUNY.
16. "Standards for Approval," *The Ounce* (BB/BSF), November 1922, 2, A&SC, The City College, CUNY.
17. Ibid.
18. "Seventh Annual Conference," *The Ounce* (BB/BSF), May 1923, A&SC, The City College, CUNY.
19. *Who Was Who in America*, vol. 2, 1943 – 50.
20. "Seventh Annual Conference," p. 3.
21. "Report of the Secretary," *The Ounce* (BB/BSF), June 1923, 5, A&SC, The City College, CUNY.
22. "Action Taken by the Executive Committee," see note 9 above.
23. "Big Sisters Meet with Big Brothers," *New York Times*, January 14, 1925, 20:8.
24. "Will Rogers Supplies Laughs Which Have a Kick in Them and Praises Federation," *The Ounce* (BB/BSF), March 1925, 6, A&SC, The City College, CUNY.
25. "Bar Publicity in Work," *New York Times*, April 12, 1925, 26:4.
26. "Federation Methods Crystallize at Denver Conference," *The Ounce* (BB/BSF), July 1925, 1, A&SC, The City College, CUNY.
27. "Charles Brandon Booth Is Dead; Headed Volunteers of America," New York Times Biographical Service, April 1975.
28. History of the Volunteers of America, pp. 170 – 171.
29. "Booth Lectures Popular," *The Ounce* (BB/BSF), June 1925, 3, A&SC, The City College, CUNY.

30. "National Field Lecturer Plans Tour," *The Ounce* (BB/BSF), August 1925, 6, A&SC, The City College, CUNY.
31. "Charles Brandon Booth Joins Federation Staff," *The Ounce* (BB/BSF), May 1925, 5, A&SC, The City College, CUNY.
32. "National Field Lecturer Plans Tour," p. 6.
33. "Dr. Williams Dies; a Psychologist, 67," *New York Times*, May 29, 1960, 57:2.
34. Herbert D. Williams, *Philosophy of Big Brother and Big Sister Service*, The Minnesota State Conference of Social Work, 1930, A&SC, The City College, CUNY.
35. "1926 Convention a Clearing House of Ideas," *The Ounce* (BB/BSF), February 1926, A&SC, The City College, CUNY.
36. "Tenth Annual Meeting," *The Ounce* (BB/BSF), August 1927, 13, A&SC, The City College, CUNY.
37. "The Selection of Big Brothers and Big Sisters," monograph published by BB/BSF, A&SC, The City College, CUNY.
38. "Campaign for Publicity," outline published by BB/BSF, A&SC, The City College, CUNY.
39. Ibid.
40. "Whalen to Extend Curb on Wayward," *New York Times*, March 9, 1930, 3:1.
41. "Early Start Is Urged in Crime Prevention," *New York Times*, November 18, 1931, 19:2.
42. Executive Committee Minutes, September 9, 1931, BB/BSF, A&SC, The City College, CUNY.
43. Law Library, American-British Law Division, Library of Congress.
44. Executive Committee Minutes, December 28, 1933, BB/BSF, A&SC, The City College, CUNY.
45. "Economic Strife Blamed for Crime," *New York Times*, April 16, 1935, 22:4.
46. Eighteenth annual report, BB/BSF, A&SC, The City College, CUNY.
47. "Anti-crime Expert Ends Life in Leap," *New York Times*, December 6, 1936, 54:3.
48. Social Work Yearbook, published by the Russell Sage Foundation, 1937.

Ruth Alexander Nichols

4

A New Federation: Big Brothers of America (1945–1957)

I n spring 1939, at the National Conference on Social Work at Buffalo, New York, a small committee of representatives from Protestant, Catholic, and Jewish Big Brothers organizations from New York City, along with Dr. Kenneth H. Rogers, executive secretary of the Toronto Big Brother Organization, sponsored a two-session conference for consideration of the national aspects of Big Brothers and Big Sisters work. At the first session, chaired by Dr. Rogers, the conference agreed on the need for a national organization to provide services along the following lines:

1. To provide authoritative advice and information about the nature and scope of Big Brother work [Big Sister work was implied here since the conference considered both areas] in reply to inquiries from individuals and interested groups throughout the country

2. To create and maintain acceptable standards of method, procedure, policy and programs for existing organizations

3. To provide an interchange of information and material concerning Big Brother work through occasional conferences, bulletins, correspondence, etc.[1]

The committee agreed that a new national organization must serve the needs of member agencies, as well as solicit active agency participation in the organization's activities. Dr. Rogers appointed a steering committee, consisting of Joseph H. McCoy, Big Brother Movement of New York, and several others, to draw up recommendations, as well as to complete an agenda for a second session.

National Study

When the committee met again, McCoy reported that the steering committee felt that there was a definite need for a national organization, but that insufficient information was available on which to base recommendation for its establishment. The steering committee then recommended that a National Study and Planning Committee be formed, consisting of five representatives from Big Brothers agencies and five representatives from Big Sisters groups, with selection to provide for regional representation.

The purpose of the National Study and Planning Committee would be to prepare and distribute a comprehensive questionnaire in order to determine the type of new federation that would best serve local organizations. Dr. Rogers was named general chairman and McCoy was cochairman. Named to the committee were Big Brothers representatives from Brooklyn (N.Y.), Minneapolis, Denver, St. Louis, and Cleveland. Big Sisters representatives came from New York, Peoria, and Minneapolis.

Representatives of the Protestant, Catholic, and Jewish Big Brothers agencies in New York City were to act as a consulting committee. As it turned out, this group did most of the work in the preparation, distribution, compilation, and analysis of the questionnaire.

It was the most comprehensive survey ever conducted by the Movement up to that time. There were separate forms for Big Brothers and Big Sisters organizations. Part one of each form dealt with local structure, including organization, historical background, finances, and scope of work; part two covered personnel practices, including the selection of board members, agency staff, and the selection and training of volunteers; part three concerned services and how they were administered; part four solicited information on needs; and part five tried to determine how local groups thought their needs could be met and how they felt about a new national federation.

The survey was distributed to fifty-six Big Brothers groups and thirty-eight Big Sisters agencies in the United States and Canada. Only twenty-eight Big Brothers, twenty-two Big Sisters, and one combination agency replied. The results of the survey were reported by the National Study and Planning Committee at a special meeting held during the National Conference on Social Work at Grand Rapids, Michigan, in May 1940.

Unfortunately, the committee concluded that a viable national organization was not feasible at that time. Dr. Rogers reported his thoughts and those of the committee on the pros and cons of forming a new federation.

On the positive side, he indicated that there was a need for a central clearing function to answer inquiries from local commmunities about the Movement. He mentioned that 318 such inquiries had been received during the past year (although he did not indicate to whom such inquiries had been directed). He said that there was an expression of need for a national organization, evidently referring to the fact that forty-three of the fifty-one respondents had indicated a desire for national services. However, only thirty-four agencies had indicated a desire for a new Big Brothers/Big Sisters federation, with nine expressing a desire to affiliate with some other existing national group. The committee felt that this level of interest would not support a national effort, and recognized several totally negative factors. Dr. Rogers cited the fact that only 56 percent of existing agencies had responded to the questionnaire. He noted many differences among local groups.

Although plans for a federation were deferred, the committee did decide to continue discussions each year during the annual meeting of the National Conference of Social Work. A National Committee on Big Brother and Big Sister Service was created to answer inquiries about the Movement, prepare and publish an informational manual for use in answering such inquiries, and arrange for the annual discussion groups. The new committee was headed by Donald Q. Watson of Minneapolis.

In concluding the Grand Rapids discussion meeting, Dr. Rogers urged the participants to "get busy and strengthen our individual agencies and service, build a sound and dependable reputation in our local communities, publicize our efforts and services . . . correspond with other Big Brother and Big Sister agencies frequently . . . build, think and plan through local growth toward the day of opportunity for the establishment of a National Office."[2]

America would soon be involved in a world conflict. Severe personnel shortages on the home front would place many agencies in holding patterns, at best, for the duration. A new (and successful) attempt to form a national organization would not come until 1945.

Since the 1940 study represents the only known body of knowledge about the Movement on a national scale just prior to America's involvement in World War II, it seems appropriate to present certain of its findings before discussing later organizational efforts. For the social researcher and historian, who may wish to do local agency research, a complete list of known local agencies during the period is included in appendix 2.

The twenty-eight Big Brothers agencies that responded to the questionnaire were located in twenty-one cities in twelve states and in Canada. The cities and the number of agencies in each were: Denver,

Jacksonville (Fla.), Chicago, Danville (Ill.), Evanston (Ill.), Peoria (Ill.), Baltimore, Minneapolis, Boston, St. Louis, Cincinnati, Cleveland, Philadelphia, Pittsburgh, Scranton (Pa.), Dallas, and Houston, all with one agency each; Los Angeles, New York, and Toronto, with three each; and Columbus (Ohio) with two.

The twenty-two Big Sisters organizations that replied were located in seventeen cities in thirteen states and in Canada. The cities and number of agencies in each were: Los Angeles, Denver, Stamford (Conn.), Washington (D.C.), Savannah (Ga.), Detroit, Minneapolis, St. Paul, St. Louis, Brooklyn (N.Y.), Cleveland, Columbus, Scranton, and Seattle, with one each; New York and Toronto, with three each; and Chicago with two agencies.

Of the Big Brothers groups, three were affiliated with Catholic organizations, seven were sponsored by Jewish groups, two had Protestant associations, and three represented another or other religious groups. Thirteen were nonsectarian. Seventeen agencies were independent, sixteen were incorporated under state laws, and eleven were dependent on parent organizations.

Of the Big Sisters groups, five represented Catholic groups, four Jewish, five Protestant, one represented another denomination, and seven were nonsectarian. Twelve of the Big Sisters agencies were independent, twelve were incorporated, and ten were dependent. Parent organizations of the dependent groups ranged from multifunctional social-service agencies and casework agencies to child guidance clinics and welfare institutions.

The annual income of Big Brothers organizations that were studied for the year 1939 ranged from a low of $75 to a high of more than $63,000. Big Sisters agency income for the same year ranged from under $100 to a high of only $21,000. The data are from the reports of forty agencies. As is the case today, most agencies participated in a number of fund-raising activities, either as a means of independent support or to supplement community chest support. Of twenty-nine Big Brothers and Big Sisters agencies reporting such activities, two conducted organized campaigns, six made direct appeals, sixteen sponsored benefits, nineteen raised funds through dues, nine looked to foundations and organizations, nine benefited from individual contributions, and two reported other sources.

The scope of Big Brothers and Big Sisters activity was apparently much wider than it is today. As already mentioned in chapter 2, several agencies provided clients with such services as vocational guidance, employment, medical and dental care. Both the agency's facilities and those of the community were utilized. For example, state and federal employment services as well as the then National Youth Administration (NYA) provided vocational guidance and employment referrals. Although many agencies operated their own summer camps, the facilities of other organizations, as mentioned in chapter 1, were also used. In addition to the benefits noted above, agencies also offered such diverse services as casework, which was the most predominant service, group work, optical care, farm placement, psychiatric care, clubs, scholarships, school clothing and supplies, recreational facilities, allowances, loans, and outright relief. Whereas Big Brothers agencies made wide use of outside resources, Big Sisters groups appeared to be more self-sufficient.

Autonomous agencies were generally governed by a group known either as the board of directors, board of trustees, board of managers, or an executive committee — with each of these groups having final authority. Dependent groups were generally governed by an executive committee, which was responsible to a parent organization. Most governing groups were elected and consisted of from ten to twenty members. A governing group with more than thirty members was rare.

Agency professional employees included the person in charge, who was known as the director, executive secretary, or supervisor depending on the size of the organization, an assistant to the administrator, and one or more caseworkers. Only those agencies with an annual income of over $8,000 per year employed more than two professionals. Agencies in the $5,000-to-$8,000 category employed two professionals, and those with annual incomes of only $2,000 to $5,000 employed only one. Clerical support varied with agency size, but generally included one or two full- or part-time employees.

The 1940 study noted that 33 percent of all professional employees were graduates of schools of social work. However, only 20 percent of the Big Brothers professionals had graduate degrees, whereas nearly 50 percent of the Big Sisters professionals had this qualification. Twenty-three percent had other college degrees, 13 percent had experience that was supplemented with courses in social work. Thirty-one percent had no academic training.

The study reported that there was probably a higher percentage of social work graduates among Big Sisters personnel because more women than men entered that field. The study also reported that the level of professionalism in lower-income Big Sisters agencies was higher than in corresponding Big Brothers organizations, and suggested that this was true because women received lower salaries than men for comparable work.

As to volunteers, most agencies required that applicants be at least twenty-one years of age. A few agencies set an age minimum of twenty-five and one agency would not consider a volunteer under thirty-five. Forty-five or fifty was usually mentioned as the top limit. Volunteers of sectarian groups had to be of the same religion as the sponsoring agency. Twenty-seven percent of nonsectarian organizations required the volunteer to be of the same faith as the child, 42 percent reported a nonsectarian policy (the volunteer could be of any religion), and 31 percent had no requirement. Character and personality were noted as the most desirable characteristics in a volunteer. Volunteers were appointed in 64 percent of the groups that were surveyed; most of the remaining organizations chose to elect volunteers. Personal contact was the most prevalent method of volunteer recruitment. Appeals were also made through church and service clubs.

Three Big Brothers agencies and three Big Sisters groups had fewer than 25 volunteers each. In the remaining organizations, about one-third had between 25 to 50 volunteers, a third had between 50 and 100, and the remaining third had between 100 and 250. One agency had 924 volunteers.

Volunteers who offered professional services were known as Big Brothers and Big Sisters as well as those who were actually matched with children. In fact, according to the survey, of 3,615 Big Brothers who were active in 1939, only 60 percent were then currently matched, whereas 19 percent were assigned to older, semi-active cases. The remaining 21 percent rendered such services as medical, psychiatric, optical, or dental care, legal assistance, or engaged in fund-raising activities. Only 40 percent of the 1,484 Big Sisters reported were actually matched with a Little Sister at that time.

No racial restrictions on referrals were reported by one-third of the groups surveyed. Most of the remaining agencies took only white children. Noteworthy is the fact that, with one exception, Catholic-sponsored groups had no racial restrictions. Sectarian agencies limited themselves to children of the faith of the agency's affiliation. In 1939, agencies did little matching of the physically or mentally handicapped, and most indicated that referrals should be limited largely to potentially normal children. Most agencies probably felt that they were not equipped to handle such cases.

Two of the agencies served fewer than 50 children each, seven agencies reported 50 to 100 referrals, eleven groups served 100 to 250 children, whereas ten agencies reported 250 to 500 referrals each. Seven agencies indicated that they had served from 500 to 1,000 children, and six agencies said that they each served more than that number. The average number of children referred by children's courts in 1939 was 31 percent. Court referrals ranged from one percent to as high as 90 percent. Weekly visits between the volunteer and the Little Brother or Little Sister during the first year were favored by approximately 50 percent of those surveyed. Twenty-five percent preferred bimonthly visits, and 25 percent reported that they required monthly visits or stated that frequency was indicated by the need in each case. Fifty percent of the agencies did not require visits at periodic intervals during the second year, but rather at times indicated by the need in each case.

Twenty-three out of forty-eight groups surveyed were affiliated with other national organizations. Sectarian agencies belonged to sponsoring national organizations such as the Catholic Welfare Association and the National Council of Jewish Women. Nonsectarian, but dependent, agencies also belonged to national groups through parent organizations. For example, several agencies that were sponsored by child welfare organizations were affiliated with the Child Welfare League.

Independent Big Brothers and Big Sisters agencies also had national affiliations. One agency was affiliated with the Boys Clubs of America, Inc., as were two dependent agencies. The American Prison Conference, the American Camping Association, and the National Probation Association each had one Big Brothers agency among its members. Both dependent and autonomous agencies were members of the National Conference of Social Work, the National Jewish Conference of Social Workers, and the National Conference of Catholic Charities.[3]

Other national organizations were concerned with their own specific goals and objectives. They could not help Big Brothers and Big Sisters agencies to disseminate information that could lead to the formation of new BB/BS groups, nor could they be of assistance in other areas essential to agency growth, such as volunteer training, establishment of standards, evaluation, and staff development. Big Brothers and Big Sisters agency needs were too specialized, too peculiar to the one-to-one concept. They could be met fully only by the Movement's own federation. As mentioned earlier, one would be formed only after the war and then, unfortunately, it would not include Big Sisters.

Toward a National Organization

The National Committee on Big Brother and Big Sister Service, formed in Grand Rapids, was discontinued in January 1944. In May 1944, at the National Conference of Social Work in Cleveland, representatives of the Toronto, Denver, and New York agencies met to discuss the possibility of forming a national association. They decided that if several Big Brothers organizations started working together on an informal basis and others joined them, it might be the beginning of a new federation.

Then, finally, on November 19 and 20, 1945, Joseph H. McCoy hosted a meeting in the offices of the Big Brother Movement of New York, which was attended by representatives of four Big Brothers agencies. The purpose of the gathering was to explore the possibility of forming a federation to represent only Big Brothers. Attending the meeting were Archie L. Rankin of Big Brothers of Denver, Charles G. Berwind and George W. Casey of the Big Brother Association of Philadelphia, Edward L. Roxborough and Kenneth H. Rogers of Toronto, and Alonzo Potter, Earle S. Thompson, and McCoy of the New York organization.

A committee known as the Temporary Big Brother National Committee was created, and Charles G. Berwind of Philadelphia was designated as its chairman. Temporary headquarters was established at 50 Union Square in New York. The group's first objective was to determine how many Big Brothers agencies existed at that time and how they felt about forming a national federation. They decided to conduct a study, but instead of a questionnaire mailed to all known groups (such as the one used in 1940), they employed an investigator to visit a group of agencies and prepare a report on which recommendations could be based.

The committee, now enlarged to include representatives from agencies in Hamilton (Ontario), Chicago, Minneapolis, Dallas, Cincinnati, Columbus, Scranton (Pa.), Baltimore, and Boston, retained the services of Robert E. Wynns to conduct the study. Wynns held a master's degree from Columbia University and had been employed as a field representative of the Big Brother Movement of New York before serving in the armed forces. Wynns visited fifteen agencies in the above cities and in the four cities represented at the meeting called by McCoy, and conducted intensive interviews to determine the practices and policies of the organizations, as well as how they felt they could benefit from a national association.[4]

Wynns's traveling expenses were borne by the agencies that had agreed to take part in the survey; other expenses of the study were borne entirely by the New York and Philadelphia agencies. Although personal interviews replaced a questionnaire, the format of the 1945 study was similar to the one in 1940, and the type and content of information derived appeared not to differ significantly, with one notable exception. There now appeared to be strong support for a national organization. Perhaps the earlier absence of support was because of the country's economic condition at that time or perhaps it was because of the gathering war clouds. Then, too, many of the agencies could have recalled the weaknesses of the old, ill-funded, ill-fated Big Brother and Big Sister Federation.

The enthusiastic, positive response now encountered could have occurred because the war had ended and it was a time of new beginnings everywhere, a time to look ahead and move ahead. Americans had just participated successfully in the greatest cooperative effort in the nation's history, and they shared a new appreciation for the concepts and benefits of team effort, sharing, and mutual aid.

According to the study, needs that might be met through an association were better techniques for recruiting, a means for the exchange of ideas and information, effective ways to publicize the Movement, increased respect and prestige, effective volunteer training materials, and general improvement in methods, programs, and services.

The agencies also mentioned several other general, yet fundamental, needs that would benefit not only them but the entire Movement. For example, they expressed a need for a formal, generally acceptable definition of Big Brothers work. They felt that the concept should be more accurately defined with respect to its philosophy, methods, and purpose. They expressed a need for generally recognized standards by which to evaluate their work and also for a set of principles that would support and lend credence to the Big Brothers idea. They knew the idea worked, but they could not adequately explain why it did. Agency people thought that they should be able to explain their successes in terms of other well-accepted disciplines, such as psychology, philosophy, and sociology.

Agencies felt that there should be a comprehensive history of the Movement, which was then less than forty-five years old. Such a history, they thought, would help them gain perspective and determine future goals. Finally, they felt that Big Brothers groups should take a greater interest in community affairs. Wynns observed that agencies had tended to be isolationists with respect to other Big Brothers agencies as well as other social-service organizations. He felt that they should work together in matters of mutual interest in order to continue to grow and develop. In noting the many differences among agencies with regard to structure, organization, program, and scope, Wynns pointed out that there existed an inherent unity of purpose in furthering the concept of one-to-one friendship between a man and a boy in order to help the boy at a critical time in his life.[5]

Big Brothers of America

The Wynns study was published and released in June 1946 at a conference of eleven Big Brothers organizations, held at Camp Wyomissing — the summer camp of the Philadelphia Big Brother Association — near Stroudsburg, Pennsylvania. It was at this gathering that the foundation was laid for the creation of Big Brothers of America (BBA). The new organization was incorporated on December 24, 1946. The seven incorporators became the temporary board.

Soon a national executive secretary was required. Gilbert H. Gendall became the first person to serve in that position. Gendall, a former regional executive for the Boy Scouts of America, had retired but agreed to accept the post on a temporary basis. An office was opened at the headquarters of the Philadelphia Big Brother Association.[6]

Wynns's study revealed that seven of the fifteen agencies surveyed felt that the national headquarters should be in New York City. None of them suggested Philadelphia. However, from the time that Charles G. Berwind was named chairman of the Temporary Big Brother National Committee to the time of the Wyomissing conference (Berwind picked up the tab for the conference) and afterward as the fledgling organization came into being, it was undoubtedly assumed that Berwind, a well-known and influential Philadelphia businessman, would be its first president, and that the headquarters would be in Philadelphia. Not only did Berwind become the first president, he retained that position for twenty-five years, also becoming the organization's chief architect, mentor, and financial supporter. A biographical sketch of Berwind appears in chapter 7.

Eleven of the Big Brothers agencies that participated in the Wynns survey became charter members of Big Brothers of America, as did two other agencies. The thirteen charter members were Jewish Big Brother Association of Boston; Big Brother Association of Cincinnati; Jewish Big Brother Association of Cleveland; Big Brother Association of Columbus, Ohio; Dallas Big Brothers, Inc.; Big Brothers, Inc., Denver, Colorado; Big Brother Association of Hamilton, Inc., Hamilton, Ontario; Big Brothers, Inc., Minneapolis; Big Brother Movement, New York; Jewish Big Brothers, New York; Big Brother Association, Philadelphia; Big Brother Organization, Inc., St. Louis; and the Big Brother Movement, Toronto.

A later compilation of the original thirteen members, prepared by Big Brothers of America in 1967, includes the Jewish Big Brother League of Baltimore, but does not mention St. Louis.[7] However, it is now generally accepted that St. Louis, not Baltimore, was a charter member, although the Jewish Big Brother League of Baltimore was a member of the Temporary National Big Brother Committee. Records indicate that the Baltimore agency joined BBA in 1949.

The new federation's proposed first-year budget totaled $10,200 including a $5,000 salary for the national executive director, $2,000 for a stenographer, $960 for rent, $1,200 for traveling expenses, and $1,040 for telephone, stationery, postage, and office expenses.[8] A funds-solicitation campaign was launched, an informational brochure was developed, and plans were begun for a meeting of affiliates, which was held on Saturday, November 8, 1947, at Buffalo, New York.

Council of Delegates Meets

Each of the thirteen agencies certified two persons to attend the Buffalo meeting. This group was known as the Council of Delegates. Its function was to elect the first board of directors (to replace the interim board) and conduct other business necessary for creating a viable organization. If one considers that it only met for one day, the amount of work that was accomplished is amazing. It elected a board, which consisted of one person from each of the thirteen agencies represented, plus two members-at-large. It authorized a maximum number of members of thirty-six subject to its approval, and gave the board latitude to appoint up to twenty-four members at its discretion. It was understood that an effort would be made to attract prominent and widely known nonagency men to the board (up to the approved limit) in order to improve the organization's financial base and also to give it credence.

The Council of Delegates also discussed agency personnel policies, training, and standards of admission for agencies. Committees were appointed to prepare reports for the board on standards and to draft a proposed constitution for local agencies. The new board met, with the Council of Delegates as guests, and elected Charles Berwind as president. Four vice-presidents were elected and an Executive Committee was created. The board also created a Technical and Advisory Committee (TAC), consisting of the executive director of each agency, to review and act on professional matters affecting the national organization, and established a Board of Sponsors, whose members would consist of major financial contributors as well as others whose names might lend prestige to Big Brothers of America.

The newly created Technical and Advisory Committee then met, appointed a temporary chairman, and discussed various matters relating to agency operations. Items for the agenda of future meetings were suggested.

President Berwind announced that a Big Brothers symbol was being developed, and that an effort would be made to develop a newsletter. The delegates discussed how they could raise the funds necessary to meet the condition of the first matching grant — a $5,000 gift from John D. Rockefeller III that had to be matched with $25,000 before December 31, 1948.[9]

The proceedings of the meetings in Buffalo have been covered in considerable detail because of their historical significance. Although the preliminary plans for the new organization were made at Camp Wyomissing, and certain developmental work was done during the following months, it was at Buffalo that the basic framework was established for Big Brothers of America (BBA) and its successor, Big Brothers/Big Sisters of America (BB/BSA).

BBA Moves Ahead

Many activities took place in 1948, as developmental activities continued at a rapid pace. President Berwind issued the organization's first annual report on January 31, 1948, in which he discussed the activities of the past year, while cautioning the members to avoid the weaknesses of the old Big Brother and Big Sister Federation.[10] After receiving a copy of this report, Ernest K. Coulter, then seventy-six years old and recovering from a serious heart attack at his home in California, wrote to Berwind and congratulated him on the progress made during the "difficult first year," and also for his efforts to avoid the mistakes of the first national organization.[11]

On March 1, 1948, Donald Jenks succeeded Gilbert H. Gendall as BBA executive secretary and, during the year, President Berwind or Jenks visited every one of the thirteen member agencies. Also joining BBA in 1948 was Margaret M. Hanley, who was to serve the organization for twenty-seven years, first as secretary to the executive director, then as secretary to the Board of Directors, and finally as BBA director of administration. Miss Hanley, who retired in 1975, died in 1978. Her record of continuous service in the national federation will not be surpassed at least before the turn of the century.

Norman Rockwell

Artist Norman Rockwell completed this drawing for Big Brothers of America in 1948. It became one of the best-known trademarks ever used by a social-service organization.

A new brochure, *Today Marks a Crossroads*, was developed in 1948. A national symbol, which Berwind had mentioned briefly at Buffalo, was developed and completed by American artist Norman Rockwell. Showing a man with one hand on the shoulder of a boy and the other hand pointing in the direction the boy should go, the symbol quickly became identified with the Movement and became one of the most popular and successful trademarks ever utilized by a social-service organization. The national organization used it in many applications until the merger with Big Sisters International in 1977. It still has limited use among some Big Brothers agencies.

The *Big Brother Bulletin* made its debut during the second half of the year. The attractively designed and effectively produced publication carried many brief but informative articles about the Movement and its member agencies. The Rockwell symbol was used in the masthead, and from the Fall 1952 issue on, the equally famous slogan, of somewhat uncertain origin, "No Man Stands So Straight As When He Stoops to Help a Boy," was used with it. The *Bulletin* was originally issued monthly, and was mailed to approximately two thousand members of affiliated and nonaffiliated Big Brothers agencies as well as to nine thousand community leaders throughout the nation.

Publicity efforts received a boost in September, when cartoonist Ham Fisher contributed the services of his popular character Joe Palooka, who became a "Big Brother." In a panel, which appeared in the *Bulletin*, Joe admonished Little Brothers to "fight fair and always keep their punches clean." Eddie Cantor, who had supported the Movement for many years, agreed to present a Big Brothers message during one of his national broadcasts, and BBA hired its first public relations director, George A. Grossman.[12]

The Council of Delegates met again on December 14, 1948, and approved a draft of the minimum standards that had to be met by agencies that wished to affiliate. Earlier, BBA had admitted the Jewish Big Brothers Association of Los Angeles, the first agency to join the original thirteen charter members. An average of two agencies a year were admitted until about the time the national organization received its federal charter in 1958, when the pace quickened and many more agencies became affiliated each year.[13] The first agency that BBA assisted in forming was the nonsectarian Big Brother Association of Boston, which became an affiliate of the national body in late 1949.

National board members represented affiliated agencies, and provision had been made for naming prominent, nonparticipating men to the board, if their presence would add prestige to the organization. But it was still felt that all areas of the nation might not be adequately represented. In early 1949, an area director program was implemented. The country was divided into twelve areas which, for convenience, were coincided with the twelve Federal Reserve Bank districts. Each of these areas was to be represented by a board member who would oversee area activities, assist in the organization of new agencies, and serve as liaison between local groups and the national headquarters. Mason K. Knuckles of Denver was the first area or regional director, and was responsible for an area that included most of Colorado, Oklahoma, Kansas, Wyoming, Nebraska, and New Mexico.[14]

The annual meeting of the Council of Delegates and board members in 1949 was in Cleveland in conjunction with the National Conference of Social Work. Annual meetings or conferences became an increasingly important part of BBA activities. The multifunction gatherings not only provided an opportunity for delegates to hear from outstanding leaders in the field of social service, they also provided a forum for the exchange of ideas and information on agency operations, and enabled the national leaders to develop a closer relationship with local groups.

The proceedings of annual meetings (they later became known as national conferences) tell much about the fast-developing national program. Quite a bit of detailed information on these early meetings can be found in bound copies of the *Big Brother Bulletin*, available in the archives of Big Brothers/Big Sisters of America in Philadelphia, and in the Big Brothers of America holdings of the Social Welfare History Archives of the University of Minnesota. The meeting locations and their dates for the period covered by this chapter (1945 – 1957), which have not previously been mentioned, are: Atlantic City, 1950; Minneapolis, 1951; Chicago, 1952; Dallas, 1953; Cleveland, 1954; New York, 1955; St. Louis, 1956; and Hamilton, Ontario, 1957.

The first Big Brother Week was observed from January 15–21, 1950. With assistance from the Advertising Council, Inc., and several top advertising agencies, BBA was able to receive publicity on many national radio and TV shows, including those hosted by such luminaries as Ed Sullivan, Fred Waring, Paul Whiteman, Bob Hope, Garry Moore, Red Skelton, Jack Benny, Bing Crosby, Bill Stern, and Art Linkletter. Newspapers gave the Movement wide coverage, and a television public service announcement (PSA), starring actor Gene Lockhart, was reportedly aired on most of the nation's then ninety-six TV stations.[15] This high level of exposure was maintained for several years thereafter during Big Brother Week. Probably not before or since has the Movement received so much national publicity during such brief periods. The results were predictable: local agencies received many inquiries from prospective Big Brothers.

The practice of naming a national figure as Big Brother of the Year (since discontinued) also began in 1950, covering the period of the previous year. The first person to be so designated was Associate Justice Tom Clark of the U.S. Supreme Court, who had previously been

Big Brother Bulletin

BIG BROTHERS OF AMERICA, INC.   UNITED STATES & CANADA

VOL. I, NO. 7   PHILADELPHIA, PA.   APRIL, 1949

Many Plan Attending Big Brother Annual Meeting in Cleveland

Indications are that the annual meeting of Big Brothers of America, scheduled for Cleveland on June 15-16, will be well attended by Big Brother executives and officers from all parts of the United States and Canada.

Staff members and officers of many of the 14 organizations affiliated with Big Brothers of America already have filed with the national office their hotel reservations for the Cleveland sessions, and others are expected to do so shortly.

Since the Big Brother meetings will be as an associate group of the National Conference of Social Work, some of the Big Brother executives are planning to attend Conference sessions as well. These include many meetings on juvenile delinquency.

The national office is arranging an exhibit booth, which will be open during the entire week of the National Conference of Social Work from June 12 to 18.

The first session of the Big Brother meetings, as tentatively planned, will be a visit and luncheon on June 15 at Bellefaire, a children's agency, with the Cleveland Jewish Big Brothers as host.

At 2:30 that day, in the penthouse of the Allerton Hotel, the first of two panel discussions will be held. It will deal with "Training the Volunteer for Work With Boys," and the speakers will be Reg. D. Scott, Executive Secretary of the Hamilton Big Brothers, and Donald S. Leaf, Executive Secretary of the Minneapolis Big Brothers. There will be open discussion following.

At 4 p. m. in the same location, the second panel discussion, "The Volunteer in Case Work With Boys," will be held. Joseph H. McCoy, general secretary of the Big Brother Movement, New York, will be one of two speakers.

On June 16, at 2 p. m. the Council of Delegates will meet in Parlor C, of the
(Continued on page 4, column 3)

DEAF LITTLE BROTHER HEARS THROUGH HANDS

Carl Hanson, a little brother of Minneapolis, who has been completely deaf for nine years, is able to sense voice and music vibrations with his hands. With him is Carl Balander, his Big Brother, who is helping the boy realize his school ambitions and his plans to become a printer.

Minneapolis Big Brothers Help Deaf Little Brother Realize Work Plans

Minneapolis Big Brothers, extending the guidance and friendship traditional with Big Brother organizations, have brought happiness and a chance to enter upon his chosen lifework to a boy afflicted with total deafness.

Because of an old deformity, Carl Hanson became completely deaf nine years ago. He was a B student in a class for deaf children. When he was fourteen in 1947, his school referred Carl to the Big Brothers for summer camp.

COLUMBUS BIG BROTHER RESCUES CHILDREN FROM ICY LAKE

Dr. D. Orval Kraner, an optometrist, and a Columbus Big Brother, is being commended for his rescue of a boy and his small sister from an ice-filled lake.

The children had fallen through the ice on the way to school.

Carl, who could speak and had learned lip-reading, was accepted at the Big Brother camp, but was given no special privileges because of his deafness. He held his own with the other boys in every respect, even earning honorable mention for his camp activities.

At the end of camp, Carl asked for
(Continued on page 4 column 2)

An early copy of the *Big Brother Bulletin*

Beginning in 1950, prominent Americans were honored by being named "Big Brother of the Year." The awards were often presented by other prominent persons. The practice had been discontinued by 1970.

Comedian Danny Kaye receives his Big Brother of the Year Award from President Eisenhower, himself a BBOY recipient, as a smiling Charles G. Berwind looks on.

Famed flying ace Capt. Eddie Rickenbacker looks on as auto pioneer and BBA benefactor Charles Stewart Mott receives a BBOY Award from President Eisenhower.

J. Edgar Hoover, director of the FBI, receives Big Brother of the Year Award from BBA President Charles G. Berwind.

John F. Kennedy made Award presentation to Comedian Danny Thomas.

Presenting a BBOY Award to President Johnson is Comedian Dick Van Dyke, as Charles G. Berwind looks on. Others in photo are not identified.

121

named an honorary board member. J. Edgar Hoover, director of the FBI received the honor in 1951. Other national figures who were honored included war hero Captain Eddie Rickenbacker, auto pioneer and philanthropist Charles Stewart Mott, comedian Danny Kaye, Francis Cardinal Spellman, President Dwight D. Eisenhower, comedian Danny Thomas, President Lyndon B. Johnson, basketball star Bob Cousy, evangelist Billy Graham, and a husband and wife team, famed criminologists Eleanor and Sheldon Glueck, both associated with the Harvard Law School. Sheldon Glueck had been the last president of the old Big Brother and Big Sister Federation in the mid-thirties. Both Gluecks were internationally known for their research in the areas of delinquency, crime prevention, and treatment.

Not only were famous people named, an effort was also made to have the award presented by other famous people. Thus, Danny Kaye received a scroll, setting forth his designation as Big Brother of the Year, from President Eisenhower. Danny Thomas's scroll was presented by President John F. Kennedy, and actor Dick Van Dyke, who later became a BBA vice-president (chapter 5), participated in the presentation to President Johnson. Eleanor and Sheldon Glueck received their award from then Vice-President Richard M. Nixon. Later, after he had become president, Nixon was designated as the "First Honorary Big Brother" by BBA.

As word of the Movement's effectiveness spread, its work was acknowledged and praised by more and more people of national prominence. Writing to BBA in 1950 from his headquarters in Japan, General of the Armies Douglas MacArthur said:

> I am in complete accord with the aims of any group which seeks to lead the young people of our country, or of any country, to a full realization, understanding and grateful acceptance of those God-given principles of living which offer to all men and all nations a path to universal peace and understanding. The safeguarding for our children of the way of life which we as free men enjoy demands of us all a tolerance, sympathetic understanding and helping hand for those young people who, during their formative years, have failed in their early responsibilities to society . . . to the extent that the Big Brother program . . . contributes toward the realization of these principles, the cause of freedom, integrity and decency among men and among nations will be strengthened and gangsterism, whether individual or international, will decline.[16]

The Board of Sponsors, recommended at the Buffalo meeting in 1947 by Berwind, now included such names as band leader Paul Whiteman, actor Jimmie Stewart, comedian Eddie Cantor, and drug magnet Justin Dart. Big Brothers of America apparently experienced little difficulty in getting popular entertainers to endorse the program. Public

Seventeen agencies were affiliated with BBA by 1951, when this annual meeting convened in Minneapolis. Charles G. Berwind is seated behind the lectern.

service announcements for radio and television were contributed by such personalities as Jim Nabors, Merv Griffin, the Amazing Kreskin, Henry Gibson, Andy Williams, Bill Cosby, David Frost, Mike Douglas, Ray Charles, Jack Klugman, and Tony Randall. The organization has always been held in high esteem by government officials and politicians, and an article in the December 1956 *Reader's Digest* titled "They Give a Boy a Break" provided the Movement with wide visibility as well as added prestige.

As in any social-service organization, fund raising was and continued to be a major problem. Much of the funding was supplied by Berwind himself. Board members contributed, gifts and donations were solicited, and each affiliated agency paid a small annual fee, but the need for new sources was ever present.

The BBA Board of Directors passed up an investment opportunity in 1949 that could have put the organization on easy street for many years, according to a story in the *Philadelphia Bulletin* for February 26, 1950. To help alleviate the postwar housing shortage quickly, Levitt & Sons, Inc., was in the process of building the first of its famed developments, Levittown, Long Island, New York. Of the 10,000 houses that had been completed at that time, more than 4,000 were rental units. Levitt decided to divest itself of the rental properties, worth an estimated $30 million. It was possible for a nonprofit organization to obtain the houses with little investment and a huge loan from the Federal Housing Administration, with attractive tax advantages for both seller and buyer.

After BBA directors considered the deal and failed to act, officials of a Philadelphia nonprofit adult education association, the Philadelphia

Junto, with which BBA executive director Donald Jenks and later BBA board member Philip Klein were associated, obtained the Levittown property for their organization. In a complex financial maneuver, involving practically no out-of-pocket cash, the Junto obtained a property with a potential of $75,000 per year in rental income—an astronomical figure by 1950s standards. The school later sold the property.

In a 1954 effort to raise funds, the BBA directors decided to offer individual membership on a national basis. Several levels of such membership were approved. For $100 a person could become a "contributor," $50 was required to become a "sponsor," $25 to be a "sustaining" member, $10 for an "associate" membership, $5 for a "regular" designation, and for only $2 a "special" membership was available. The plan was never successful, possibly because of the burden of administration. It could not be determined when the program was abandoned.[17] At about the time that the individual memberships were approved, a plan to create "Associate Big Brothers" was announced and approved. Associates were to be well-known men who could effectively solicit large gifts. Captain Eddie Rickenbacker, among others, served in that capacity.

By 1957, BBA had grown to thirty-three agencies, and Charles G. Berwind had been elected to his eleventh term as president (he would serve for yet another fifteen years). Although nearly everyone in the field of social service expressed admiration for Berwind's leadership and many contributions, some felt that the organization's future growth and success depended upon a widening of executive responsibility.

One of Berwind's closest friends and associates in the Movement, G. Ruhland Rebmann, a Philadelphia lawyer, BBA organizer and board member, once chided him for not delegating more of his functions. He told Berwind, "If it is your ambition, desire, and willingness to contribute $25,000 to $30,000 a year to the national organization and run it more or less as an individual charity, there is no question . . . but that an effective job can be done and that you will be able to raise, in addition, $15,000 or $20,000 a year from other sources." Otherwise, Rebmann told Berwind, "your Board of Directors must be given and must assume full responsibility for practically everything that is done." Continued Rebmann, "There is no question in my mind that practically all of the other directors consider that this is your show." He reminded Berwind that as long as Berwind was financing practically the entire program and making almost all of the decisions, the other board members were not going to step in and voluntarily assume more responsibility. He urged Berwind to entrust the functioning of the organization to an active executive committee, empowered to act in the board's absence.[18]

Although Berwind may have endeavored to heed his friend's advice to some extent, the evidence indicates that he continued to retain a firm grip on the rudder, and the attitude of the board, for the most part, seemed to be one of benign, friendly acceptance. Rebmann's admonishment apparently did have one positive effect. The Executive Committee, which had been created nearly four years before, and which had never met, was activated and began meeting on a regular basis. The first meeting of this group was in Philadelphia on September 20, 1951.[19]

Vital to the success of day-to-day operations — administration, services, and agency relations — was the key role of the BBA executive director, who sometimes had the title of executive vice-president. Donald Jenks, the first permanent BBA executive director, was succeeded in 1950 by Benjamin Van Doren Hedges, who was elevated to executive vice-president. Hedges had been personnel administrator for Bankers Trust Company in New York. Hedges apparently never moved to Philadelphia during the time he held the top post, preferring instead to continue living in Manhattan. Hedges had been active in the New York Movement and had been a Big Brother.

He was succeeded in 1952 by Felix Gentile, the first professional social worker to become the BBA chief administrator. Gentile, whose title was executive director, served with distinction in that capacity until his sudden death in May 1957. Stanley B. Adams, a former advertising agency executive, was appointed executive vice-president to fill the vacancy left by Gentile. However, Adams resigned after serving for only a few months. He was succeeded by Goesta Wollin, with the title of executive director. Goesta, both a scientist and a social worker, had been serving as BBA's director of programs and services. Whether or not the position was filled by an executive director or an executive vice-president apparently depended upon the personal qualifications of available candidates. By the end of 1957, the headquarters' staff of BBA consisted of approximately six persons.

The next twelve years would be characterized by rapid change for BBA, heralded by the obtaining of a federal charter, election of a successor to President Berwind, and many developmental and structural changes.

* * * *

Big Brothers—
The Art
of Friendship

Official Guidebook for Big Brothers

Notes to Chapter 4

1. Study of the Big Brothers and Big Sisters organizations of the United States and Canada on the basis of a Survey of Local Organizations, folder 7, Big Brothers of America (BBA) records, Social Welfare History Archives (SWHA), University of Minnesota.
2. Ibid., p. 55.
3. Ibid., p. 35.
4. Transcript of taped interview with Joseph H. McCoy, executive director of the New York Big Brother Movement, May 28, 1957, Big Brothers/Big Sisters of America (BB/BSA) Archives, Philadelphia.
5. Study and Report of Fifteen Big Brother Organizations in the United States and Canada, June 1946, BB/BSA Archives, Philadelphia.
6. Interview with McCoy, p. 5.
7. Big Brother Movement — History, statement on file in the BB/BSA Archives, Philadelphia.
8. A Statement and Appeal from the Big Brother National Committee, folder 104, BBA records, SWHA.
9. Papers related to the Council of Delegates meeting held at Buffalo, N.Y., on November 8, 1947, BB/BSA Archives, Philadelphia.
10. Informal Report, First Year's Operation, Big Brothers of America, Inc, BB/BSA Archives, Philadelphia.
11. Letter from Ernest K. Coulter to Charles G. Berwind, April 28, 1948, BB/BSA Archives, Philadelphia.
12. "President's Report Details Work Done, Tells of New Plans," *Big Brother Bulletin*, January 1949, 1.
13. Agency and budget data, 1947–1964, folder 5, BBA records, SWHA.
14. "Mason Knuckles New Area Director in Denver for National Big Brothers," *Big Brother Bulletin*, February 1949, 1.
15. "Big Brother Week TV Radio Shows Created Wide Interest in Work," *Big Brother Bulletin*, February–March 1950, 1.
16. Letter from General of the Armies Douglas MacArthur to Benjamin Van Doren Hedges, December 4, 1950, BB/BSA Archives, Philadelphia.
17. "Campaign to Enroll Big Brothers as National Members Underway," *Big Brother Bulletin*, Fall 1954, 2; see also *BBB*, Spring 1955, 7.
18. Letter from G. Ruhland Rebmann, Jr., to Charles G. Berwind, May 29, 1951, BB/BSA Archives, Philadelphia.
19. Minutes of first meeting of Executive Committee, September 20, 1951, folder 5, BBA records, SWHA.

5

A Federal Charter and Rapid Growth for Big Brothers (1958–1970)

Although an attempt by the old Big Brother and Big Sister Federation to obtain a federal charter had failed, an effort by Big Brothers of America would now be successful. Legislation introduced by Missouri Senator Thomas C. Hennings, Jr., to incorporate the organization in the District of Columbia was passed by both houses of Congress and signed into law by President Eisenhower on September 2, 1958, as Public Law 85-870 (72 Stat. 1691). Senator Hennings was a longtime supporter of the Movement, and had been honored as Big Brother of the Year in 1955. His father, Judge Thomas C. Hennings, had founded the St. Louis agency in 1914.

The new corporation assumed all of the assets and liabilities of the former national organization, which had been incorporated in the State of New York. A federal charter meant that BBA, and its member agencies, now had full and exclusive rights to the name Big Brothers of America, Inc., as well as such rights as the use of emblems, seals, and badges that had been used previously. The incorporators, named in the act, were Charles G. Berwind and Mark Willcox, Jr., both of Philadelphia, and Earle S. Thompson, Archie O. Dawson, and Isadore A. Wyner, all of New York City.

Accelerated Growth

Activity at the national level, as well as in local communities, increased sharply during BBA's second decade, as new agencies were formed and agency affiliations grew. During BBA's first ten years, 20 additional agencies had joined the 13 charter members. During the next ten and a half years, these 33 agencies grew to 150 affiliated groups, a more than fourfold increase by mid-1969.[1] In 1963, 68 affiliated agencies reported 10,500 Big Brother – Little Brother matches. By 1968, 128 affiliates reported 27,000 matches. During that five-year period, the BBA national budget grew from $113,770 to $200,000 annually.[2]

Goesta Wollin had resigned in 1960. He was succeeded as executive director by Thomas E. O'Brien, also a social worker, with a master's degree in the field from Boston College. O'Brien, who had served as executive director of two local agencies before coming to BBA, held the top administrative post for twelve years — longer than any other person in the federation's history thus far. Under his administration, during the turbulent 1960s and early 1970s, BBA enjoyed its greatest period of growth and development up to that time, becoming an organization of truly national stature and renown by the time of his resignation at the end of 1972.

Many innovative and effective projects involving service delivery, fund raising, public awareness, and professional staff development were implemented by O'Brien, with the support and guidance of Charles G. Berwind and other board members. By far the most ambitious and far-reaching of such activities was the multipronged Era of Growth (EOG) Program, which was launched in 1965.[3]

Coordinated by board members Ernest G. Fritsche, as chairman, and Solo A. Blank, as vice-chairman, Era of Growth embraced a five-year program designed to double the organization's size by the time the program ended in 1970. To involve more volunteers, make possible needed research, and increase BBA's annual budget dramatically, twelve major EOG projects were developed. Eight of these endeavors were designed for agency implementation, and four were earmarked for completion by the national board. Agencies were expected to select one or more projects to be completed within one year and to select and complete new ones in subsequent years. National project chairmen assisted and kept track of results.

Agency projects involved responsibility for the creation of new agencies in neighboring cities, solicitation of funds from local industries, local recruiting and recognition of volunteers who could not serve as Big Brothers but who could contribute financially, solicitation of additional United Way funds, the sponsoring of fund-raising testimonial dinners, a stepped-up Big Brothers recruiting program, the solicitation of Big Brother volunteers for additional funds in the form of dues, and the utilization of past agency board presidents in current activities.

National board projects were designed to raise funds by sponsoring benefit activities, such as sports or entertainment spectaculars, the solicitation of foundations for funds, the seeking of research grants, and the creation of a "Chair of Philosophy" which would be established for any board member who contributed at least one thousand dollars.

The projects, announced in a special edition of the *Big Brother Bulletin*, and geared to the immediate needs of the Movement, generated considerable enthusiasm. An elaborate recognition and awards program for both individuals and agencies provided additional incentive. An agency that selected and completed one project received a BBA award plaque. An agency that completed two projects received a medallion award. A "Presidential Citation" was awarded for three accomplishments, and any agency that completed more than three projects received the "Charles G. Berwind" Trophy.

During EOG's first year, 51 agencies selected a total of 116 projects. Nineteen agencies completed projects, with one, Columbus, Ohio, receiving the Berwind Award. By late 1967, it became apparent that several of the projects were either too similar to others or impractical. In early 1968, a revised program involving only five agency projects was announced. Two of these appeared to be new: the involvement of Big Brothers alumni and the creation of Women's Auxiliaries. A new chairman, John Heller, attempted to breathe new life into the program.[4] Although EOG apparently ran its projected five-year course, and although such project-related activities as volunteer recruitment and fund raising continued to be emphasized, it appears that it commanded increasingly less attention. The last EOG awards were presented at the BBA annual meeting in Detroit on April 25, 1969.

Fund-Raising and Publicity Efforts

When it became apparent near the end of the 1960s that volunteer fund-raising efforts were inadequate, either in meeting current needs or projected expenditures for increasing services to agencies, the federation turned to a professional fund-raising consultant for the first time in its history. It retained a Columbus, Ohio, firm, R. H. Goettler and Associates. At a December 8, 1967, meeting of the BBA Executive Committee, Goettler representatives outlined a four-phase development-fund campaign designed to raise $3.5 million over a five-year period. It was not to be a broad-based campaign. Rather, it would focus on obtaining funds from a few wealthy individuals, foundations, and corporations. The drive actually got underway in January 1969.[5]

Despite a significant pledge from President Berwind, a large pledge from board member William S. Fishman, then president of Automatic Retailers of America (now known as ARA Services), and eventually total pledges of more than $200,000 from other board members, the program encountered formidable difficulties. The board became disillusioned with the Goettler organization, and the latter blamed the board for many of the campaign's failings.

The consultant also cited other negative factors. The economy was experiencing new inflationary pressures, corporate profits were declining, the stock market was experiencing a decline, a new tax reform bill was having an unfavorable impact on foundation bequests, and the Boy Scouts were concurrently conducting a nationwide drive to raise $65 million. Even the death of Washington columnist Drew Pearson, a BBA Board member, affected the effort. Pearson had agreed to assist in solicitation of the Ford Foundation as well as make a personal contribution.[6]

On January 15, 1970, the services of R. H. Goettler were terminated although the firm agreed to serve on a per diem basis when needed. Berwind returned control of the drive to BBA in Philadelphia and named Executive Director Thomas O'Brien as its director.[7] However, inside administration proved no better, as solicitation efforts continued to abate. The futility of the effort was recognized when the board on February 12, 1972, turned its attention to other means of support and ordered that all development fund monies be transferred to BBA's regular operating account.[8]

An effective fund-raising idea was implemented in 1966, possibly as part of the EOG program. BBA held two successful fund-raising dinners that year—affairs that have continued to the present time on an annual basis. A dinner in Los Angeles on April 21, 1966, hosted by popular actor and comedian Dick Van Dyke, netted more than $25,000 for BBA. A similar dinner in Philadelphia on December 13 of that year grossed nearly $40,000. The formula for these annual affairs is simple, yet effective. Severely limit the invitation list, charge several hundred dollars per person, and invest a substantial portion of the proceeds in expensive door prizes, which usually include a new automobile. Today, four such dinners are held annually for the benefit of Big Brothers/Big Sisters of America. In addition to the Los Angeles event, now known as "Show Biz Bash West," and "The Epicurean Club," in Philadelphia, the "250" is held in Cleveland, and New York is the host city for "Show Biz Bash East." The New York affair has, for several years, been successfully headlined by comedian Alan King, who is often joined by funnyman Buddy Hackett.

Many agencies have also found such dinners to be excellent fund-raisers. One noteworthy agency event during the 1960s, with a different format, was the annual barbeque hosted by Drew Pearson at his Maryland farm for the benefit of Big Brothers of the National Capitol Area. At the 1966 affair, which raised $12,000 for the agency, more than 2,600 guests were entertained by then popular TV star Mitch Miller. Pearson, in addition to being a national board member, served as president of Big Brothers of the National Capitol Area agency for ten years. When he retired from that post, he was honored at a giant agency benefit, at which Vice-President Hubert Humphrey spoke, and the "chairman of the board" himself, Frank Sinatra, sang for the guests.

Many other unique and innovative fund-raising ideas were tried or proposed by BBA. One of the most unusual and appealing was a plan considered by the board in 1972, which involved the creation of "Big Brothers Sports Ambassadors," and the formation of a "1001 Club." Well-known professional athletes were to be asked to contact affluent businessmen around the country and ask them to join the club by contributing $1,001 to Big Brothers each year. In turn, the sports personages would present donors with personal, autographed mementos, such as sports equipment used by the stars in crucial games. Although the board was enthusiastic about the proposal, and authorized a pilot study to determine its feasibility, the program apparently was never implemented.[9]

it takes a man to help a boy

Be a BIG BROTHER
Call 000-0000

Actor and comedian Dick Van Dyke, shown on this poster, was a BBA vice-president during the 1960s and participated in many Movement activities.

The Movement had long looked to business and industry for financial assistance. In 1967, BBA decided that this sector could also be helpful in other ways. Early in that year, an agreement was reached with the Kresge Company, in which the nationwide, nine-hundred-store retailer was to help recruit Big Brothers among its employees, help publicize the program through store displays and through the distribution of Movement literature, and help organize new Big Brothers agencies.[10]

In late 1967, a similar agreement was reached with the Thom McAn Shoe Company, which also operated nine hundred retail units. In a memorandum to the company's management and store personnel, John Riefler, Thom McAn vice-president for personnel, said, "We are proud to offer our personnel the opportunity to contribute their services to an organization of such demonstrable worth as the Big Brothers of America." Said Lawrence McGourty, the company's general manager, "We will do everything in our power to further the cause."[11] Despite initial enthusiasm on the part of BBA and the two firms, they apparently achieved few tangible results, possibly because of inadequate follow-through by both BBA and the companies.

Even though the Movement was held in high esteem by many celebrities, support by such personages was generally limited to an occasional public endorsement, the contribution of a public service announcement (PSA), or perhaps attendance at a fund-raising dinner. One popular entertainer insisted on doing more. Dick Van Dyke, mentioned earlier in connection with the first Los Angeles benefit dinner for BBA, became a member of the BBA Board of Directors in either 1963 or 1964 (the board minutes for those years have been lost). By 1965, he was a national vice-president. Although it was probably the busiest period in his career — he was at the height of his popularity as star of the CBS "Dick Van Dyke Show" with Mary Tyler Moore — he participated actively in many BBA affairs. Included were fund-raising solicitations, participation in award presentations, and liberal contributions of his time and talent for the production of BBA promotional materials. On posters, billboards, and car cards (for use in streetcars, buses, and subways) Van Dyke will be remembered for his re-creation of the famous Norman Rockwell BBA man and boy symbol. It is not known how Van Dyke first became interested in the Movement, although it could have been through Abe Lastfogel, an official of the William Morris Agency, or through the influence of Meredith Willson, both of whom were then members of BBA's board. Meredith Willson, of course, is remembered for his creation of the hit Broadway musical, and later film, *The Music Man*. Van Dyke was last elected to the BBA board in 1970. There is no mention of his activities on behalf of the Movement after that time.

Enthusiasm for a new recruiting film, A *Friend for Joey*, premiered at the meeting of members in 1970, quickly dimmed when Dr. C. Randolph Taylor, a black board member, protested that the picture was totally unacceptable to the black community in spite of its excellent technical characteristics. Dr. Taylor, as a child in Harlem, was the Movement's first black Little Brother (chapter 2). The film had been authorized by the board in October 1969, at a cost of $34,500. After being admonished by Dr. Taylor, the board adopted a resolution that urged the producer of the film to include "all of the many ethnic and religious groups that are presently involved in the Big Brother Movement."[12] But this was not done to Dr. Taylor's satisfaction. The board then authorized an additional expenditure of $8,000, when and if funds became available, to produce an acceptable revision of the film.

Dr. Taylor is believed to be the first black to serve on the BBA national board. The first woman to serve on the BBA board was Eileen Hart McMichael of Villanova, Pennsylvania; she was elected to that post on May 19, 1959.[13] McMichael subsequently established the National Women's Committee, which functioned as a special BBA fund-raising arm for many years. The committee sponsored various benefits, including — for several years — an annual AAU-sanctioned swim meet. Although the scope of this committee was supposed to be national, most of the activity centered around Philadelphia. The organization apparently dissolved during the early 1970s.

Joyce Black, a director of Big Brothers of New York, was elected to the BBA board around 1970, becoming the first woman to serve as a national director, who was also active in local agency work. Black later became president of the New York agency. As of 1985, she was continuing to serve in both capacities – as head of the New York agency and as a member of the national board (now BB/BSA). Black has made many valuable contributions to the progress of both organizations.

Esther Edwards, a senior vice-president of Motown Records Corporation, is believed to be the first black woman to serve on the BBA board. She became a director in May 1972, but resigned shortly thereafter.

Before leaving the discussion of fund raising, publicity, and recruitment during the period covered by this chapter, mention should be made of the continuing contributions of the *Big Brother Bulletin* in those areas. The *Bulletin* not only served as the major link between the national organization and its affiliated agencies, it also functioned as an effective, though limited, liaison with community leaders. Discontinued because of limited funds in 1960, the *Bulletin* was reactivated in 1964 as a quarterly, and had a national circulation of twelve thousand copies. Twenty thousand copies were being distributed by 1966. By 1973, after its name had been changed to the *Big Brothers Ambassador*, the publication had reached a circulation of forty thousand, and had made an unsuccessful effort to solicit support through advertising.[14] Around 1974, the *Ambassador* was discontinued. Agencies, national board members, and other friends of the Movement were kept informed by a newsletter, the *Communicator*, which had a greatly reduced circulation. Today, a publication, with the same format, is known as the *Correspondent*.

That the Movement's efforts to achieve public recognition were successful was indicated by a survey made by National Family Opinion, Inc., involving a sample of 10,000 respondents, and made available in December 1969. The results indicated, however, that although most people had heard of Big Brothers of America, only 11 percent of those questioned indicated that they were aware that no costs were involved in becoming a Big Brother, and only about 20 percent indicated that they were familiar with the fact that BBA provided professional supervision of its matches.[15]

B**i**G BROTHERS
AMBASSADOR

VOL. XXII—No. 6   MAY, 1973

Atlanta Getting Ready for 25th Annual Meeting

LEWIS P. READE
BBA Executive Vice President

All roads will lead to Atlanta early next month as Big Brothers of America holds its 25th Annual Meeting in the jewel city of the South. And more than 400 Big Brothers' volunteers and professionals are expected to make the Meeting the best in history.

The Meeting will feature a variety of sessions designed to share information and provide insight into many of the major concerns challenging our society today, according to Harrington Witherspoon, general chairman.

In addition to the work sessions, which will begin with a full day for professionals only on Wednesday, June 6, and continue for both professionals and laymen through Saturday, there will be two top social events and leisure time for enjoying the attractions of Atlanta.

Headquarters for the Meeting will be the fabulous Hyatt Regency House which is world famed for its sweeping architectural innovations, including a 23-story lobby, glass elevators operating at speeds up to 700 feet per minute, and a kaleidoscopic view of fountains, suspended metal sculpture and live trees.

Joining the Regency as a special attraction to visitors to the Meeting are a host of noted landmarks including Georgia's Stone Mountain, Underground Atlanta, the Atlanta Memorial Arts Center and others.

BBA President Vic Gelb is encouraging a large attendance of volunteer board members from local Agencies in the hopes of having "the best representation of volunteers ever at a Big Brothers' meeting."

(Continued on Page 14)

Lewis P. Reade New BBA Exec

The national staff of Big Brothers of America recently has been reorganized with the appointment of Lewis P. Reade as executive vice president and chief operating executive.

Formerly chairman of the board and chief executive officer of the Kellett Corp., a diversified manufacturing, distribution and services company in Willow Grove, Pa., Mr. Reade was named to his new post in January. Since assuming the position, Mr. Reade has made many systems changes at BBA de-

(Continued on Page 14)

Downtown Atlanta Is a Spectacle of Light

By 1973, the *Big Brothers Ambassador,* formerly the *Big Brother Bulletin,* had a circulation of 40,000 copies.

136

Professional Organization Gains

Agency relations with the national BBA staff and board were greatly improved in 1969, when the board approved several proposals made by the Professional Staff Conference Committee (PSCC), the professional organization that represented agency executive directors and other non-clerical agency personnel.

The functions and concerns of the PSCC were those relating to casework and service delivery, as distinct from the purely administrative aspects of agency operations. Thus, the PSCC was concerned with educational programs and materials, professional development activities at BBA's annual conferences, and the maintenance of professional standards and research. The committee was founded in May 1961 after a predecessor, the old Technical Advisory Committee (TAC), known earlier as the Technical Planning Committee (TPC) (chapter 4), had been discontinued. The earlier organizations had similar functions.

The PSCC had proposed that an effective agreement of affiliation between BBA and each member agency be developed, and that it provide for a periodic agency program evaluation. It had further proposed that BBA hire a director of agency services. The board agreed to these proposals. The board also established a Committee on Agencies Services, and authorized the PSCC to change its name to the Professional Staff Council (PSC), its name today.[16]

Some BBA board members apparently considered the PSCC requests presumptuous. However, the remedies sought appeared to be long overdue, and the PSCC felt that better communication with the board needed to be established. Its members also sought to affirm that BBA regarded its relationship to its agency professionals as important to the success of the entire organization.

In practice, agency executives and other casework professionals are involved with all facets of agency operations, not just those of a professional nature. In fact, the first executive institute hosted by BBA was concerned with management and administration, not casework. The week-long institute was held in Flint, Michigan, and was made possible by a grant from the Mott Foundation. Charles Stewart Mott himself, the benefactor and well-known automotive pioneer, presented certificates of accomplishment to the twenty-four agency executives who attended.[17]

The person most responsible for obtaining Mott Foundation aid for BBA training programs was Joseph T. Ryder, director of the Flint (Mich.) Youth Bureau, which was affiliated with BBA. Ryder joined the bureau in 1944. He also helped organize many new agencies throughout Michigan and Ohio, where he became known as "Mr. Big Brother". Today, there are more Big Brothers and Big Sisters agencies in Ohio than in any other state. Michigan ranks second in number of agencies. The high degree of activity in these two states is reportedly because of Ryder's early work. Ryder died in 1979.

A more comprehensive and far-reaching training program, begun during the early 1970s, was made possible by a $287,000 grant from the W. K. Kellogg Foundation of Battle Creek, Michigan. The program, covering a four-year period, offered both administrative and professional casework training for appropriate personnel of the then more than two hundred member agencies.[18]

National conferences continued to be an important vehicle for the development of agency people. The 1958 conference was held in Philadelphia. In 1959, the delegates met in Los Angeles. Subsequent locations and dates, for the period covered by this chapter were: Cincinnati, 1960; Flint, 1961; New York City, 1962; Columbus, 1963; Chicago, 1964; Boston, 1965; Baltimore, 1966; Anaheim, California, 1967; Toronto, 1968; Detroit, 1969; Cleveland, 1970. The practice of holding regional meetings began around 1960, and the first ones were held in Columbus, Dallas, and Hamilton, Ontario. Such meetings were patterned after earlier meetings held in Michigan on a statewide basis.

New Leadership

In 1970 the era of BBA President Charles Berwind, as the dominant figure, came to an end. A new national president, Victor Gelb, was elected. As far back as 1959, Berwind had urged the board to find someone to replace him. At that time, he had said that it is a mistake for one person to stay in office too long in any organization and that the time had come for the directors to seek a person who could be groomed for the office of president.[19] Although he continued to insist that a successor be found, apparently no serious effort was made in that direction until Gelb was considered. Gelb was president of a Cleveland chemical manufacturing company, had long been involved in local Big Brothers activities, and was a member of the national board.

Elected to serve with Gelb were three vice-presidents, whose names have already been mentioned in connection with various activities — William Fishman, C. Randolph Taylor, and Dick Van Dyke. Berwind was elected chairman of the board, a role he increasingly, and probably correctly, viewed as that of a race horse turned out to pasture. On April 20, 1972, in a letter to President Gelb, he wrote: "I have felt for some time that my title of Chairman of the Board of Big Brothers of America has no real significance and that my role as such is serving no useful purpose."[20] He then tendered his resignation and asked that the board elect a new chairman. Berwind died on November 9, 1972.

138

Biographical sketches of both Berwind and Gelb appear in chapter 7.

Citing a communication gap between the national headquarters staff in Philadelphia and both the national board and local member agencies, Gelb visited many areas of the country during his first year as president in an effort to remedy the situation. He also initiated a new newsletter directed to all agency presidents and executives.[21] Inadequate communication between any organization and its constituencies is a perennial problem, but the problem appeared to be somewhat pronounced within BBA at the beginning of the 1970s. At a board meeting on October 24, 1970, member Walter Kingsley went so far as to suggest that the "national staff . . . declare a temporary hiatus on its regular functions and instead spend . . . time visiting boards of present member agencies explaining the services of national and their value to the local agency. There is a lack of understanding on the part of local agencies on the interrelationship of national with the locals," concluded Kingsley.[22]

During the early 1970s Irvin F. Westheimer began pursuing his claim of having conceived the idea of Big Brothers in 1903. Westheimer was over ninety years old at the time. It was puzzling to many why he had waited until then. The story he told of seeing and befriending a hungry boy had been published in a Cincinnati newspaper in 1911 (see chapter 1), Westheimer had organized the Cincinnati agency that year, he had been a lifelong supporter of the Movement, and at the time he asserted his claim, he was a member of the national board. However, he had not been so active in the Movement during his mid and later life as he had earlier. Perhaps it was his other major activities during these periods that had diverted his interest. According to various accounts, he had been a co-founder of Junior Achievement in Cincinnati and had participated in many Jewish charitable activities and civic endeavors.

The recognition he now sought generated considerable controversy among BBA board members and others within the Movement. Until then, Ernest K. Coulter, founder of the first organized program, had been regarded as the originator of the Big Brothers concept. However, on January 21, 1974, the BBA Executive Committee, in consideration of Westheimer's long service and strong financial support, voted to recognize his earliest reported activity as the official beginning of the Movement.[23]

Armed with this new credential, Westheimer reentered the Movement's activity arena with an uncommon zeal, all the more remarkable because of his advanced age. He was the subject of several magazine and newspaper interviews, appeared and spoke at a BBA annual meeting, and made public appearances with Presidents Nixon and Ford. He participated in the signing of the merger agreement between BBA and Big Sisters International (chapter 6), and remained active in Movement affairs until near the time of his death in 1980.

In early 1971, President Richard M. Nixon was designated by BBA as the First Honorary Big Brother. At the award presentation are, *left to right,* Joseph M. Zamoiski, representing Big Brothers of the National Capitol Area; Victor Gelb, president of BBA; President Nixon; Irvin F. Westheimer, and Dr. C. Randolph Taylor, a BBA vice-president.

Incidentally, the early activity of the Catholic Big Sisters of New York as well as that of an early New York judge (chapter 1) must be taken into account when the originating activities of both Westheimer and Coulter are considered, although both men made significant contributions. In perspective, the efforts of no individual — during the entire history of the Movement—can match the zeal, loyalty, dedication, and support of Charles G. Berwind.

Foreign Participation

Although it is not within the scope of this book to explore the Movement in other countries, what is known of foreign activities, during this period and later, may be of interest. Big Brothers work was begun in Canada shortly after getting underway in the United States during the early part of the century. Canadian agencies participated in the first Big Brother and Big Sister Federation as well as in the formation of Big Brothers of America. Until 1972, Canadian agencies were affiliated with BBA as well as with a Canadian federation, which was also known as BBA's Northern Region. In May and June of that year, the U.S. and Canadian federations, at their respective annual meetings, approved proposals that recognized the autonomy of each organization.

Reports of activities in other parts of the world have surfaced for years, and several well-established programs are known to exist. The foremost authority on foreign Big Brothers work is John R. Cohan, a Los Angeles lawyer and longtime director of BBA and BB/BSA. Cohan began a one-man campaign to generate foreign interest in Big Brothers work in 1966. A year later he reported that he had made contacts in fifteen countries on behalf of the Movement. In only two of those countries, Korea and Japan, had programs already been established. It was later reported that the Korean program included both Little Brothers and Little Sisters. The current Japanese program, begun in 1946, is administered by Japan's Department of Justice.

Cohan's early contacts included officials and organizations in Italy, India, Venezuela, England, Yugoslavia, Formosa, Israel, and Denmark, according to articles in the *Big Brother Bulletin* published during the late 1960s. He has continued to spread the one-to-one philosophy in foreign lands for nearly two decades, through correspondence and extensive foreign travel. John Cohan's knowledge of the breadth and scope of foreign activity is probably unequaled. The number of agencies formed as a result of his contacts is unknown. In early 1984 he reported that Big Brothers agencies now existed in Germany, Mexico, Jamaica, Ghana, Puerto Rico, England, Israel, Holland, and Bermuda, in addition to Japan and Korea.

From time to time other Americans have helped organize or assisted foreign groups. For example, in 1973, Conrad Nathan, executive director of the Jewish Big Brother and Big Sister League of Baltimore, helped organize a Big Brothers agency in Haifa, Israel.

By 1970, efforts were underway to create a new federation exclusively for Big Sisters, as BBA continued to move ahead. Big Sisters International (BSI) was chartered and, finally, the two federations were merged to create Big Brothers/Big Sisters of America.

* * * *

No matter how good a mother you are, you can't be a father, too.

Notes to Chapter 5

1. "17 New Agencies Bring Organization Total to 150," *Big Brothers Ambassador*, July 1969, 1.
2. "This Is the Start of Something Big," a recruiting and fund-raising brochure on file in the BB/BSA Archives, Philadelphia.
3. "Era of Growth Program, 1965 – 1970," *Big Brother Bulletin*, September 1965, 1 – 4.
4. Report issued by John H. Heller, chairman, Era of Growth Program, contained in the minutes, BBA Board of Directors, Philadelphia, February 9, 1968.
5. "$3.5 Million Fund Drive Blasts Off!" *Big Brother Bulletin*, January 1969, 1.
6. Report issued by R. H. Goettler and Associates, contained in the minutes, BBA Board of Directors, Philadelphia, October 25, 1969.
7. "Development Fund Drive Regearing for $3.5 Million," *Big Brothers Ambassador*, Winter 1970, 1; see also minutes, BBA Board of Directors, Philadelphia, January 31, 1970.
8. Minutes, BBA Board of Directors, Philadelphia, February 12, 1972, p. 8.
9. Ibid., p. 10.
10. "Kresge Company Aids Big Brother Movement," *Big Brother Bulletin*, March 1967, 8.
11. "Thom McAn Shoe Co. Works for BB," *Big Brother Bulletin*, December 1967, 8.
12. Minutes, BBA Board of Directors, Philadelphia, October 25, 1969.
13. Minutes, BBA Board of Directors, Philadelphia, May 19, 1959; see also *Big Brother Bulletin*, Fall 1959.
14. Letter from Victor Gelb, president of BBA to All National Board and Advisory Board Members, dated July 31, 1973, on file in the BB/BSA Archives, Philadelphia.
15. "People Know Us, But How Well?" *Big Brother Bulletin*, Winter 1970, 2.
16. BBA Minutes, October 15, 1969.
17. "BBA First Executive Institute," *Big Brother Bulletin*, Summer 1968, 7.
18. "W. K. Kellogg Grant to Aid BB Training," *Big Brothers Ambassador*, November 1973, 11.
19. Minutes, BBA Board of Directors, Philadelphia, May 22, 1959.
20. Letter from Charles G. Berwind to Victor Gelb, dated April 20, 1972, on file in the BB/BSA Archives, Philadelphia.
21. Report presented by Victor Gelb, president of BBA, at the organization's annual meeting in San Francisco, June 24, 1971, on file in the BB/BSA Archives, Philadelphia.
22. Minutes, BBA Board of Directors, Philadelphia, October 24, 1970, 9.
23. Proceedings of BBA Executive Committee meeting, Philadelphia, January 21, 1974.

6

A Big Sister Federation and Big Brothers/ Big Sisters of America
(1971–present)

Both Big Sisters and Big Brothers were part of the first federation, which had its beginning in 1917. Big Sisters were not included when Big Brothers of America was formed in 1945–1946, because the leaders at that time felt that a national program could not be geared to what was considered the diverse needs of both boys and girls. Joseph H. McCoy, general secretary of the New York agency and an organizer of BBA, had even attributed the demise of the early federation to its dual membership (chapter 3).

Of course, many agencies had combined programs which had operated successfully for years. Some of these were members of BBA; however, in accordance with a policy adopted by the BBA Board of Directors on May 23, 1964, such affiliates could not include "Big Sisters" in their name, and they had to maintain a sharp distinction between their Big Sisters and Big Brothers programs.[1]

Clearly, many BBA board members were not ready to think in terms of serving both sexes. Big Sisters agencies, whether independent or as part of a Big Brothers organization, continued to function as best they could, without the benefit of a national organization—a major handicap in all areas of their work.

For example, BBA had little difficulty in attracting the attention of the national media, with its well-organized public relations function and assistance from such organizations as the Advertising Council. Without a national voice, Big Sisters groups received little nationwide publicity. An exception was an article in the *Ladies' Home Journal* for January 1953. But even then, it was only an ancillary feature, included with a major Big Brothers story, and titled "Big Sisters Needed Too."[2]

During the early 1970s, the philosophy of the BBA Board of Directors regarding Big Sisters began to change, slowly at first, then with increasing momentum. The person most responsible for turning the tide was a former Big Sister and a founder of Big Sisters of Rhode Island—Winifred Derry.

Mrs. Derry had moved to Washington, D.C., during the late 1960s. Under her leadership the idea for a Big Sisters federation was developed. Seventy agencies and interested individuals that were engaged in Big Sisters work were invited to an exploratory meeting in Washington, D.C., on June 20, 1970. Forty-five responses were received and eighteen persons actually attended, including representatives from one state organization — Big Sisters of Michigan, which had a membership of twelve Big Sisters agencies. The Big Sisters agency in New York City, founded by Mrs. William K. Vanderbilt, Sr., and considered by many to be the nation's first Big Sisters organization, was not represented.

After the Washington meeting, at which the nucleus for a new organization was formed, organizational activity proceeded at a fairly rapid pace, especially for a group that had extremely limited resources. In fact, the fledgling federation had no funds at all during its first year. It may well not have survived if it had not been for the Council of

Before forming Big Sisters International, Mrs. Winifred Derry had organized Big Sisters of Rhode Island. She is shown with Rhode Island Governor John H. Chafee, who had just proclaimed April (1966) as Big Sister Month in that state.

National Organizations for Children and Youth (CNOCY). Through the kindness of Mrs. Isabella J. Jones, then CNOCY's executive director, CNOCY provided Mrs. Derry and her fellow organizers with free office space and staff services during their first year of activity. During that period, a constitution and bylaws were framed, a proposal for a charter was prepared, and a temporary board was selected, with Mrs. Derry as president.

Big Sisters Receive Charter

On August 3, 1970, the organization was incorporated in the District of Columbia, becoming Big Sisters International (BSI). The first name considered was Big Sisters of America. That name was discarded when the group's attorney mentioned that the initials might be confused with those of Boy Scouts of America.

At a BSI Board of Directors meeting on January 23, 1971, held in Washington, D.C., where the national headquarters had been established, the delegates wasted no time in attending to as many items of business as possible during the one-day session. They proposed a suggested fee schedule for agencies, reviewed agency affiliation forms, ratified the constitution, asked a committee to recommend a method for selecting board members, approved a quarterly newsletter, discussed a "Big Sisters Week," and approved the location of the next meeting in Chattanooga, Tennessee.

The delegates even discussed such accouterments of organization as mottos, seals, and official colors. Several agencies presented their own slogans for consideration. An Arizona group suggested "Better Guidance Builds Better Girls." A Baltimore agency presented "For There Is No Friend like a Sister." The Chattanooga agency's motto presented for consideration was "A woman shall conserve the dignity of womanhood by reaching forth her hand to a young girl." The Lansing (Mich.) agency suggested "An Adventure in Friendship."[3] No selection was made that day, but the Lansing agency's suggestion was later chosen.

Mrs. Derry summarized her remarks to the delegates at the January meeting by reminding them that, even though they had a dream, dreams take hard work and money to bring to reality. She said that it was up to them to take the dream and build it into a reality. With little more than that dream with which to work, the members began the task of building a new organization.

BBA Shows Interest

Almost from BSI's beginning, BBA officials were concerned about its activities. The reason or reasons for this interest are not clear. It could have been that BBA officials and board members felt that it was time again for a combined national federation, that two federations meant much duplicated, wasted effort, or that a Big Sisters federation would seriously compromise and dilute BBA fund-raising efforts.

In any event, when BBA Executive Director Tom O'Brien reported to the BBA board on October 24, 1970, that he was aware of an interest on the part of Big Sisters in establishing a new national organization, the reaction was immediate. He was asked to investigate and report back at the next board meeting.[4]

Later, George Katz, a BBA staff member, met with Mrs. Derry and Susan Dexter, BSI secretary, to discuss the new organization and its implications, and on a separate occasion Katz talked with Mrs. Jones of the CYOCY about Big Sisters activity.

Then, on May 25, 1971, Katz, joined by three BBA board members, met again with Mrs. Derry and Ms. Dexter to establish a continuing dialogue and discuss a possible merger of the two organizations. The meeting took place in Washington at the offices of the Big Brothers of the National Capitol Area, a BBA-affiliated agency.

Each side kept its distance on the merger question, especially the Big Sisters. Both agreed that such a move should be considered only after a thorough study, and both agreed to refer the question to their boards for further consideration. Big Sisters International was concerned that being required to embrace Big Brothers standards for affiliation, in the event of a merger, would discourage or eliminate many small Big Sisters agencies which did not have the financial resources to meet them. The parties did acknowledge that funding sources did not look with favor on the proliferation of social-service organizations. Both probably felt that they might gain financially through a combined federation. The Big Sisters representatives also acknowledged that the established framework of BBA would be an advantage to BSI. The BSI officials indicated that the new national organization, as well as many local Big Sisters agencies, had benefited from the advice and guidance of BBA, which had made its literature available to BSI. The representatives of both organizations agreed to continue to cooperate.[5]

At a meeting of the BSI temporary Board of Directors in Washington on July 24, 1971, the structure of the new organization was further strengthened. A new temporary board was elected (permanent board structure had not yet been formed), Winifred Derry was reelected as president, Sue Dexter approved as secretary-treasurer, and Mildred Moon Montague, a Chattanooga, Tennessee, area community leader and supporter of Big Brothers of Chattanooga (which later became a combined agency) was elected vice-president. The board approved a permanent board structure, a board committee structure, and a fund-raising plan. It authorized an agency-affiliation agreement and established a committee to study and explore the possibility of a future merger with BBA.[6]

Just over a month later, on August 26, 1971, the Movement was shocked and saddened by the unexpected death of Mrs. Derry, who died after surgery. Although her death represented a temporary setback for BSI, Mrs. Montague, having just been elected vice-president, provided effective continuity and assumed the presidency. There was one major problem. Unlike BBA, Big Sisters International did not have a paid executive at this early stage. All work was done by the volunteer, nonpaid, officers. The national headquarters was in Washington only because Mrs. Derry had lived there. Mrs. Montague lived in Chattanooga. If she were to perform her duties effectively, it would be necessary to move the headquarters there, and the move would require extra funding.

BSI Moves to Chattanooga

The problem was solved when Big Brothers/Big Sisters of Chattanooga volunteered not only to provide free office space for BSI for three years, but to contribute $5,000 per year for operating expenses for the same period. Headquarters were quickly established in the Big Brothers/Big Sisters building in that city, and a part-time clerk was employed.

A previously planned board meeting and the first annual conference of BSI were held in Chattanooga on June 22-23, 1972. Thirty-nine representatives from Big Sisters agencies, representing fifteen states and Canada, registered for the conference. A permanent board of directors was elected and, under the leadership of Mrs. Montague, considerable planning for growth and development was accomplished. Mrs. Montague announced that she would be unable to serve a second term as president, and the group created a new position — chairwoman of the board — to which she was elected. Leola (Lee) Meyer, of Big Sisters of Arizona, Phoenix, was elected president.[7]

George Katz represented BBA at the Chattanooga meeting, as BBA continued its increasing interest in BSI. Although its relationship with the new federation was never far in the background, BBA also had many other vital concerns.

As BBA observed its twenty-fifth anniversary in 1971, Executive Director Tom O'Brien reported that it had 208 affiliated agencies, which included 114 full members, 46 associate member, and 48 provisional members, in 91 communities.[8] In his report at the BBA annual conference held in San Francisco on June 22-26, 1971, President Gelb cited the need to establish agencies in twenty other major population areas, and O'Brien, in his report, cited fund shortages and resultant staff shortages as obstacles to continued growth.

Lewis P. Reade, a Willow Grove, Pennsylvania, businessman, became executive vice-president and chief operating executive of Big Brothers of America on January 15, 1973, succeeding O'Brien.[9] Reade's immediate application of the techniques, methods, and principles that he had utilized as a business executive, as well as a somewhat aggressive manner, incurred a negative response from a number of people in various parts of the organization. However, no one could fault his enthusiasm. In a four-and-one-half month period, during his first six months on the job, he visited eighty-three agencies in twenty-eight states, soliciting comments and recommendations on their needs and requirements. Responding to his critics, Reade admitted that the transition from business to social service had been difficult. However, he soon adapted to his new environment, and went on to become one of the Movement's most effective executives.

Determining that BBA's greatest needs at that time were improvement of service to agencies, improved public relations, including better government relations, and the establishment of new agencies, Reade developed or created many new ideas and programs designed to deal with these deficiencies.

Major Changes at BBA

It was under Reade's administration that a major revision of the BBA constitution and bylaws occurred. He directed the reorganization of the regional governing structure, wherein the nation was divided into twelve new areas or regions for administrative purposes, each with a president and vice-president, who were members of the national board. The same structure is in effect today. Occurring under his administration, and not without controversy, was the adoption of a new National Agency Development Program.[10]

This program outlined two important new concepts. One involved the establishment of Agency Service Communities. Implicit was the idea that each agency should be responsible for a specific, well-defined geographical area, and the entire country was to be covered by either existing agencies or new ones to be established. The program's goal was to serve every single-parent boy in the nation who needed a Big Brother. Using data from the 1970 U.S. Census, BBA divided the United States into 595 Service Communities, with each one containing a minimum of 1,000 single-parent boys. It was found that only 159 of the areas were then being served by affiliated agencies. In forming the areas, BBA recognized that certain natural characteristics bound communities together. For example, a large city and its surrounding suburbs were joined in a single Service Community. Areas served by a single United Way organization were not divided. Such factors as transportation systems, mass media coverage, and other service facilities were taken into consideration.

Noting the difficulties that many small agencies had experienced in the past, BBA determined that if a Service Community, as defined above, were to be adequately served, its agency should have an annual budget of at least $50,000, have at least three full-time professionals, and be able to handle a caseload of at least 200 to 250 boys. This, of course, did not mean that agencies not then meeting these requirements would be eliminated.

The second important concept of the National Agency Development Program had to do with the manner in which BBA became involved with the creation of new agencies. Before 1973, the national federation merely acted in a volunteer advisory capacity when a community indicated a desire to form a new unit. Literature, guidelines, and helpful suggestions were provided to local leaders, but BBA did not become officially involved until the new agency was organized and operating, and had met certain minimum standards for its type of operation. Then it could apply for a particular class of membership.

Inherent in the National Agency Development Program was the assumption that the involvement of BBA, on an official basis, is more important to a new organization during its critical embryonic period than at any other time. The program called for a formal, signed agreement between BBA and any local interest group as soon as the latter indicated a desire to form a Big Brothers agency. As organization progressed, other signed agreements were required, until full membership had been attained.

Reade hired the first two BBA field representatives. One was based in the South and the other in the West. Later, others were added. Under his administration, a training director was hired and an extensive executive training program was launched. A new publication, the *Communicator*, mentioned in chapter 5, was begun and a professional journal, although short-lived, was launched. Reade supervised the issue of the first BBA Standard Operations Manual for agencies, and was responsible for the first professionally produced annual reports, which resembled those issued by industry. It was during Reade's tenure that Vice-President Gerald R. Ford became BBA's honorary chairman.

Reade's influence was widely felt in many Movement activities, but probably in no other endeavor was it so evident as in the move to merge BBA with BSI. During his first six months in office, he—together with President Vic Gelb — met with BSI President Lee Meyer and BSI Chairwoman Mildred Montague. They agreed that it would be desirable to establish a formal liaison — perhaps exchanging observers on the respective boards, and arranging annual meetings at the same locations and times, to enable members of each organization to attend the other's sessions. When BSI held its annual meeting in Fond du Lac, Wisconsin, in July 1973, Lew Reade was on deck as a guest. By the following year, as relations between the two national federations strengthened, he would be named "acting executive vice-president" of BSI.

Lilly Endowment Fund Grants

At the time of the Fond du Lac meeting, BSI had only four affiliated agencies. Both Mildred Montague, chairwoman of the board, and Lee Meyer, president, were elected to second terms. The prospects for rapid growth at that time were not encouraging. Then in late 1973 an event occurred that had an immediate, profound effect on BSI activities and all but assured its eventual merger with BBA. In its quest for financial support from foundations, BSI had submitted a request for funds to the Lilly Endowment Fund. Later, when Lew Reade met with Lilly Endowment officers to request support for a BBA project, he was asked about BSI. He then arranged for Endowment officials to meet with BSI representatives. As a result, in December 1973, Lilly approved a grant of $150,000 to BBA, to be used by BBA and BSI for the development of Big Sisters activities, and to investigate the possibility of a merger of the two organizations. Subsequent grants for the same purposes, of $122,206, $102,535, $20,000, and $25,000, were made in February 1975, November 1975, August 1976, and March 1977, respectively. Altogether, Lilly Endowment assistance totaled $419,741.[11]

Big Sisters International's headquarters was moved from Chattanooga to Philadelphia in early 1974, sharing quarters with BBA. A staff was hired and new promotional and organizational materials, including a twenty-three-minute movie, were developed. The first BSI coordinator was Sharyn Forrest, a social-service worker from Philadelphia. Although Forrest did not function at the level of the BBA chief executive, she had many similar responsibilities in connection with BSI. She served in that capacity until just before the merger.

The Lilly grant and the move to Philadelphia had a significant effect on BSI growth. It grew from 4 affiliated agencies in July 1973 to 6 by March 1974, 11 by May 1974, and had skyrocketed to 42 member agencies by April 1975, with an additional 30 applications in process. As of September 1973, only 38 of the more than 200 BBA agencies had Big Sisters programs. By February 1974, President Vic Gelb reported that nearly half of BBA full-member agencies either had Big Brothers/Big Sisters programs or were in the process of creating them.

At a BSI board meeting in Oakville, Ontario, in June 1974, Montague became honorary chairwoman of the board, Meyer became chairwoman, and Judy A. Weill, active in Big Sisters work in Omaha, Nebraska, was elected president. The 1974 BSI annual meeting was held in Scottsdale, Arizona, on October 18-19. In June 1975, when Montague, Meyer, and Weill were reelected to their posts, BSI's annual meeting was scheduled concurrently with that of BBA in Denver. The first BSI meeting of members also took place during the June gathering.

BBA and BSI Merge

The question of merger was undoubtedly uppermost in everyone's mind at Denver. The previous February, both organizations had appointed special merger study committees. A major obstacle appeared to be whether or not BSI could generate enough revenue to support its own operations. The chairman of the BBA Merger Committee, speaking to members of his organization at Denver, emphasized that committee members were keeping an open mind on the question, and that considerable additional information was needed before a decision could be made.

Most of the opposition to a merger appeared to come from the BBA board. However, at the BBA National Conference in 1974, a new president, Maurice Schwarz, Jr., had been elected and the joining of the two federations was one of his prime objectives. Given the earlier support of President Vic Gelb, the strong support and enthusiasm of Lew Reade, and the continuing commitment of Schwarz, the outcome was predictable. In February 1976, the BBA board overwhelmingly approved, in principle, the concept of merger and a few days later the board of BSI took similar action.

At the annual meeting of members of the two organizations, held concurrently at Indianapolis, Indiana, on June 18, 1976, the memberships also voted to endorse, in principle, the idea of joining the two bodies.[12] Both BBA and BSI then appointed committees to meet as a joint committee to study and recommend methods and procedures for effecting the merger, with such recommendations to be due no later than the following year's meeting of members. At the BSI meeting in Indianapolis, Hilda Patricia Curran, a social worker and former Big Sister, who had long been active in BSI affairs, was elected president of that organization, succeeding Judy Weill.

As mentioned earlier, many local agencies were already offering both Big Brothers and Big Sisters services, and the BBA and BSI national offices were sharing the same quarters. Now the legal aspects had to be handled, including the formulation of an agreement and plan of merger. The Joint Merger Committee worked hard throughout the following year. The plan called for merging Big Sisters International, Inc., a District of Columbia corporation, into Big Brothers of America, which had been chartered by Congress, as the surviving corporation.

Former BBA Honorary Chairman Gerald R. Ford prepares to sign a special ceremonial resolution commemorating the merger of BBA and BSA in June 1977, when he became Honorary Chairman of BB/BSA. Participating in the ceremony are, *left to right*, BB/BSA Executive Vice-President Lewis P. Reade, representing BSI officers and BBA board members Mildred Montague and Hilda Patricia Curran, Mr. Ford, Maurice Schwarz, president of BBA at the time of merger, former BSI official Judy A. Weill, and John Frank, chairman of the Merger Committee.

The major details had been worked out by the time BBA and BSI met concurrently at Orlando, Florida, on June 17, 1977. The members of each organization approved unanimously their resolutions of merger, as well as the agreement and plan of merger.[13] The members of each group also approved a new slate of at-large directors, which had been proposed by a joint nominating committee. A new national federation had been created — Big Brothers/Big Sisters of America (BB/BSA).

A special ceremonial resolution congratulating the new federation was signed by former President Gerald R. Ford, formerly BBA honorary chairman, who became honorary chairman of the new organization. Ford spoke at the historic merger meeting, telling the delegates, "There can be no argument that a strong family life is the heart as well as the backbone of this nation. I know what my family has meant to me — the strength my children and my wife have given me to face the crises my role in government thrust upon me."[14]

Ford said that he wished that all Americans could enjoy a good family life, but that a staggering divorce rate, desertion, and untimely death have made that impossible. He said he would be proud to do whatever he could to forward the work of Big Brothers and Big Sisters, who are helping children to become adults who will lead responsible, productive, fulfilled lives.

Also signing the special resolution was Maurice Schwarz, Jr., president of BBA; Victor Gelb, past BBA president; Mildred Montague, honorary chairwoman of BSI; Hilda Patricia Curran, BSI president; Judy Weill, past BSI president; Leola Meyer, a founder of BSI and an earlier president; and Irvin F. Westheimer.

A bill (H.R. 7249) was introduced to amend the BBA charter to include the new name. After approval by both the House and Senate, President Jimmy Carter signed the bill into law on November 11, 1977, becoming P.L. 95-167.

The merger created a total of 357 agencies in all classifications. These included 231 Big Brothers agencies, 25 Big Sisters groups, and 101 combined Big Brothers/Big Sisters organizations.[15] A new symbol and logotype were developed to identify the new organization — a symbolic, semi-abstract depiction of an adult embracing a child, with the new name set in Bookman bold italic with swash. It identifies the organization today. The symbol and type style have also been adopted by many BB/BSA – affiliated agencies.[16]

Don A. Wolf, a Fort Wayne, Indiana, association executive, became the first president of Big Brothers/Big Sisters of America. Wolf was elected at the merger meeting. Before the merger, both BBA and BSI had, in addition to their regular boards, such special bodies as honorary and advisory boards. Now, a new honorary board and a new advisory board were created for BB/BSA; in addition, to recognize past service to BBA and BSI, several individuals were designated as "trustees for life." They were Victor Gelb and Maurice Schwarz, Jr., past presidents of BBA; Maimie Gimble of BSI and G. Ruhland Rebmann, Jr., of BBA, early leaders and supporters of these organizations; Mildred Montague and Leola Meyer, past presidents of BSI; and Irvin F. Westheimer. Since that time, a few others have been accorded this honor. All directors, officers, staff members, and special boards and councils are now listed in the BB/BSA annual report each year.

The locations and dates of all BSI meetings have been discussed. Even though several BBA meetings have been mentioned, here for easy reference is a complete listing of all BBA and BB/BSA annual meetings for the period covered (1971-present), including all BB/BSA meetings scheduled for the foreseeable future. In June 1971, BBA met in San Francisco. Subsequent BBA locations and dates were: Richmond, Virginia, May 1972; Atlanta, June 1973; Lake of the Ozarks, Missouri, June – July 1974; Denver, June 1975 (concurrent with BSI); Indianapolis, June 1976 (concurrent with BSI); and Orlando, June 1977 (concurrent with BSI). Big Brothers/Big Sisters of America held annual meetings in Washington, D.C., June – July 1978; San Francisco, June 1979; Louisville, June 1980; Philadelphia, June 1981; St. Louis, June 1982; San Diego, June 1983; and Memphis, June 1984. Meetings have been scheduled for Cleveland, 1985; Clearwater, Florida, 1986; Spokane, Washington, 1987; and Milwaukee, 1988.

Funding

Now that the merger had been consummated and organizational restructuring completed, new funding sources were urgently needed. During the late 1970s and early 1980s, several new fund-raising techniques were tried, including a direct mail campaign which failed. Activities involving sports events were tried. A golfing promotion was unsuccessful, but a bowling fund-raiser, which had been successful for Big Brothers of Canada, proved highly effective in generating revenue for both agencies and the national organization. Known as Bowl For Millions in Canada, the program became Bowl For Kids' Sake (BFKS) in the United States. Annual bowling events are now sponsored by local agencies, and BB/BSA furnishes promotional materials on a revenue-sharing basis.

In another effort to raise revenue, BB/BSA entered into an agreement with a West Coast producer of TV programs, Ed Friendly Productions, in which the Friendly organization was given the rights to produce movies, teleproductions, and perhaps a television series based on Little Brothers and Little Sisters case records furnished by BB/BSA. A schedule of fees provided payments for various uses. National board member

Walter Kingsley was to act as the BB/BSA consultant, to ensure that the Movement was properly depicted. Friendly Productions encountered difficulties with the various television networks and the program never got off the ground.

The late 1970s and early 1980s was also a time of intensive grant-seeking. As a result, several highly innovative activities were funded, and ongoing programs received added assistance. Several new programs, created by short-term grants, have become permanent activities. An example is the Citizen Board Development Program (CBDP), a training program for new national and local agency board members, launched by a three-year grant from the Kellogg Foundation in 1978. A grant from the Green Island Foundation in 1980 made possible the founding of the BB/BSA Education Institute, which now has the responsibility for all BB/BSA training activity. A grant from the U.S. Office of Juvenile Justice and Delinquency Prevention (OJJDP), an agency of the Law Enforcement Assistance Administration (LEAA) of the Justice Department, in mid-1979, made possible five additional field representatives.[17]

Large grants from the U.S. Department of Labor, beginning in 1979, made possible two special national-agency studies involving youth employment. The first, termed the Career Aspiration Project (CAP), was designed to determine how the Big Brothers/Big Sisters concept affected the employability and job performance of the youths involved. Three BB/BSA–affiliated agencies participated. The second, the Youth Employment Project (YEP), called for employing Little Brothers and Little Sisters in industry in a manner that would enhance their career development. Seven agencies participated in the fifteen-month program.[18] BB/BSA obtained both CAP and YEP grants through the National Collaboration for Youth.

Other significant grants or gifts to BB/BSA, came from AVCO Corporation, Glenmede Trust of Philadelphia, and the Lilly Endowment Fund, the last making funds available for support of BB/BSA field representatives and for a special task force to study services to girls.

In October 1978, the Independent Order of Foresters, a Canadian-based fraternal organization, with wide representation in the United States, allocated $100,000 to produce a twenty-six-minute Big Brothers recruiting film.[19] The organization also produced recruiting literature and announced that it was launching a major campaign to help enlist Big Brothers. Not since the activities of the Elks before the 1920s (chapter 1) had such a substantive commitment been made by a large fraternal group.

The year 1979 was especially significant for BB/BSA. An evaluation of the organization's effectiveness by the management consulting firm of Touche Ross was completed and distributed. The evaluation covered national board organization, budgeting and planning, staff roles and functions, resource development, communication effectiveness and other vital areas, and resulted in a number of significant changes. Later, to improve communications, two new publications would be launched: the *Executive Newsletter* for agency executives and the *Presidents Letter* for local board presidents.

In 1979, BB/BSA moved to new, larger quarters in the Architects Building in Philadelphia. Rented quarters in the Suburban Station Building, several blocks away, had become crowded since the merger. In 1978, the federation had purchased a former large residence for a permanent national home. But adequate financing could not be obtained, and the purchase agreement had to be terminated.

Early in 1979, Lew Reade, who had joined BBA as executive vice-president in January 1973, submitted his resignation, indicating that he thought the time had come for him to pursue other interests. In a comprehensive five-page letter to BB/BSA President Don A. Wolf, Reade cited many of the accomplishments under his administration, and indicated that he would remain with the organization until a successor was chosen.[20]

President Wolf appointed a search committee, which began the task of finding a new chief operating officer. The coming 1980s would present many new and formidable social and economic problems. The new leader would not only have to be a strong, growth-oriented, problem-solving administrator, who could deal with the complexities of a fast-growing national organization and its relations with funding sources, governmental bodies, and the social-service community, he or she would also have to be an expert in diplomacy and human relations in order to promote harmony and maintain a sense of unity among the organization's mushrooming family of affiliated, yet autonomous local agencies. Agency relations had been a recognized weakness for some time.

Although the committee retained a Princeton, New Jersey, executive recruiting consultant, conducted a nationwide search, and received more than four hundred applications, the candidate who appeared to be the best qualified, and who was selected, was already a member of the national board. He was David W. Bahlmann, an Indianapolis attorney and chairman of the board's External Affairs Committee. Bahlmann assumed his new post as executive vice-president and chief operating officer on September 14, 1979. He was well qualified from the standpoint of both education and experience, having previously served as director of youth services for the Indiana Lawyers Commission, Inc., and in other social-service capacities. He was also uniquely fitted for the job because, over the years, he and his wife, Joan, had either adopted or provided foster home care for twenty-five children.

Bahlmann announced a new three-year plan designed to prepare BB/BSA for the 1980s. Emphasized were an improvement in field services, national board development, the development of a computerized national data bank and information system, and the creation of increased public awareness. Field service was greatly improved in 1981, when twelve geographical regions were grouped into four administrative districts, each headed by a district director responsible for the field representatives in his or her district. Board development received a boost in 1980 with the publication of a Regional Officers manual. William Mashaw, also of Indianapolis and, like Wolf, an association executive, was elected national president in June 1980. Mashaw was the first lawyer to head the organization. Succeeding Mashaw, in June 1982, was Albert L. Brown, Jr., a Cincinnati insurance executive. Mark K. Kessler, a Philadelphia lawyer, was elected to the top post in June 1984. However, because of a restructuring of board and staff positions at the time of Kessler's election, he became chairman and chief executive officer, rather than president. The title of president was assumed by David W. Bahlmann, who was also chief operating officer of BB/BSA.

To evaluate the results of the Citizen Board Development Program, funded earlier by the W. K. Kellogg Foundation, as well as to obtain other current agency data, a comprehensive study of 375 local units was made in 1981. Known as the Yanoff Study, after Dr. Jay M. Yanoff, the Philadelphia consultant who compiled and evaluated the data, the study covered agency demographics, staffing, finance, and operations. It was probably the most comprehensive survey of the Movement since the 1940 study (chapter 4) to determine if a new federation was warranted. A copy of the Yanoff report may be inspected at BB/BSA headquarters in Philadelphia and a summary is available for distribution.

As BB/BSA entered the 1980s, it continued to attract the attention of many celebrities. Lynn Swann, popular wide receiver for the Pittsburgh Steelers became a spokesperson, as did super star Burt Reynolds and popular actress Dyan Cannon. On November 30, 1982, the CBS Television Network presented a feature-length telemovie based on a Big Brother match, which attracted a wide audience. Famous cartoonist Charles M. Schultz created a special cartoon for BB/BSA, featuring several "Peanuts" characters, which was highly effective in publicizing the Movement. In late 1984, nationally-known cartoonist Ted Key, creator of "Hazel," also contributed a cartoon that was widely used in recruiting materials.

Also during the early 1980s, Young & Rubicam, the world's largest advertising agency, created a new print and electronic media campaign for BB/BSA, donating all of its services.

To recognize efforts by print media journalists to portray the problems of children from single-parent homes, BB/BSA began a National Journalism Awards Program in 1982. BB/BSA also used attractive, professionally produced annual reports in its efforts to raise funds and gain greater public recognition.

Cartoonist Charles M. Schulz created this cartoon exclusively for Big Brothers/Big Sisters of America .

In February 1982, President Ronald Reagan received a BB/BSA delegation at the White House, marking the first time since 1971 that Movement representatives had visited the Oval Office. The delegation included BB/BSA national President William G. Mashaw and national Communications Director Betty Larkin. Also in the group were B. C. Hallum, president of the Independent Order of Foresters, and several agency representatives, including both Big and Little Brothers and Sisters.

In February 1982, President Ronald Reagan received a Movement delegation in the Oval Office. The group includes several Big and Little Brothers and Sisters. *Left to right:* Big Sister Doris Collins; Independent Order of Foresters President B. C. Hallum; Little Sister Lisa Brown; William G. Mashaw, then president of BB/BSA; President Reagan; Betty Larkin, BB/BSA director of Communications; Little Sister Diana Muniz; Big Brother Sam Freeman, and Little Brother Alex Dvoretsky.

The longtime dream of BB/BSA for its own national headquarters building was realized in 1983, when a 20,000-square-foot, brick and marble structure was acquired at 230 North Thirteenth Street, Philadelphia. After extensive renovations to create a modern headquarters and national service center, the facility was occupied in late 1984. At that time, more than 460 agencies were affiliated with BB/BSA.

Shortly before occupying its new headquarters, BB/BSA received word from William F. Bolger, postmaster general of the United States, that the organization would be honored with a commemorative postage stamp in 1985.

Why has the Big Brothers/Big Sisters Movement flourished for more than eighty years? Why is it today one of the most admired social-service organizations in America? Possibly because it seeks to satisfy the basic need that occurs anew with each generation—the need that many children have for an older friend. The approach is unique, of course, in that an adult volunteer befriends only one child. He or she

The Big Brothers/Big Sisters of America national headquarters building in Philadelphia was occupied in late 1984.

Shull Photo Service

is that child's friend exclusively, and that personal friendship is also a reason for the Movement's success.

One writer, referring to the success of a Big Brothers program, put it this way:

> It is more than simply one more charitable agency in co-operation with the rest and caring for a special class; it is an idea, simple and well known, yet elastic and far-reaching in its possibilities of application . . . . It is one man taking up one boy as his little brother and trying in truth and in fact to be a big brother to him . . . the whole genius of the movement is personal and individual.[21]

Those words were written more than seventy-seven years ago in reference to the Big Brother Movement of New York, but they could be used in describing the reasons for the success of the Big Brothers/Big Sisters Movement today, and they will be just as applicable tomorrow.

* * * *

Notes to Chapter 6

1. Policy adopted at the annual meeting of the Board of Directors, May 23, 1964.
2. Margaret Hickey, "Big Sisters Needed Too," *Ladies' Home Journal* (January 1953).
3. Minutes, Big Sisters International, Philadelphia, January 23, 1971.
4. Minutes, BBA, Philadelphia, October 24, 1970.
5. Record of BBA and BSI meeting, May 25, 1971, found in BSI minutes, vol. 1, Philadelphia, 1971–76.
6. Minutes, BSI Board of Directors, Philadelphia, July 23–24, 1971.
7. Minutes, BSI Board of Directors, Philadelphia, June 22–23, 1972.
8. Executive Director's Report, filed with BBA minutes, Philadelphia, October 30, 1971.
9. "Lewis P. Reade New BBA Executive," *Big Brothers Ambassador*, Philadelphia, May 1973, 1.
10. Draft of BBA's new National Agency Development Program, on file in the BB/BSA Archives, Philadelphia.
11. Information based on telephone conversation between author and Susan Houk, Lilly Endowment, Inc., Indianapolis, Ind., on November 21, 1983.
12. Minutes, BBA Board of Directors, Philadelphia, June 18, 1976.
13. Minutes, BBA annual meeting of members, Philadelphia, June 17, 1977.
14. "Big Brothers of America and Big Sisters International, Inc., Merge," *BB/BSA Correspondent*, Philadelphia, June-July-August 1977, 1.
15. Minutes, BSI annual meeting of members, Philadelphia, June 17, 1977.
16. "New Logo for Big Brothers/Big Sisters of America," *BB/BSA Correspondent*, Philadelphia, June-July-August 1977, 15.
17. Minutes, BB/BSA Executive Committee, Philadelphia, June 20, 1979.
18. Minutes, BB/BSA Board of Directors, Philadelphia, June 20, 1981.
19. Minutes, BB/BSA Executive Committee, Philadelphia, October 27, 1978.
20. Minutes, BB/BSA Board of Directors, Philadelphia, February 23 – 24, 1979.
21. "The Big Brothers Movement," *Work with Boys*, vol 8, no. 2, April 1908. (Few copies of this publication exist. One is available in the Minneapolis Public Library, Minneapolis, Minn.)

PART TWO

7

Modern Leaders of the National Movement
(1945–present)

Because of space limitations, the persons discussed in this chapter will be for the most part those who have served as either national board presidents or in the capacity of executive director of either Big Brothers of America (BBA), Big Sisters International (BSI), or, after the merger, Big Brothers/Big Sisters of America (BB/BSA).

What kind of people were the men and women who organized, led, and sustained the modern Movement? Were they social workers, association executives, business or industrial leaders, lawyers or scientists? Were they Protestant, Catholic, or Jewish? Were many of them from one section of the country, or did they come from widely dispersed geographical areas? Had they served as Big Brothers or Big Sisters themselves, or did they learn of the Movement just before being employed? Were they wealthy individuals or persons of modest means? Did they include people of national renown, such as those listed in *Who's Who in America*, or were most of them largely unknown outside of their communities and occupational areas?

In all seriousness, the answer to every single question above can be answered with a resounding yes. In fact, except for their intense concern for the welfare of children, these leaders appear to have had no more in common with each other than individuals in a randomly selected group from the general population. It may be surprising to many to learn that of the nine persons named to the top administrative post in BBA and its successor, BB/BSA — that of executive director or executive vice-president (title changed to president in 1984) — only three had backgrounds in social work, and only two others had had previous experience in association work. The others came from various

Joseph H. McCoy

business backgrounds. The six past presidents of BBA and its successor, BB/BSA, have been businessmen or business association executives (although one had a degree in law). The current chairman (title changed from president to chairman in 1984) is a lawyer. Of the four past presidents of BSI, two were active in community volunteer activities, one had been an educator, and one was a social worker. Many of these leaders first served as Big Brothers or Big Sisters themselves. Many of them also served in various agency capacities before becoming national executives.

JOSEPH H. McCOY
A Leader Whose Work "Spanned the Eras"

It is appropriate that the late Joseph H. McCoy be included in this list of modern leaders of the national Movement, and that he head the list. In reality, he never held a top national post. He spent most of his professional life as executive secretary and executive director of the Big Brother Movement of New York. But he was active in the affairs of the old Big Brother and Big Sister Federation. In the interim between the demise of the old federation around 1937 and the formation of Big Brothers of America in 1945, McCoy, as administrative head of the New York agency, assumed several of the functions of a national organization leader by answering inquiries and supplying information to communities that were interested in establishing Big Brothers agencies.

He certainly was not required to assume such responsibilities. He did so only because of his strong belief in the principles and effectiveness of Big Brother work, and because of his deep concern for the welfare of children everywhere. He later recalled that although his office was over-burdened with a heavy case load and many administrative and financial problems, he felt that he simply could not ignore requests for assistance from other communities. To do so would give the impression that no one was interested in perpetuating the work.

McCoy was especially concerned that, in the absence of a central coordinating body, Big Brother activities were occurring that did not conform to established methods, standards, and practices. Through trial and error, well-meaning groups were developing programs that varied widely from the original concept of Big Brother work. He cited several examples. In one city, men who paid for Y.M.C.A. memberships for needy boys were known as Big Brothers. In another city, members of a service club who provided a party for under-privileged children once each year were also known as Big Brothers. McCoy felt a personal sense of responsibility for the misconceptions such activities caused. He believed strongly that a national organization was necessary if the Movement were to survive.

He played an active role in the two exploratory surveys during the early 1940s to determine if a new federation was feasible. He arranged the meeting in 1945 during which Charles G. Berwind and several other influential men formed the Temporary Big Brother National Committee, which led to the formation of BBA. Thus, Joseph H. McCoy, more than any other person, served as a bridge between the early and modern Movement, providing perspective and much needed continuity while helping to preserve the rich heritage of one of America's most successful social-service endeavors.

McCoy believed that there is no such thing as a bad boy. In the absence of physical, emotional, or mental trauma, he believed that a boy got into trouble only through his natural, normal reactions to unnatural situations encountered in society. Thus, it was the environment, not the boy, that was to blame for delinquency.

To prove his point, McCoy told the story of a boy, referred to only as "George B," who was arrested and brought into Children's Court for climbing a pillar of New York's Third Avenue "L." George became a Little Brother and, several months later, at a Big Brothers camp, he volunteered to climb a flag pole and re-thread the pulley rope, becoming an instant camp hero. George's natural inclination to scale heights was the same in both cases, bringing condemnation in one situation and praise in another.

McCoy retired in 1957, after thirty-five years of service with Big Brothers of New York. At the Big Brothers of America annual meeting that year, he was presented with a specially designed BBA scroll in recognition of his long service to the Movement, including his leadership role in bringing about the formation of the new federation.

After retirement, McCoy and his wife, Beulah, moved to Sherman, Connecticut. He died on February 9, 1979. McCoy was often referred to as "Mr. Big Brother," and "Dean" of all Big Brothers — titles that were richly deserved.

CHARLES G. BERWIND
President, BBA, 1947–1970; Chairman of the Board, 1970–1972

Charles Graham Berwind, Philadelphia industrialist and founder of Big Brothers of America, "more than any other individual, epitomized the dedication and resourcefulness of volunteers associated with the Big Brothers program throughout its distinguished history. He left an indelible legacy that provides a challenge and a pathway for those who are engaged in the unique service that is Big Brothers."

Thus, after Berwind's death on November 9, 1972, did the *Big Brothers Ambassador* (Winter 1972–73) describe his nearly twenty-five years of service to the Movement. Volumes would be required to detail

Charles G. Berwind

and describe fully his countless contributions as president and chairman of the board of BBA. Possibly no more profound statement can be made than that he was responsible for making the name *Big Brothers* a household phrase throughout America. Although he was president and later chairman of one of the nation's largest mining companies, he contributed freely of his time, as well as of his somewhat substantial financial resources to further the Movement's work. He promoted the Big Brothers cause at the grass roots community level as well as in the nation's halls of power. He was a frequent guest in the Oval Office.

Berwind first became interested in Big Brothers work in 1931, when he became a director of the Big Brother Association of Philadelphia. He served as president of that organization from 1941 to 1946. He became interested in forming a national organization around 1945. Later, Joseph McCoy, then executive director of the New York Big Brother Movement, and heads of several other agencies, held a national organization exploratory meeting in New York which was attended by Berwind, who assumed the responsibility for spearheading a new federation.

Berwind was born in Philadelphia on October 26, 1894. He received his early education at the Delancey School (no longer in existence) in Philadelphia, and at the Army and Navy Preparatory School in Washington, D.C. In 1912, he entered the U.S. Naval Academy. He was graduated in 1916, and served in the Navy until 1920. Honorably discharged as a lieutenant, he joined the Berwind-White Coal Mining Company, a family-controlled concern. He served as a vice-president of that company, which later changed its name to the Berwind Corporation, from 1923 until 1960, and as its president from 1960 until 1967, when he became chairman of the board.

At various times during his career, Berwind served as a director of the First Pennsylvania Banking and Trust Company, and the Pennsalt Chemicals (now Pennwalt) Corporation, as a vice-president and board member of the Philadelphia Orchestra and the World Affairs Council of Philadelphia, and as a director of the Crime Prevention Association. In 1960, he received the Boys' Club of America Bronze Keystone Award for fifteen years of distinguished service in the Crime Prevention Association. Berwind received many awards and citations, both locally and nationally, for his many Big Brothers achievements.

He married the former Ellen McMichael, and they had four children and fourteen grandchildren. Berwind was also fond of designing, making, and refinishing furniture, designing jewelry, gardening, and painting. He was active in the Philadelphia Union League, the Midday Club, and the Racquet Club of Philadelphia.

Big Brothers was more than a major interest in his life. Service to disadvantaged youths was a prime cause, which occupied most of his time and thought. What motivated this man to dedicate a major portion of his life to social service? A clue might be found in a lengthy, detailed philosophy of life which Berwind formulated and recorded in writing, evidently somewhat early in his adult life. Although highly ideological, his treatise emphasizes, again and again, the importance of brotherhood and service to others as basic to man's development. Illustrative is this excerpt:

> *Only by immersing himself in the human stream, preferably in an atmosphere which encourages liberty and freedom, can (man) appreciate that brotherhood is the only answer to the ills of the world. Brotherhood not of family, class or kind, but based on his experience with and sympathy for mankind.*

As indicated in a biographical sketch of Berwind, distributed by BBA during the early 1950s, the BBA founder felt that the practice of such brotherhood is basic to the survival of democracy; according to the sketch:

> *He believes that through the expansion and extension of the Big Brother Movement there can result a moral and spiritual regeneration, which is so much needed in the world today, if we are to successfully meet the problems that have resulted from the highly industrialized character of living, and the highly centralized form of our government.*

VICTOR GELB
National President, BBA, 1970–1974

Victor Gelb, of Cleveland, Ohio, was elected national president of BBA in 1970, and served until 1974. He succeeded Charles G. Berwind, who had held the post for twenty-five years. Gelb had been a Big Brother since 1948, had served as president of Jewish Big Brothers of Cleveland, and had been a regional vice-president of BBA for several years. In 1984, he was named co-chairman of the BB/BSA development council along with retired Admiral Elmo R. Zumwalt, Jr., former chief of Naval Operations.

Gelb, forty-three years old when he assumed the helm of BBA, had a reputation as an energetic and tireless executive. He was then president of Woodhill Chemical Sales Corporation of Cleveland, a company he had joined as sales manager in 1953. Before that time, he was an advertising executive. When Woodhill was sold to the Loctite Corporation in 1974, Gelb remained as president and chief executive officer until 1978. Today, he heads his own company, Victor Gelb, Inc., which processes fibers and fabrics. Gelb also serves or has served

Victor Gelb

on the boards of several Cleveland-area companies and financial institutions.

But his business commitments never prevented him from finding time for a wide variety of social-service activities. He has served as national vice-chairman of United Jewish Appeal, as a vice-president of United Way Services of Cleveland, as president of the Bellefaire Child Care Center and the Jewish Children's Bureau of Cleveland, as chairman of the Mayor's (Cleveland) Council on Youth Opportunities, vice-president of the National Federation of Settlements, vice-president of the Jewish Community Federation, and president of the Greater Cleveland Neighborhood Centers Association.

Gelb has been honored many times for his civic and community work. He has had three Little Brothers, all of whom are now grown. He attended Western Reserve University in Cleveland and, during World War II, he served in the U.S. Merchant Marines. Gelb is married, and he and his wife, Joan, have four children. In a recent interview, he said that his only avocation was that of helping people, a statement well validated by his excellent track record.

MAURICE SCHWARZ, JR.
National President, BBA, 1974–1977

Maurice Schwarz, Jr., was elected national president of BBA at its annual meeting of members in 1974. He served until 1977, when BBA and BSI were merged. Schwarz had been a strong proponent of the merger and worked diligently to bring it about. He first became interested in the Big Brothers Movement during the early 1930s. He has had two Little Brothers and has remained a friend to each of them in their adult lives. One former Little Brother is now a school psychologist.

Before assuming the top BBA post, Schwarz was a BBA vice-president and director. He had served as a director and president of Jewish Big Brothers of Los Angeles, and as a director of Big Sisters of Los Angeles.

Maurice Schwarz, Jr.

Schwarz was also a founder of Big Brothers of Los Angeles. He tells this story:

> *When Walt Kingsley (BB/BSA board member and West Coast advertising executive) first came to Los Angeles from New York, he noted that there was a Catholic Big Brothers and a Jewish Big Brothers here, but no nonsectarian group for those who might prefer to deal with such an agency. He called me and we got together and laid the groundwork for such an organization, holding the first meetings in my living room. Meredith Willson of* The Music Man *and* The Unsinkable Molly Brown *fame became interested, later became president, and the agency grew very quickly.*

Schwarz has served on the Planning Council Board and the Community and Government Affairs Committee of the United Way of Los

Angeles as well as on the board of the Mental Health Association of Los Angeles County. As of 1984, he was a director of VOLUNTEER: The National Center for Citizen Involvement, an Arlington, Virginia, based organization, which encourages more effective volunteerism as a solution to community problems. When his term on the BB/BSA board ended in June 1984, Schwarz had been involved with the Movement continuously for about fifty years. He has been named to the BB/BSA honorary board for life. He initiated and has been a strong supporter of this effort to produce a Movement history.

Schwarz is a senior vice-president in the Los Angeles office of the San Francisco–based investment banking-brokerage firm of Sutro and Company, a firm that he joined in 1942. He has served as a trustee of the Pacific Stock Exchange and as vice-chairman and a director of the National Association of Securities Dealers.

Participation in the Los Angeles area Welsh Terrier Club, tennis, and travel are Schwarz's major recreational interests. He and his wife, Marjorie, reside in Los Angeles and have two children and four grandchildren.

DON A. WOLF
National President, BB/BSA, 1977–1980

Don A. Wolf, a Fort Wayne, Indiana, hardware executive, became the first president of Big Brothers/Big Sisters of America, after BBA and BSI merged in 1977. He held the top post until 1980 and currently serves as a national director.

Wolf has a special empathy for fatherless and motherless children. He lost his father when he was in the fifth grade and his mother two years later. He lived with various relatives after that, even living alone for a time as a fourteen-year-old. He first became interested in the Movement around 1970. He founded Big Brothers of Fort Wayne in 1972, and was elected president in 1973. He also served as a Big Brother for several years.

Wolf was a member, vice-president, and then president of Big Brothers of Indiana, a state federation which was formed to qualify for certain funding and which no longer exists.

In 1947, Wolf joined Hardware Wholesalers, Inc., Fort Wayne, becoming purchasing manager in 1957, and advancing to vice-president and general manager in 1967. He later became executive vice-president and, in 1980, he was named president of the company, which is one of the largest hardware distributors in the nation.

Recognized nationally in his field, Wolf was named Hardware Wholesaler of the Year in 1973. He is a member of the National Wholesale Hardware Association, has served as a director of that orga-

Don A. Wolf

nization and as a director of the Russell Mueller Retail Hardware Research Foundation. He has served as adviser to several trade publications, as well as to the National Hardware Packaging Institute.

In addition, Wolf has served on the boards of several Fort Wayne area companies. He has been a director of the Indiana State Chamber of Commerce and the Fort Wayne Chamber of Commerce, and has been active in Junior Achievement of Fort Wayne. Wolf was born in Allen County, Indiana, on June 18, 1929. He and his wife, Virginia, have four children.

WILLIAM G. MASHAW
National President, BB/BSA, 1980–1982

William G. Mashaw of Indianapolis became the second president of BB/BSA in 1980. Before that time, he had been a vice-president and member of the national board. He first became interested in the Movement in 1971, when he was elected to the board of Big Brothers of Indianapolis. He subsequently served on that agency's finance, personnel, and benefits committees.

Mashaw became interested in the field of social service after an early career as an FBI agent. In FBI work, he later explained, "you had to be concerned with collecting evidence to convict a malfeasant rather

William G. Mashaw

than help him with his problems, and I found this extremely frustrating." Several years after leaving the FBI, Mashaw became active in Public Action in the Corrections Effort (PACE), an organization concerned with corrections reform. He was a member of the PACE board from 1963 to 1977, and served as president of the group from 1967 to 1969. Mashaw also has long been active in Indianapolis-area school, community, and church activities.

In 1954, Mashaw joined the National Retail Hardware Association (NRHA) as director of trade relations. He later became executive vice-president and was named publisher of *Hardware Retailer*, now known as *Hardware Retailing* magazine. Today, he is managing director of NRHA. Mashaw is also a lawyer, and he feels that his legal background together with his business association experience were excellent preparation for his role as national president of BB/BSA, especially since the National Retail Hardware Association is organized along similar lines.

Active in other business activities, Mashaw has served as a member of the board and executive committee of the American Retail Federation, as chairman of the Central Council of the National Retail Associations, and as a member of the board of the American Society of Association Executives.

One of eight children, Mashaw is a native of Arkansas. He attended Arkansas A & M College and is a graduate of the Columbia University School of Law. During World War II, he served as a pilot in the U.S. Naval Reserves. Spare-time interests include hunting, backpacking, and golf. Mashaw and his wife, Dorothy, have four daughters.

ALBERT L. BROWN, JR.
National President, BB/BSA, 1982–1984

Albert L. "Buzz" Brown, Jr. of Cincinnati was elected national president of BB/BSA in 1982, and served until 1984. A veteran of more than thirty years of service to the Movement, Brown became a national director of BBA in 1965, and has served continuously in that capacity (BB/BSA after 1977) until the present time.

A member of the Executive Committee for many years, Brown has also served on almost every other national board committee. He has been chairman of the Operations and Fund Development committees and, several years ago, headed a special study on agency dues structuring.

Described by associates as quiet and unassuming, Brown is recognized for his leadership qualities, including his ability to motivate others, and has been responsible for the success of many Movement activities over the years. Said a fellow board member recently, "When there is a job to be done, you can always count on Buzz, and he isn't concerned about whether or not he gets the credit for what he does. He has played a major role in organizing support for the new national headquarters building, and it is largely due to his leadership that we have obtained this facility."

Brown was matched with a Little Brother in 1953 by the Big Brothers/Big Sisters Association of Cincinnati. His Little Brother later became

Albert L. Brown, Jr.

a doctor. He was a member of that agency's board for many years and has served as board president. He has also served on the board of Big Brothers/Big Sisters of Greater Cincinnati, Inc., and Catholic Big Brothers of Cincinnati.

For many years, Brown has been associated with Frederick Rauh and Company, a Cincinnati insurance firm, where he is chairman of the board. He is, or has been, active in many area health, charitable, and community organizations. Part-time interests include skiing, tennis, fishing, jogging, and travel. He and his wife, Marian, have three children.

MARK K. KESSLER
Chairman of the Board and Chief Executive Officer, BB/BSA, 1984–present*

Mark K. Kessler, a Philadelphia attorney and BB/BSA board member, was elected chairman of the board and chief executive officer of the national federation in June 1984, becoming the first Philadelphian

Mark K. Kessler

to head the organization since Charles G. Berwind. Kessler had served on the board since 1973, and has served as board legal counsel. He is a former Big Brother.

Long active in Philadelphia-area community affairs, Kessler has served on the boards of the Albert Einstein Medical Center, the Federation of Jewish Agencies of Greater Philadelphia, the International House of Philadelphia, Jewish Family Service, and St. Peter's School. He served as division chairman, Special Gifts Department, of the United Way of Southeastern Pennsylvania in 1980.

Kessler attended Brown University, where he received a bachelor of arts degree in 1957. In 1960, he graduated from the University of Pennsylvania School of Law. He is presently a partner in the Philadelphia law firm of Braemer and Kessler. After graduating from law school, Kessler served as a law clerk to the Honorable Herbert B. Cohen, a Pennsylvania Supreme Court judge. In 1962, he joined the staff of the Securities and Exchange Commission (SEC), Washington, D.C., later becoming legal assistant to a SEC commissioner.

Kessler entered private practice in 1964. Today, he is a widely recognized specialist in the field of securities law. He is a member of the American Law Institute, the American Bar Association, and the Philadelphia Bar Association, where he has held several chairmanships. Kessler is married and he and his wife, Constance, have two sons.

---

*Until June 1984, the person holding the top volunteer position was known as the national president.

GILBERT H. GENDALL
National Executive Director, BBA, 1947–1948

Early in 1947, after the nucleus of Big Brothers of America had been formed, President Charles Berwind needed an experienced association executive to establish the administrative framework of the new organization. Robert E. Wynns, who had conducted the national study that led to the creation of the new federation, was a likely candidate, but he was not available. Joseph H. McCoy, of the New York Big Brother Movement, recommended Gilbert H. Gendall, a recently retired Boy Scout executive, who was living in nearby Chalfont, Pennsylvania. Gendall, who agreed to accept the position on a temporary basis, was a fortunate choice. He had been engaged in youth work for nearly forty years, first with the YMCA, then with the Boy Scouts of America. He had retired in 1941, but came out of retirement to become director of the Rochester, New York, USO during World War II. He had retired a second time when he received the call from Berwind in 1947. Gendall opened the first BBA national headquarters office in space made available by the Philadelphia Big Brother Association, and established the necessary practices and procedures to insure the smooth functioning of the new organization. He left BBA when Donald Jenks, the first permanent national executive director, was hired in 1948.

Gilbert H. Gendall

Gendall's Scouting career began in 1916, when, at the age of thirty-seven, he organized the third Scout Council west of the Mississippi in Des Moines, Iowa. As executive of that council, he organized the first formal training course for scoutmasters in Iowa. In 1920, he was named executive of the Scout Council in Omaha, Nebraska, where he was also active in community and social-service affairs. The first training course for Scout executives took place in Omaha in 1925 under Gendall's supervision.

From 1925 until his first retirement in 1941, Gendall was regional executive for the New York and New Jersey Scout Region, in charge of seventy-two councils. It was here, as one of twelve regional executives in the United States, that he did some of his finest work, including the securing of thirty-nine new Scout camp sites. In 1941, the New York–New Jersey Scout councils were serving 170,000 boys.

Gendall's work with the YMCA began in 1907, when he became confidential secretary to Richard C. Morse, then general secretary of the YMCA International Committee. He later held several YMCA posts in New York City.

Gendall was born in Newtown, Pennsylvania, on April 4, 1883. He spent two years at Wyoming Seminary in Kingston, Pennsylvania, but could not take advantage of a scholarship to Syracuse University because of home obligations. Before beginning his life of social service, Gendall worked for several mining companies. He and his wife, the former Mary

Francis, had three children. Gendall died in Chalfont, Pennsylvania, in December 1963, at the age of eighty.

DONALD JENKS
National Executive Director, BBA, 1948–1950

The first permanent executive director of BBA was Donald Jenks. Jenks joined BBA in March 1948, when he was fifty-four years old. Little in his background was predictive of a career in social-service work. However, as he had in several previous endeavors, he quickly adapted and apparently became an excellent administrator. He was operating his own public relations and fund-raising firm in Philadelphia, when he was tapped by Charles Berwind for the BBA post.

It was as a worldwide shipping and transportation expert that he was best known. He entered this field at an early age when he dropped out of St. Paul's School, Concord, New Hampshire, before graduation, to begin an adventure that most boys his age only dreamed about. He became a merchant seaman and traveled all over the world. At one time, he commanded a two-masted hospital ship in Labrador and, before his twenty-first birthday, he was in command of a supply ship that operated between Newfoundland and the mainland of Canada. He studied steam transportation in Europe, North Africa, and the Far East.

Donald Jenks

During World War I, Jenks was an officer in the Army Quartermaster Corps. Reportedly, he also worked for the Pennsylvania Railroad and the Army Transportation Corps during this period. After the war, he became a steamship agent in New York. The most significant period of his shipping career came during World War II, when he served as district director of the Port of Philadelphia for the U.S. Office of Defense Transportation (ODT). During this time, he also served as liaison officer between the ODT and the British Ministry of Shipping and the British Ministry of War Transportation, which served all American ports. In addition, Jenks was director of the Russian relief effort in Philadelphia, when Russia was a U.S. ally. He entered the public relations field after the war.

Jenks had a strong interest in adult education and in 1941, together with the late Philip Klein, who later became a BBA director, founded the Philadelphia Junto—one of the nation's first independent schools for adults. Jenks maintained a lifelong love for the sea and, in 1962, he and his wife, Edith, moved to Vineyard Haven, on Martha's Vineyard, Massachusetts, where he had maintained a summer home for many years. He died there, after a brief illness, on June 1, 1968, at the age of seventy-five.

BENJAMIN VAN DOREN HEDGES
National Executive Vice-President, BBA, 1950–1952

Benjamin Van Doren Hedges was named executive vice-president of BBA in September 1950. He had previously been associated with the Big Brother Movement in New York on a volunteer basis, serving as chairman and as a trustee of that organization. He had also been matched successively with several Little Brothers. To accept the full-time position with BBA, he resigned his post as personnel administrator with the Bankers Trust Company of New York, where he had been employed for the past eighteen years, although he maintained his residence in New York.

An outstanding athlete in his youth, Hedges was a silver medalist in the 1928 Olympic games at Amsterdam. In the Olympic running high jump event, he finished in a second-place tie for the United States. He was a 1930 graduate of Princeton University, having been elected president of his class for all four of his undergraduate years. He was also captain of both the freshman and varsity track teams.

During World War II, Hedges served in the Navy as an air combat intelligence officer, and attained the rank of commander. Hedges was born in Plainfield, New Jersey, on June 8, 1907. He attended the Loomis School before entering Princeton. He and his wife, the former Alice-Marian Hecht, had two children, a son and a daughter. Hedges

Benjamin Van Doren Hedges

joined BBA at the age of forty-two and left two years later, when he was succeeded by Felix Gentile. It is not known what he did after that time, although he presumably continued to live in New York. He died there in December 1969, at the age of sixty-two.

FELIX M. GENTILE
National Executive Director, BBA, 1952–1957

Delegates to the 1957 BBA National Conference in Hamilton, Ontario, were shocked and saddened by the death of Felix M. Gentile, forty-seven, who had served as BBA's national executive director since 1952. Gentile, who had been largely responsible for planning the conference, died of a heart ailment on May 12, 1957, just a few days before the event was to get underway.

Gentile, a social worker and the fourth person to serve as chief executive after BBA was organized in 1946, was an energetic and innovative administrator. During his tenure the federation grew from twenty-three to thirty-three affiliated agencies.

Gentile joined BBA after serving as executive director of the Mayor's Commission on Community Relations in Toledo, Ohio, which he joined in 1947. After receiving a bachelor's degree from Manhattan College in 1932, and before receiving a diploma in social work from Fordham University in 1934, Gentile began his career as a social worker with the New York State Department of Social Welfare in 1933, becoming a senior social worker in 1935.

In 1936, he joined the Works Projects Administration (WPA) as a social research analyst. In 1937, he was employed by the Social Security Administration as an associate technical adviser, being promoted to public assistance analyst in 1941. In 1942, he became executive secretary of the Louisiana Mental Health Association. He also lectured at the School of Social Work of Tulane University and at Louisiana State University. In 1944, Gentile began a tour of overseas duty with the United Nations Relief and Rehabilitation Association (UNRRA), serving in Italy.

Gentile joined the Russell Sage Foundation as a research associate in 1946, and in 1947 he accepted the community relations position in Toledo, which he held before joining BBA. He was a member of the American Association of Social Workers, the National Conference of Social Work, and contributed articles to various professional publications. Gentile was born in the Bronx, New York, on February 16, 1910, the son of Michael and Carmelina Gentile.

Gentile spent his entire life in the field of social welfare. In a December 1956 *Reader's Digest* article on Big Brothers work, Gentile was quoted as saying:

Felix M. Gentile

Over one million children between the ages of 10 and 17 are dealt with by the police every year, and half a million children of the same ages are brought to the attention of the juvenile courts. Yet, bad as this is, the overt delinquent isn't our main problem. What must concern us even more is the boy who, instead of striking out against society, turns his hostility inward, silently destroys himself and lands in a mental institution. We can save them, and the overt delinquents, only by rescuing them when they are children. This is a job for every man who looks upon our children as our most precious national resource.

STANLEY B. ADAMS
National Executive Vice-President, BBA, 1957–1958

The tenure of Stanley B. Adams as BBA's chief executive and administrative officer was the briefest of all of those who have served in that capacity. A former advertising executive, Adams was named executive vice-president after the sudden death of Felix Gentile; the appointment was announced in the September 1957 issue of the *Big Brother Bulletin*. He apparently resigned the following spring, possibly serving no more than ten months.

Stanley B. Adams

The reason for his departure is not known, other than a brief notation in the *Big Brother Bulletin* that he wished to return to the field of advertising. His credentials were indeed impressive. According to the announcement of his appointment, he was an engineer, advertising agency executive, former federal government official, and a business leader. He held a degree in metallurgical engineering, having graduated from Lehigh University in the class of 1929.

During World War II, Adams served in a number of high-level capacities with the War Production Board (WPB) in Washington. A 1944 news item in the *New York Times* tells of his promotion from deputy director of the metals and minerals division of the WPB's Office of Civilian Requirements to director of WPB's Consumer's Durable Goods Division.

After the war, he worked for a brief period with the War Assets Administration. In 1947, he joined Edward R. Stettinius, Jr., and others, in the formation of a company organized to develop agricultural, mineral, and commercial projects in West Africa. Stettinius, a former Big Brother (chapter 2), had been secretary of state under Franklin D. Roosevelt. Adams accepted a government post in Korea in 1949. Later, he worked for the Ray-O-Vac Company, serving as assistant to the president and manager of the firm's Washington office. After Ray-O-Vac, he joined the advertising firm of Ruthrauff and Ryan, Inc., where he worked before coming to Big Brothers of America. Adams was married to the former Mary Semmes Gambrill. They had a daughter and a son. According to the Alumni Records Office of Lehigh University, Adams died on May 9, 1979.

GOESTA WOLLIN
Executive Director, BBA, 1958–1960

Goesta Wollin, now of Palisades, New York, was executive director of BBA from 1958 until 1960. He had served as director of program and services for the national organization before that time, a post he assumed in 1957.

He can, without contradiction, be characterized as the most unusual, multitalented person ever to be associated with the federation. Wollin is both a social scientist and a physical scientist. A graduate of Hermods College in his native Sweden, where he received a bachelor of science degree in 1939, he subsequently received a master's degree in social work from Columbia University.

In addition to a multifaceted career in social work and criminology, he can also lay claim to the titles of author, oceanographer, geologist, journalist, and inventor.

Wollin was born in Ystad, Sweden, on October 4, 1912. He came to the United States in 1942 and was naturalized in 1943. During World War II, he served as a paratrooper in the U.S. 82d Airborne

Goesta Wollin

Division, and took part in the invasion of Normandy and Holland, and in the Battle of the Bulge.

Before joining BBA, Wollin was a journalist in Sweden, Germany, and the United States, a research assistant at Columbia University, and executive director of the Mental Health Association of Union County, New Jersey. He had also been a caseworker with the Community Service Society in New York City, and had been associated with the Welfare and Health Council of Greater New York. After leaving BBA, he became project director for the National Council on Crime and Delinquency. He later became a consultant at the Lamont-Doherty Geological Observatory, Columbia University, with which he is presently associated.

At various times, Wollin has lectured at the University of Rome, Italy; City College of New York; the New School of Social Research; and Fordham University. He is the author of two book-length novels, published in Sweden, and coauthor of two nonfiction volumes titled *The Ever-Changing Sea* and *The Deep and the Past.*

He has been a member of the Council of National Organizations on Children and Youth, the White House Conference on Children and Youth, and he was the U.S. representative at the 3d United Nations Congress on the Prevention of Crime. He has held membership in the

British Glacial Society, the Swedish Colonial Society, and the New York Academy of Science.

His scientific achievements include the invention of a snow-making machine for ski slopes, discovery of a method for dispelling fog, and the synthesizing of amino acids and peptides from gases. Wollin and his wife, Janet, have one daughter. Reflecting on his interests and associations, he indicated recently that he considers BBA to be the most important work with which he has ever been associated.

THOMAS E. O'BRIEN
Executive Director, BBA, 1960–1972

Thomas E. O'Brien, now of Los Angeles, was the first executive director who "came up through the ranks" in Big Brothers work, having served as a caseworker for Big Brothers of Boston and as executive director for Big Brothers of Saginaw, Michigan, and Big Brothers of Greater Los Angeles, before assuming the national post in 1960. He served BBA until the end of 1972 — longer than any other person in that position to date.

Thomas E. O'Brien

During his tenure, the number of affiliated agencies increased from approximately 50 to more than 200 — a fourfold increase, and the number of boys being served reportedly increased from 4,000 to more than 50,000. O'Brien was responsible for greatly increasing the national awareness of the federation by helping to obtain the endorsements of a number of national figures, including Robert Kennedy, Danny Thomas, basketball star Bob Cousy, Billy Graham, and Bob Hope. O'Brien implemented many innovative fund-raising, recruiting, and administrative programs of lasting value.

A native of Boston, O'Brien graduated from the Cathedral of the Holy Cross High School in that city. He obtained a degree in sociology from Boston College, then entered the Navy, where he received a commission as an ensign and served until the end of World War II. He returned to Boston College after the war, and earned a master's degree in social work in 1949. He was employed by the Massachusetts Society for the Prevention of Cruelty to Children until 1951, when he joined Big Brothers of Boston. He went to Saginaw in 1953, and to Los Angeles in 1956.

For a brief period after leaving BBA in 1972, O'Brien operated a counseling service in Los Angeles. Then he joined Catholic Social Services in that area, where he currently serves as a caseworker at the organization's Vernon, California, facility. O'Brien and his wife, Louise, have seven children and five grandchildren.

LEWIS P. READE
Executive Vice-President, BBA & BB/BSA, 1973–1980

Lewis P. Reade, presently director of the U.S. agency for international development in Kingston, Jamaica, came to Big Brothers of America, as executive vice-president in 1973, after an extensive, technically oriented background in business and industry. As indicated in chapter 6, he brought to BBA a number of practices that he had found useful in the field of commerce and that ultimately proved to be of considerable value to the federation. Reade was executive vice-president of BBA and acting executive vice-president of BSI at the time the organizations merged in 1977, and served as executive vice-president of the new organization, BB/BSA, until 1980.

Before joining BBA, Reade was chairman of the board, chief executive officer, and treasurer of the Kellett Corporation, Willow Grove, Pennsylvania, a manufacturer of precision aerospace assemblies. An engineer by training, Reade received a bachelor of science degree in mechanical engineering from the University of Miami (Fla.) in 1953, where he was an honor student. He did graduate work at Hofstra University and attended the University of Baltimore School of Law for a brief period.

Lewis P. Reade

Between 1953 and 1957, Reade was a project engineer for several companies and the U.S. Army Ordnance Corps. In 1957, he joined the Westinghouse Electric Corporation, where he advanced through several engineering and management positions, becoming a group vice-president in January 1967. In 1970, he joined Tyco Laboratories, Inc., Waltham, Massachusetts, as vice-president for corporate planning and development, the position he held before coming to the Kellett Corporation.

Reade is and has been a member of numerous technical, social-service, educational, and community organizations. He and his wife, Peggy, are the parents of three children.

DAVID W. BAHLMANN
Executive Vice-President, BB/BSA, 1979–1984,*
President and Chief Operating Officer, BB/BSA,
1984–present

David W. Bahlmann, of Philadelphia, joined BB/BSA as executive vice-president in September 1979, and presently serves as national president and chief operating officer. Both a lawyer and experienced association executive before assuming the top administrative post, Bahlmann had served as director of Youth Services for the Indiana Lawyers Commission, Inc., Indianapolis, from 1975 until 1979.

He was a member of the BB/BSA board at the time of his appointment as executive vice-president, and was serving as chairman of its

---

*The title of this position was changed from executive vice-president to president in June 1984.

External Affairs Committee. Reared in a single-parent home, he has the distinction of being the first person in his position to have been associated with a Big Brothers program as a child.

David W. Bahlmann

Bahlmann is a graduate of Hillsdale College, Hillsdale, Michigan, where he received a degree in economics in 1961. He received a law degree from Valparaiso University in 1965. From 1967 until 1970, he engaged in the private practice of law in Valparaiso, Indiana. Also during this period, he served as deputy prosecuting attorney for the state's 67th Judicial Circuit and acted as legal adviser to the speaker of the House of Representatives of the Indiana General Assembly.

In 1971, Bahlmann was elected prosecuting attorney for the 67th Judicial Circuit, a post he held until 1973, when he became executive secretary of the Indiana Prosecuting Attorneys Association in Indianapolis. He held the last post concurrently with that of executive director of the Indiana Prosecuting Attorney's Council, a state agency for prosecuting attorneys, their deputies, and support personnel. In 1975, Bahlmann moved to the Indiana Lawyers Commission, the position he held before joining BB/BSA.

Long active in national youth-service activities, Bahlmann is a director of American Humanics, participates in the affairs of the National Assembly of Health and Social Welfare Organizations, and is past chairman of the National Collaboration for Youth. He is also a director of the National Adoption Exchange.

His memberships in professional organizations include the American Society of Association Executives, the National Council of Juvenile and Family Court Judges, the National District Attorneys Association, and the American Judicature Society. An accomplished and popular speaker, Bahlmann is often called on to address civic, community, and professional groups on matters concerning child welfare.

Bahlmann was a member of the U.S. Air Force Reserves from 1963 until 1969. He and his wife, Joan, have one child of their own, and have either adopted or provided foster care for twenty-five other children, as indicated in chapter 6.

WINIFRED DERRY
Founder and First President, BSI, 1970–1971

Winifred Derry, founder of Big Sisters of Rhode Island, was the founder and first president of Big Sisters International, Inc. (BSI). The organization was incorporated in Washington, D.C., on August 3, 1970. Before that time, Derry had assembled a group of interested

Winifred Derry

individuals, who represented independent Big Sisters organizations, and one state organization, to determine the feasibility of forming a Big Sisters federation. The response had been positive, and immediate steps were taken to create the organization's framework. Unfortunately, Derry died in August 1971, before many of her plans could be implemented. She was succeeded by Mildred Montague, who had been elected BSI vice-president.

Although three of Derry's nephews had been Little Brothers, it was as a member of the Providence, Rhode Island, Zonta Club, an organization of business and professional women, that she first became interested in forming a local Big Sisters group. Under her direction, and with the support of the club, Big Sisters of Rhode Island was organized in 1965.

An employment counselor, Derry was assistant manager of the Sterling Employment Service of Providence until the late 1960s, when she became the manager of an employment service in Washington, D.C., where BSI was founded. Derry was a licensed pilot, enjoyed travel, and, according to friends and associates, was a lively, outgoing, energetic person who loved to help others. Her death was a tragic blow to the fledging Big Sisters federation. Derry was survived by her husband, Jasper, and two daughters.

MILDRED MONTAGUE
President, BSI, 1971–1972; Chairwoman, 1972–1973;
Honorary Chairwoman, 1973–1977

Mildred Montague, of Lookout Mountain, Tennessee, became BSI president in August 1971, after the untimely death of BSI founder Winifred Derry. Montague had been a BSI vice-president before that

Mildred Montague

time and had served in several other capacities. She was elected chairwoman in 1972, and became honorary chairwoman in 1973. Montague had been elected to the board of Big Brothers of America in June 1971. She continued to serve on the BB/BSA board after the merger, and has been designated a BB/BSA Honorary Member for Life.

Long active in the affairs of Big Brothers of Chattanooga, she served on its Building Fund Committee, was instrumental in merging the Big Brothers and Big Sisters organizations in Chattanooga, and was later elected a vice-president of that combined agency.

Widely known in the mid-South for her charitable and philanthropic work, Montague has served as secretary of the Tennessee division of the American Cancer Society, as well as a regional vice-president and crusade chairman for that organization. She is a past president of the Junior League of Chattanooga, has served as the women's advance gifts campaign for the Community Chest, as building campaign chairperson for the Little Theatre of Chattanooga, and as a vice-president of that organization.

Montague has been associated with the Chattanooga Symphony Guild, has been a trustee of the Bachman Home, a Presbyterian residence for children in Cleveland, Tennessee, a trustee of the Caldsted Foundation, which operates a home for the elderly, and has served as a member of the Salvation Army Advisory Board in her area.

A graduate of the Bright School and the Girls Preparatory School in Chattanooga, Montague received a bachelor of arts degree in sociology and economics from Sweet Briar College. She and her husband, William, have three sons and two grandsons.

LEOLA E. MEYER
President, BSI, 1972–1974

Leola "Lee" E. Meyer has been involved in Big Sisters work since 1967, when she was named to the board of Big Sisters of Arizona, Inc. She served as vice-president of that group from 1969 to 1970, and as president from 1970 to 1972. An active Big Sister herself, she has served the Arizona agency in almost every capacity, and was a founder of three Big Sisters auxiliaries in the Phoenix area which support the agency.

Meyer was active in Big Sisters International, Inc., almost from its inception. She became a director, was elected president in 1972, and became chairwoman of the board in 1974. Meyer remained on the BSI board until the 1977 merger. She was a member of the Merger Committee. After the merger, she was accorded life membership on the Honorary Board of BB/BSA.

Meyer continued to play an active role in the affairs of Big Sisters of Arizona after assuming her national duties. This group was the first to be accepted as a full-member agency by BSI, which recognized the Arizona organization as having the strongest Big Sisters program in the nation. Meyer was instrumental in bringing the BSI annual meeting to Scottsdale, Arizona, in 1974.

Leola E. Meyer

Movement activities account for only part of Lee Meyer's social-service activity. Over the years, she has been active in Girl Scout and Boy Scout work. She has served as a local coordinator of Catholic Charities, as a director of the Inter-Club Council of Arizona, and as a representative to her local Community Council. She has been active in Phoenix-area musical theater, symphony, and museum activities.

A native of Ohio, Meyer has lived in Phoenix since 1952. She attended Phoenix College, where she majored in home economics. She and her husband, John, have two children.

JUDY A. WEILL
President, BSI, 1974–1976

Judy A. Weill, Omaha, Nebraska, was elected president of Big Sisters International, Inc., in 1974, and served until 1976. She had previously served on the BSI board, had served on several of its committees, and had been chairperson of the Membership, Agency Relations, and Promotion committees. Weill was a member of the Merger Committee and later served as an at-large director of BB/BSA. She is a life member of the BB/BSA Honorary Board. She was responsible for developing the BSI symbol that identified the organization before the merger.

Judy A. Weill

Before becoming involved with the national Big Sisters organization, Weill had participated in Big Sisters activities in the Omaha area, and had served as acting chairwoman of Big Sisters of Omaha – Council Bluffs, Inc.

A practicing attorney with the Omaha law firm of Kutak Rock & Huie, Weill graduated from the Creighton University School of Law in 1979. She received an undergraduate degree from the University of Nebraska in 1964, and did graduate work at New York University and at the University of Nebraska. During the mid-1960s, Weill taught speech and English at Oyster Bay High School, Oyster Bay, New York. She and her husband, Richard, have two children. Weill is a member of the Omaha and Nebraska Bar associations and the Junior League of Omaha.

HILDA PATRICIA CURRAN
President, BSI, 1976–1977

Hilda Patricia Curran, of Lansing, Michigan, was elected president of BSI in 1976, and served until 1977, when BSI was merged with BBA to form BB/BSA. She was the first professional social worker to head the Big Sisters organization. Curran is currently an active member of the BB/BSA board, and has served on the Executive Committee.

She was named to the board of BSI in 1973. Before becoming president, she served as BSI treasurer and as a member of the BSI-BBA Merger Committee. Long active in the affairs of Big Brothers/Big Sisters of Greater Lansing, Michigan, Curran served that organization as a Big Sister, volunteer caseworker, secretary, and chairperson of several key committees. She served on the board of the Greater Lansing Agency from 1976 until 1981.

Hilda Patricia Curran

Curran is currently director of the Office of Women and Work of the Michigan Department of Labor, which seeks to identify and solve the problems of Michigan's working women. A graduate of Hiram College, Hiram, Ohio, she has a master of social work degree from Ohio State University, and has been certified by the School of Social Work of Michigan State University.

From 1963 until 1965, Curran was employed by social agencies in Springfield, Massachusetts. She then joined the United Community

Centers, Inc., Brooklyn, New York, as a program development specialist, before becoming a consultant to the Michigan Department of Education's Division of Vocational Rehabilitation, Lansing, in 1967. In 1970, Curran became the program developer for the Bureau of Community Services, Michigan Department of Labor, the position she held before assuming her current post.

A member of many professional and civic organizations, Curran has served on a number of social-service commissions and task forces, including the Ingham County (Mich.) Housing Commission, the Ingham County Board of Social Services, the Michigan Task Force on Sexual Harassment, and the Michigan Women's Commission. She is a founding member, and served as the first president, of Women in State Government. Curran has also been associated with the Lansing Model Cities Program, the Retired Senior Volunteer Program Advisory Council, the Adult and Continuing Education Advisory Council of the Michigan Department of Education, and the Greater Lansing Food Alliance, as well as the Michigan Capital Girl Scout Council, the Zonta Club of Lansing, and the Michigan Women's Political Caucus.

Curran is a popular speaker, workshop presenter, and panelist. She is listed in *Who's Who of American Women, Who's Who of the Midwest*, and in 1977 was selected as "Social Worker of the Year" by the Lansing-Jackson Chapter of the National Association of Social Workers.

SHARYN FORREST
Coordinator, BSI, 1974–1977

Before the merger of Big Sisters International, Inc., and Big Brothers of America, BSI never had an executive vice-president or director-level staff position as had BBA, largely due to lack of funds and an organizational structure that would support such a position.

However, after the Lilly Endowment Fund grants during the early 1970s to investigate the possibility of a merger of the two federations as well as to enhance BSI services to girls, staff support at an executive level was clearly indicated. On February 21, 1974, Sharyn Forrest, until then an administrative assistant to BBA Executive Vice-President Lewis P. Reade, was named to the post of BSI coordinator. Forrest had joined BBA in 1973. Immediately before that time, she had been a business education teacher for the Neighborhood Youth Corps.

Forrest is a graduate of Goddard College, Plainfield, Vermont, and has completed a number of leadership and training institutes. Before assuming the BSI managerial position, she did a wide range of consulting for such clients as Hamilton College, Mohawk Valley Community College, the YWCA, and the Episcopal Diocese of Pennsylvania. She

Sharyn Forrest

has been involved in several projects for various educational organizations, in the areas of curriculum development, program evaluation, and resource development for the primary grades through college.

Until near the time of the merger, when Forrest left BSI, she was responsible for developing and administering a BSI headquarters staff, gathering data on existing Big Sisters organizations, both affiliated and nonaffiliated, organizing new agencies, creating informational and training materials, and directing program development. She also found time to be a Big Sister herself.

Forrest presently resides in Uniontown, Pennsylvania, where she serves as a volunteer in a number of church and community-related youth activities. She and her husband, James, an Episcopal priest, have four children.

Countless others deserve to be featured in this chapter. During the past four decades they have served as local board members, local board officers, agency executive directors, caseworkers, and volunteers, as well as in various capacities with the national federations. It is unfortunate that space does not permit greater coverage.

* * * *

8

Today's Agencies

Many people outside the Movement are familiar with the terms *Big Brother* and *Big Sister*. They may even know that a Big Brother or Big Sister is a volunteer adult who befriends a child, generally from a single-parent home, on a one-to-one basis. Not so well known is how these matches are made or how a Big Brothers/Big Sisters agency functions.

A brief overview of a hypothetical agency introduces a general description of actual day-to-day operations in BB/BSA-affiliated agencies across the country. Finally, the actual match process, involving volunteers, Little Brothers, Little Sisters, and others, is discussed in considerable detail.

Affiliated agencies are autonomous bodies; they are not centrally controlled, "cookie-cutter" operations. Local differences exist and a significant difference is agency size. For example, Big Brothers/Big Sisters of Houston, Texas, supervises nearly seven hundred matches, has five branch offices, twenty-five employees, and a six-figure annual budget. In contrast, an agency in northern Michigan has only twelve matches, one part-time employee, and a budget of under $12,000.

But all affiliates are required to meet prescribed operating practices, and most agencies share many other characteristics. An agency that might exist in a city of 100,000 population will serve as an example although no specific organization is being described.

Hypothetical Affiliated Agency

A locally elected citizen board of, perhaps, twenty persons governs the agency. It operates under its own constitution and bylaws as well as under an affiliation agreement with BB/BSA. Its mission statement sets forth its objectives. It has a casework manual which contains written, board-approved policies and procedures, covering all phases of service delivery, in accordance with the Minimum Standard of Practice formulated by BB/BSA. Its operations are monitored and evaluated by BB/BSA on a periodic basis.

The agency is incorporated. It has obtained 501(c)(3) federal income tax-exempt status. It has obtained approval from the applicable state agency to solicit funds. Adequate insurance coverage, including liability insurance, is maintained, and it submits to annual independent financial audits required by its own board, by BB/BSA, and, perhaps, by several funding sources. It maintains a liaison with other established social-service organizations, where children may be referred for specialized services.

An executive director administers the agency's program. He or she has at least a bachelor's degree in the social sciences or humanities. This person could have a master's degree in social work and be sanctioned by the Academy of Certified Social Workers (ACSW). Typically, the agency also has one caseworker with an undergraduate or graduate degree and one clerical employee.

At any one time, the agency has a caseload of approximately seventy-five Big/Little Brother/Sister matches and a waiting list of from fifty to sixty children. The agency has an annual budget of approximately $80,000, a third to two-thirds of which is funded by the local United Way. Additional funds are raised through various agency revenue-generating activities and from gifts and donations, both monetary and in-kind. The board might have created a membership category for members of the community who wish to support the agency financially but not to volunteer their services. An auxiliary group might also exist for purposes of providing financial aid and assisting with agency activities.

A child, known as the client, and generally between the ages of eight and sixteen is most often referred by a parent. Referrals are also made by schools, courts, and other social-service agencies. Prospective volunteers either call or visit the agency, indicating their desire to serve.

In 1980, as part of a larger BB/BSA study, averages were obtained for several important agency functions, based on a responding sample of 288 groups. Findings showed that there were 22 members on an average local board, 450,000 persons in the average agency's jurisdiction, an average of 160 Big-Little matches per agency, and an average staff of 6 persons, including the support staff. Average agency income was $100,000. However, such averages can be misleading if used to depict a typical operation, since figures from very small as well as very large agencies are included. Several large cities have some relatively small agencies and some medium-sized communities have several large programs. Because of the wide ranges of such factors as annual income, board size, number of matches and staffing, no organization can truly be described as typical.

Affiliated Agencies

Today, Big Brothers/Big Sisters of America has 460 affiliated agencies. It is not known how many independent or unaffiliated groups exist, but it is believed that there may be as many as a hundred organizations that provide some type of similar service or use the names *big brother* or *big sister* or both. Several of these agencies are known to be rather large. At least one has over one hundred active matches. Big Brothers and Big Brothers/Big Sisters of America, and its symbol, are registered trademarks. The phrase, "one to one," used to describe Big Brothers/Big Sisters service, is also registered. Unauthorized usage is monitored on a regular basis, with legal measures taken when and where appropriate.

Most agencies serve both boys and girls. All new agencies must serve both sexes unless a single-gender agency already operates in the applicant's population jurisdiction (as indicated in an earlier chapter, the entire nation is divided into well-defined service areas to assure complete coverage and to avoid overlapping). Then a new agency to serve only the opposite sex may be approved.

The majority of BB/BSA affiliated agencies today are independent and governed by a board of directors. Others are sponsored by such organizations as the YMCA or YWCA, church groups, or other social-service agencies. Such agencies have a dual affiliation and are referred to by BB/BSA as "umbrella" groups. These agencies are generally governed by an advisory board or committee appointed by the board or governing body of the parent or umbrella organization. The parent bodies may also provide most of their financial support. New groups may be sponsored by sectarian bodies, but must agree to serve clients (Little Brothers or Little Sisters) of all faiths. Large agencies — both independent and umbrella — could have as many as ten satellite or branch offices.

Local agency boards are urged to provide for continuing training of agency staffs. Professional employees keep abreast of current techniques and developments in the field of social service by attending seminars and conferences, including the annual meeting of Big Brothers/Big Sisters of America and by enrolling in day or evening classes at local colleges and universities. A few agencies offer tuition reimbursement, or permit class attendance during normal working hours.

Many agency professional employees belong to one or more professional organizations, such as the National Association of Social Workers (NASW). Contributions to professional journals by agency personnel are encouraged as long as this activity does not interfere with normal duties. Agencies sometimes form state associations for training or fund raising—the latter generally involving the seeking of state grants. Such groups range from informal, infrequently held gatherings to formal organizations with elected officers. All state organizations are created through the initiative of the agencies themselves and have no official standing in the national federation (BB/BSA).

How Affiliated Agencies Are Formed

When a community-based group indicates a desire to form an agency, its leaders contact Big Brothers/Big Sisters of America. The national organization assists the interest group in completing a local audit or needs assessment. If it is determined that the group is willing to meet certain minimum requirements, including assurances of financial support, it forms a fledgling organization known as an agency-in-formation. At this stage, BB/BSA provides the new group with information, materials, and guidance to assist it in forming a local citizen board, obtaining a suitable facility, retaining a professional staff, and implementing required administrative and operating procedures. Advice and counsel are provided in the areas of fund raising, public relations, and casework.

BB/BSA evaluates the agency-in-formation at the end of its first year. If it has met previously prescribed minimum operating requirements, it may be advanced to provisional status, with more stringent operating requirements. Another BB/BSA evaluation occurs in two years, to determine if the agency is ready for full membership. Full members are evaluated every five years. Agencies-in-formation and provisional status groups pay fixed affiliation fees to the national organization. Full members pay a prescribed percentage of their annual expenditures.

Small groups, primarily in rural areas, which have limited resources and serve a limited area, may advance to associate status, rather than to full membership, where they remain. Associate agencies pay a fixed membership fee.

Big Brothers/Big Sisters agencies are not unlike other social-service organizations when it comes to meeting the challenges of ever-increasing operating costs, budget deficits, volunteer recruitment, fund raising, and staffing. All of these areas are intimately related.

Volunteer Recruitment

By far the best means of obtaining volunteers is through local word-of-mouth, involving current Big Brothers and Big Sisters. Often, only

TOUCH THE LIFE OF A BOY
AND CHANGE YOURS

I became a Big Brother after reading a story about the great difference one made in the life of a young boy. What I didn't know is how he would change my life!

School books, baseball gloves, hiking, walks on the beach all became a part of my life again. What a feeling he gave me . . . just imagine being hero, role model, trusted listener and FRIEND!

There are over 200 boys waiting to be matched to a man like you. Be a positive force in our future by becoming a Big Brother today. I promise you an experience that will change your life.

BIG BROTHERS/BIG SISTERS
of ORANGE COUNTY
150 Yorba Street, Tustin, CA 92680
(714) 544-7773

This appeal for Big Brothers appeared in 1984 in a regional edition of *Time* magazine (reprinted courtesy *Time* magazine).

a few short weeks after being matched, an adult volunteer will urge friends to become involved in the program. Local media are also an effective recruiting device. Included are institutional-type advertising in newspapers, sometimes underwritten by a local business, local and nationally-generated radio and television public service announcements, special features on television news programs, billboards, and posters displayed in local businesses and institutions. Also effective are such devices as bumper stickers, restaurant place mats, bookmarks distributed through local libraries, and announcements in church bulletins and company publications.

Agency-produced news releases, as well as reporter-generated feature articles about Big and Little Brothers and Sisters activities, almost always result in prospective volunteer inquiries. Volunteers also learn about BB/BS activities from speakers at service club luncheons, from agency personnel who work in information booths at fairs and other public events, and from agency newsletters. Many activities primarily designed for fund raising also attract volunteers.

Several negative factors deter volunteer participation. Some people believe that the Movement offers only a recreational program. They fail to perceive its therapeutic role and, therefore, feel that they can use their time better in other areas. Others believe that Big Brothers or Big Sisters must have several hours of spare time each week. Such is not the case. Volunteers are expected to include their matches in routine work and leisure activities. Elaborate, costly pursuits are discouraged. A Little Brother might help his Big Brother wash his car or help with other chores. A Little Sister might help her Big Sister redecorate her apartment. Such activity is considered beneficial as long as the child is not exploited.

Some prospective volunteers may believe that they will be required to pay a fee. This is not true. They may think that the program is only for kids who have been in serious trouble with the law and wonder if they can handle such a child. Although agencies strive to help all children that can benefit from one-to-one friendship, most Little Brothers/Sisters have never been in any kind of trouble, but merely lack adult friendship. Volunteers need to know that they are never left to deal alone with their matches. Expert assistance is available from trained caseworkers at all times.

Why do Big Brothers and Big Sisters volunteer? Some offer their services because they were once Little Brothers or Little Sisters themselves; they want to offer the opportunities they once enjoyed to others. One Big Brother, with two children of his own, volunteered because he hoped that someone would befriend his sons if anything happened to him. A Big Sister volunteered because, "I'm a child. I like to play." She and her Little Sister climb trees, play games, go ice-skating, do art projects, and join in the world of fantasy together. Others volunteer because their own children are grown and they miss sharing the world of childhood. But most serve simply because of a deep and abiding desire to help others who are less fortunate, and because the Movement provides one of the most fulfilling ways to give of oneself, instead of only making monetary contributions.

Most agencies publicly thank their Big Brothers and Big Sisters and other volunteers during some special event each year. Many choose to do this by hosting a dinner during BB/BSA-sponsored National Big Brothers/Big Sisters Appreciation Week, which is usually observed during the second or third week in February. Other events during the week publicize agency activities and enhance fund-raising and volunteer recruitment efforts.

Fund Raising

Big Brothers/Big Sisters agencies, like hundreds of other social-service groups, depend heavily on United Way and related community funding organizations. But additional funding is also needed. Most welcome are direct gifts and grants from individuals, corporations, and foundations. Since most united giving programs do not permit recipients to conduct additional, direct-solicitation campaigns, Big Brothers/Big Sisters agencies raise revenue through many other innovative activities, all of which involve extensive public relations and promotional activity.

Probably the most popular and effective is the annual dinner or dinner dance, which takes several forms. Like the fund-raising dinners conducted each year by Big Brothers/Big Sisters of America (chapter 6), agency dinners may be billed as formal, gourmet affairs, with high ticket prices and, perhaps, headlined by a nationally-known celebrity. Expensive prizes may be awarded. Additional revenue is often raised through menu/program advertising. Closely related to these events are the celebrity roasts, where a well-known actor, politician, or sports figure is kidded good-naturedly by peers. Such events have been known to result in a six-figure income for their sponsors.

Next in popularity are benefit performances by nationally-known entertainers, and various sponsored sports events, such as golf tournaments, perhaps also involving celebrities. Two nationally available agency fund-raising activities merit comment. Bowl For Kids' Sake, offered through Big Brothers/Big Sisters of America, mentioned briefly in chapter 6, is growing rapidly in popularity. Local bowlers solicit funds for points scored during special bowling events, which are generally held in February or March each year. Agencies pay a percentage of their income from this activity to BB/BSA in exchange for licensing,

Gibson

Dexter

Someone to talk with and share the day's problems, someone who is always there when needed, someone who really cares what happens to you—that's a Big Brother or Big Sister.

advisory services, and promotional materials. Agency gross income from Bowl For Kids' Sake during the mid-1980s is expected to reach $4 million per year.

The other activity, provided by a national marketing organization, DialAmerica Marketing, Inc., Teaneck, New Jersey, solicits magazine subscriptions by telephone. DialAmerica enters into revenue-sharing agreements with individual BB/BS agencies before making solicitations in their areas. Agencies increase income from this source by urging members of the community to respond favorably to DialAmerica calls. Total agency revenue from this source passed the $1 million mark during the early 1980s. According to an article in the *Wall Street Journal*, for June 21, 1984, sharing profits from designated sales with consumer products companies is the wave of the future for charitable endeavors. The article described how American Express Company raised $1.7 million for the restoration of the Statue of Liberty by pledging, during a particular period, a penny for each use of its cards and a dollar for most new cards issued in the United States. Restaurants frequently donate a portion of a day's receipts to Big Brothers/Big Sisters agencies, and amusement parks sometimes donate a portion of their gate fees for a day.

An activity that has worked well for several charities for many years is bingo. A few BB/BSA – affiliated agencies are now discovering that this long-popular game can be a continuing major source of revenue where permitted by law. One agency in a northwestern state reportedly grosses more than $4 million each year from this activity.

Agency fund-raising activities that are designed to supplement primary sources of revenue abound, and are seemingly limited only by the imagination of the sponsors. Recently noted activities across the country include tailgate and garage sales, flea markets, auctions, at times celebrity auctions, in which memorabilia donated by movie, TV, and sports stars are sold, car washes, art and style shows, bake sales, Christmas tree sales, and all kinds of athletic events in which contributions are solicited for miles walked or run or distances covered by cycling, swimming, or rowing.

Fishing derbies are popular and offer a variety of ways for raising funds. Tags, representing various amounts of money, are placed on the tails of several fish, which are then released in a lake or river. Participants pay to try to hook one of the fish and claim the reward. Many new shopping malls feature pools and fountains into which people toss pennies and other coins, perhaps thinking that it will bring them good luck. Some mall managements donate these funds to charities. Although the competition is keen, this is another source of revenue for fortunate agencies.

One agency raises funds by helping otherwise forgetful people remember birthdays, anniversaries, and other important occasions. For a small fee paid at the beginning of the year, the agency sends appropriate cards with the donor's name. At least one bank allows its savings-deposit customers to designate one percent of their interest for a local agency. The customer, however, does not lose a penny. The bank makes the payments. Sometimes local service organizations, college fraternities, and even prison groups "adopt" local agencies and provide supplementary funds on a regular basis, either directly or through a sponsored fund-raising event. Government funding — state or federal — is sometimes available for special projects. And, of course, possible income from wills, bequests, and life insurance should not be overlooked.

An Effort That Failed

What would probably have been the biggest fund-raiser in local agency history never came about. In early 1962, Floyd Patterson was the world heavyweight boxing champion. In March that year, columnist Drew Pearson, then president of Big Brothers of the National Capitol Area and a member of the board of Big Brothers of America, invited Cus D'Amato, Patterson's manager, to his home in Washington to discuss a possible title-defense fight with contender Sonny Liston, for the benefit of the Washington agency.

On behalf of Big Brothers, Pearson offered Patterson, through D'Amato, one million dollars. Liston was to receive a lesser amount, with the net proceeds going to the Big Brothers. Pearson also thought that such a match would help Liston, a two-time convicted felon, improve his image and repay society for his past malfeasance. Because of Liston's criminal record, the New York Boxing Commission had already refused permission for a title bout in that state.

D'Amato told Pearson that a million dollars was not enough, with income taxes being what they were. Instead, he proposed that Patterson be placed on the Washington agency's payroll as a public relations representative upon his retirement from boxing, at $200,000 a year for thirty years. Thus, Patterson would eventually receive a total of six million dollars. D'Amato would also have an employment contract with Big Brothers, but for a lesser amount.

An initially shocked Pearson then heard D'Amato explain that the fight would probably gross five to six million tax-free dollars for Big Brothers. After initial expenses were covered, the Washington agency could invest the remainder in high-yield, longterm investments. Only half of the interest would be needed for the salaries to Patterson and D'Amato. The agency would receive the other half, and at the end of

George Mason

Sports and other outdoor activities provide opportunities to cement friendships.

Ken Goad

Brian Harris

Robert John Mihovil

the thirty-year contract period, Big Brothers would still have the mul-timillion dollar principal. The proposal, as outlined, sounded good to Pearson, and both men parted to check out the details with their lawyers.

But all was not to go smoothly. Of late, the D'Amato/Patterson relationship, once as close as that of a father and son, had been dete-riorating. Patterson had been dealing directly with the law firm that D'Amato used instead of going through D'Amato. Furthermore, he was dealing with another partner in the firm. According to D'Amato, this partner was a secret associate of Roy Cohn, who was connected with a sports promotion organization known as Championship Sports. This is the same Roy Cohn of the infamous McCarthy hearings during the early 1950s.

D'Amato reported that, when Cohn heard of the discussion with Pearson, he decided to promote the fight himself, bypassing D'Amato and eliminating Big Brothers as a beneficiary. And that is exactly what happened. The fight was held in Chicago on September 25, 1962, under the sponsorship of Championship Sports. Liston won, becoming the new heavyweight champion.

But Pearson did not give up. He contacted Liston and proposed that a title defense fight be held for the benefit of Big Brothers. Liston's enthusiastic reply indicated that he was in favor of such a match, but that Patterson had the right to say when and where the re-match would be held. Evidently no reply was received to a similar proposal made to Patterson, who was still under contract to Championship Sports. The second fight was held in Las Vegas on July 22, 1963, with Liston again the winner.

During a 1984 conversation with D'Amato, then seventy-six years old, he told me that the first fight, proposed by Pearson, could have grossed as much as seven million dollars for Big Brothers. But, alas, it did not happen. The estrangement between D'Amato and Patterson continued to grow. Patterson fired his manager in July 1964. Drew Pearson continued to be a strong supporter of the Big Brothers Move-ment, both locally and nationally, until his death.

Staffing Problems

Staffing problems generally do not stem from shortages of social-service workers. There are more than three hundred accredited schools of social work in the United States. Altruistically motivated, thousands of young graduates enter the field each year. Rather, difficulties arise in striving to maintain a balance between the number of caseworkers on the one hand and caseload and budget on the other. BB/BSA generally recommends that no more than seventy-five matches be supervised by one caseworker. When this number is exceeded, and funds limit caseworker hiring, service to everyone is hampered and, eventually, service to new clients must be refused. It is sad when that happens. Agency people worry about what will happen to those who are turned away. What finally became of one small boy who could not be matched in time provides ample justification for their concern.

This boy was referred to Big Brothers, Inc., New York City, on December 2, 1953, by the Probation Department of the Bronx Children's Court, which indicated that he badly needed a Big Brother. He was only thirteen at the time, and had been arrested for long-term truancy. His probation officer described him as a bright, likable boy. When the officer asked him why he did not go to school, the boy replied that school was a waste of time. He said that he was not learning anything and that the kids laughed at him, making fun of his clothes and southern drawl.

So the boy withdrew into himself and had nothing to do with other children. Although he said that he had once had hobbies of clay modeling and stamp collecting and that he also liked horseback riding, he now spent most of his time in solitude, watching television while his mother worked. The probation officer said that he felt that what the boy needed most was someone who cared, especially someone who could represent a father to him, since he had never known his father.

Because of a caseworker shortage, the Big Brothers agency was unable to do anything about the case for thirteen days, even though immediate action was indicated. Then, it made contact with the boy and his mother. In all, there were six contacts, including three home visits. Before a Big Brother could be found, however, the boy and his mother disappeared. The boy's case record was filed and the Big Brothers agency heard nothing more about him for nearly ten years. In fact, not until November 22, 1963. The boy was Lee Harvey Oswald.

Would it have made a difference in this boy's life if the agency had had the resources to act sooner? Would world history have taken a different turn? In a news release issued on December 6, 1963, by Big Brothers of New York, which is on file in that agency's archives, Adalbert von Gontard, Jr., then agency president, said, "In retrospect, it is impossible to state what might have been the result if the efforts of Big Brothers, Inc., had been successful in providing the boy with a favorable adult male relationship with a volunteer Big Brother." Impossible indeed. But agency and Movement officials will always wonder what might have been, as they turn their attention to the thousands of children on current waiting lists.

Other Agency Problems

Caseworkers in small and medium agencies not only must handle professional duties, they must assist with recruiting, fund raising, public relations, and administrative activities. Difficulties arise, according to one agency executive, in maintaining an equitable balance of these additional functions. Staff members who are more proficient than others in certain areas may be unduly burdened with extra duties, causing employee relations problems.

By their very nature, Big Brothers/Big Sisters agencies for the most part are not large enough to support more than two layers of management. Unless the agency executive director position is available, the other professionals must remain as caseworkers, a situation that often fosters turnover. Larger agencies have an intermediate level, that of casework supervisor, which offers an additional opportunity for advancement.

Big Brothers/Big Sisters agencies, as well as many other social-service organizations, find it difficult to compete in the job market with various government agencies, which are generally able to offer significantly higher salaries and greater benefits. But Big Brothers/Big Sisters caseworkers report that their work is extremely satisfying. Few other areas of social work provide an opportunity to witness the effects of a specific therapeutic technique on the lives of children over a protracted period.

A social-service agency shares many of the social responsibilities of business, industry, religious organizations, academia, and the population as a whole. Big Brothers/Big Sisters agencies do not discriminate on the basis of race, creed, sex, or affectional preference in the accepting of volunteer applications. They comply fully with all federal, state, and local laws and ordinances that deal with discrimination. But all volunteers are subject to a program of intense scrutiny involving all aspects of their lives, and while protecting identities before matching, the caseworker always passes the information obtained on to the parent of prospective clients.

In November 1974, a man contacted the Big Brothers agency in Minneapolis, volunteered to become a Big Brother, and admitted that he was a homosexual. He was told that the information would be passed on to the mothers of prospective Little Brothers. Objecting to this, the volunteer filed a complaint with the Minneapolis Civil Rights Department, claiming discrimination.

A hearing examiner for the department ruled that Big Brothers should *not* ask an applicant's sexual preference, or else it must reveal the preference of all applicants. However, a district court judge ruled in April 1978 that Big Brothers not only may ask a volunteer about his sexual preference, but may also communicate this information to the mother of a prospective Little Brother. This decision was subsequently upheld by the Minnesota Supreme Court, in *Big Brothers, Inc. v. Minnesota Commission on Civil Rights*, 284 N.W. 2d. 823 (1979).

Increasing public concern about child neglect and child abuse, both physical and sexual, is welcomed by Big Brothers/Big Sisters agencies. In addition to screening techniques designed to detect potential abusers, many agencies now sponsor prevention workshops and seminars for Little Brothers and Little Sisters and their parents. Agency personnel also report any incidents of abuse or suspected abuse to local child-abuse reporting authorities for appropriate action.

How Matches Are Made

Upon referral to a BB/BS agency, a child's parent or guardian is asked to complete an application, state why a match is desired, and furnish information relating to the child's social and physical background. A caseworker then interviews the parent and child, both together and separately. There could be several interviews. At least one could take place in the child's home. Local practices vary, but there is generally a home visit at some point in the procedure. The child's school and, if applicable, the referring social agency will be contacted for additional information. The child is rejected, or accepted; when accepted, the child is put on an agency waiting list. Incidentally, many girls are not referred for matching because a parent or referral agency mistakenly believes that since Big Brothers are for boys without fathers, Big Sisters must be only for girls without mothers. Such is not the case. Girls without fathers are also eligible for matching.

Agencies may engage in various activities to make known the availability of clients on waiting lists. They might, for example, sponsor a "Big Brother or Big Sister for a Day" event. Prospective volunteers, as the event's name implies, are asked to befriend a waiting-list child for just one day, with both child and volunteer aware that a permanent commitment is not implied. An increasingly popular weekly segment on many television newscasts across the country, generally known by the day it is aired (such as "Wednesday's Child"), features children who are seeking a Big Brother or Big Sister. A daily newspaper in Illinois recently published a full page of photographs of prospective Little Brothers, together with brief biographical sketches which indicated how long they had been waiting for a Big Brother.

Prospective volunteers are subject to a more rigorous screening process. When a man or woman first indicates a desire to be a Big Brother or Big Sister, he or she is invited to a periodically held general orientation session, during which the agency's executive director, or a caseworker, discusses the program and its requirements. Until this meeting,

Jim Sieger

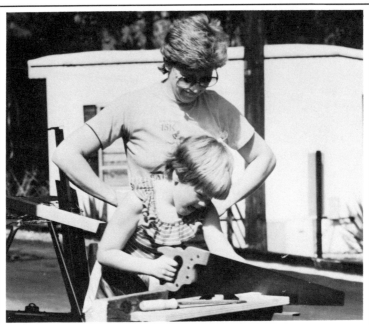

Sharing a skill with a Little Brother or Little Sister is an excellent way to instill self-confidence and build self-esteem.

many volunteers have only a vague, general idea of what the program requires or how it functions. Volunteers generally range from eighteen to forty-five years of age, but many older adults are now accepted.

Prospects are told that, if accepted, they must agree to see their Little Brother or Sister at least three hours weekly for a minimum of one year. The qualities desired in a Big Brother or Big Sister are discussed. The emotional as well as the procedural aspects of matches are covered and, finally, they are told that every facet of their personal lives will be thoroughly probed before acceptance. Spouses and friends of prospects are encouraged to attend these meetings. At the end of the session, applications are distributed, but no one is ever pressed for a decision. If the program is not what a prospective volunteer thought it was, he or she may leave without fear of intimidation. That is what orientation sessions are for.

Volunteer application forms request data from which a personal file is constructed. An employment history must be completed and three character references furnished.

The most penetrating search of a volunteer's capabilities takes place during the interview. If accepted, the volunteer will be entrusted with a stranger's minor child. It is vitally important that he or she be physically, mentally, and emotionally fit for the task. A major objective of the interview is to determine why the volunteer wants to enter the program, what he or she has to offer, what he or she hopes to gain. The caseworker also wants to learn what the volunteer wants in a Little Brother or Little Sister. Likes, dislikes, common interests, and a number of socioeconomic and demographic factors applicable to both the volunteer and child are important when a match is considered.

The interview will probably begin with a discussion of any "general impressions" the caseworker may have formed during prior meetings. Then, specific areas will be probed. Of special interest is how the volunteer was treated during childhood and adolescence. During these periods, how did the volunteer relate to his or her parents? To siblings? Other relatives and friends? Were there any incidents of child abuse or other unfortunate experiences? There will be questions relating to the prospect's marital relations, sex life, and sexual preference; experiences with drugs and alcohol and other personal habits. Finally, such areas as education, religious preferences and practices, personal finances, hobbies, favorite sports, and other spare-time activities are covered.

Where permitted, a police record check is made. Noting an alarmingly sharp increase in child abuse cases, more and more legislatures are passing laws that permit recognized youth-service agencies to obtain information relating to a job applicant's or volunteer's conviction for criminal offenses. However, having a police record does not automatically disqualify an applicant. It all depends on the offense and the nature of the applicant's rehabilitation.

A visit may be made to the volunteer's home, if deemed necessary. Volunteers who are accepted for the program are either matched immediately or placed on a waiting list. Since there are almost always more Little Brothers on waiting lists (many have been there for many months) than available Big Brothers, the latter seldom have to wait long. On the other hand, many agencies have more Big Sister volunteers than available Little Sisters.

Successful candidates have stated that their lives were subjected to more scrutiny in becoming a Big Brother or Big Sister than they were previously in obtaining top secret government clearance. Some prospective volunteers may have doubts about qualifying, which keep them from offering their services, but such fears are usually unfounded. While screening is intensive, it is mainly concerned with factors that relate directly to the safety of the child. Qualifications in other areas are extremely broad and flexible. Just as there are all kinds of children with all kinds of needs, there is a need for all kinds of Big Brothers and Big Sisters.

From time to time, the national organization, BB/BSA, as well as its member agencies, receive reports of individual strangers who approach single parents, represent themselves as Big Brothers or Big Sisters, and offer to befriend their children. Such approaches should be reported immediately to either the nearest BB/BS agency, another child welfare agency, or to local law enforcement officials. Big Brothers and Big Sisters assistance is *never* offered in this fashion.

The actual match occurs as follows. The Big Brother or Big Sister is presented with the case records of several Little Brothers or Little Sisters on waiting lists. Names of the children are not revealed and the children themselves are not aware that they are being reviewed. If a volunteer likes a particular child's characteristics, the child's parent or guardian is contacted and provided with information on the volunteer, also on an anonymous basis. As previously indicated, the parent is told everything that is known about the prospective Big Brother or Big Sister. If agreement is reached at that point, a meeting of the principals —the adult and child—is arranged.

The first meeting generally takes place in the child's home, with the parent and the caseworker present. The caseworker, with the concurrence of the parent, may then suggest that the volunteer and child spend some time together alone to become better acquainted. Several such exploratory visits could occur. When all of the parties involved are comfortable with the new relationship, it is made permanent. The caseworker carefully supervises the match and the Big Brother or Sister is required to submit periodic reports and be available for consultation.

An agency caseworker interviews a prospective volunteer.

A match is quickly terminated if difficulties arise. Matches are generally monitored for at least two years. After that, the case may be closed by the agency. But many Big-Little friendships continue for years; some endure for a lifetime.

In matching, religion as well as race may be a factor. However, cross-racial matches are fairly common and, more rarely, cross-gender matches are made. In a few cases, still considered experimental, a child is matched with a couple rather than an individual. The parent and caseworker, as well as the client, exercise considerable input in decisions involving these factors.

The Volunteer's Role

A Big Brother or Big Sister is not a surrogate parent, nor is he or she expected to assume the prerogatives of a parent. Rather, a volunteer provides counsel and guidance, provides emotional support, encourages the child to pursue areas of special interest, and helps build the child's self-esteem and self-confidence. Most importantly, the volunteer is a personal friend—someone in whom the child can confide, someone to talk with, someone who is always there when needed.

For a match to be successful, it is vitally important that the child know that the volunteer is his or her special friend alone. Difficulty is sometimes encountered when several children in one family are in need of an adult friend and, because of a shortage of volunteers, only one can be matched. But the one-to-one relationship *must* be maintained. It is what makes the match special to the child; it is the unique feature on which the Movement is built. Sometimes, agencies do provide for group activities, such as camping trips or picnics, and unmatched children are generally included in these activities.

* * * *

Steve Hulbert

Steve Olsen

Courier-News, Richard A. Chapman

9

One-to-One Friendship:
Selected Cases

W hen seeking material for feature stories, writers often ask agency caseworkers for examples of children who, because of the Movement, have overcome backgrounds fraught with despair, deprivation, and encounters with delinquency, to go on to become distinguished, well-known adults.

Such examples are to be found in case records, to be sure, but the prime objective of one-to-one friendship is not to effect startling rags-to-riches, Cinderella-like changes. Rather, volunteer adults, under the guidance of agency caseworkers, endeavor simply to aid children to develop into normal, happy, well-adjusted adults.

There are many Little Brothers today who, before referral, experienced difficulties every bit as great as those encountered by Ernest K. Coulter's Little Brother, Latsky (chapter 1). And there are a few such failures. But there are thousands of cases where a boy or a girl, because of a Big Brother or Big Sister, overcame severe environmental and family difficulties, as well as almost unsurmountable personal problems. If they were dependent on drugs, they overcame their habits. If their education had been interrupted, they returned to school, perhaps even completing college and graduate school. They gained self-confidence and developed self-esteem, as well as concern for others. They obtained good jobs, married, raised families, and became not movie stars or brain surgeons but respected participating members of their communities. Such success stories are what the Movement is all about.

All of the following case summaries have been compiled from Big Brothers/Big Sisters agency files. Each case record is, in most instances, longer than this entire chapter. Except where noted (last three cases), names, locations, dates, and other likely identifying elements have been changed or modified to protect both the individuals and the integrity of the Movement. In a few instances, use of dramatization emphasizes points. None of the cases is atypical.

Scott and Alex

To mask his feelings of inadequacy, eight-year-old Scott became the neighborhood bully. He picked on children who were much smaller. He broke neighbors' windows and deliberately vandalized flower beds. His every unsocial act appeared to be a cry for attention. To make matters worse, his long, unkempt hair, mottled complexion, and several broken teeth contributed to an overall appearance that left much to be desired. No wonder he was an unwelcome visitor in almost every yard for several blocks around his home.

Scott lived with his grandmother. Several brothers and sisters lived with other relatives. His mother was in a mental institution and the whereabouts of his father was unknown. Scott had above average intelligence, but he did not like school, did not do well, and his grandmother did little to change his attitude. He was referred to Big Brothers/Big Sisters in the mid-South town where he lived by a family social agency that had long tried to help his relatives.

He did not want a Big Brother. He was surly and uncooperative when the BB/BS caseworker talked with him. However, he did agree to attend a group function — in this case, an all-day picnic — that the agency was having for both matched and unmatched children. It was at this event that he was observed by Alex. Alex had been a Big Brother for the past four years. His previous match had been terminated when his Little Brother left for college, but he agreed to be re-matched if someone really needed him. Everyone agreed that Scott needed him badly.

Things did not go smoothly for many months, but Alex did not give up and he was glad that he did not. Knowing that someone really cared about him gradually changed Scott's attitude. His appearance improved, as did his grades. He developed a happy, outgoing disposition, and a dentist friend of his Big Brother helped Scott create a smile that he could be proud of. Today, two years later, he enjoys good peer relations, was recently elected captain of his school's baseball team, and, of course, no longer has to draw attention to himself in socially unacceptable ways.

Mark and Ray

Not all kids need a Big Brother or Big Sister because they have been in trouble with the law. As indicated throughout this book, the emphasis today is on preventive measures. Mark's trouble was simply that he had no one to talk with about things that troubled him. After divorcing his mother, his father had remarried and lived several miles away. He did not see Mark on a regular basis, and Mark's mother was too occupied with earning a living to give much time to him and his two older sisters. As a result, Mark was more or less left on his own after school. With no one showing much concern about his academic progress, he began to skip classes and finally, at age seventeen, he realized he was not going to graduate with his class the following year.

The school counselor knew that Mark had a high IQ. He did not have a drug problem, or severe emotional difficulties. His problem was lack of motivation. He was the most lethargic person the counselor had ever seen. He was also just the type of person Big Brother Ray could help. Ray was a local real estate broker. Friendly, outgoing, and empathic, Ray had achieved excellent results with two previous matches. The school counselor knew about Ray and arranged for him to meet Mark at the Big Brothers/Big Sisters agency. It is somewhat unusual for an agency to receive a seventeen-year-old referral.

A match was effected, and Ray decided that his first priority was to help Mark catch up in school. This was accomplished through a number of evening sessions at Ray's house, as well as a term of summer school, with Ray closely following Mark's progress. Ray then decided that his approach would be to expose Mark to as many life experiences as possible. He wanted him to know that there was a big world out there and that a good education was a prerequisite for success in any endeavor.

On weekends they visited a local marine museum, the art museum, the public library, and attended football games. Ray took Mark with him on several business trips. He even let him sit in on a house closing (real estate closing). Mark developed an interest in real estate, completed high school, and later obtained a real estate sales license. Today, he and Ray are friendly competitors, as well as lifelong friends. But for Ray, Mark readily admits, he would have never even finished high school.

Amy and Jane

Amy had been sexually abused by her alcoholic father when she was seven. Previously, her mother had been admitted to a sanitarium for the chronically ill. Removed from the home by a family service agency when she was eight, she and an older sister and brother spent the next three years in a succession of foster homes. Now, at age eleven, Amy was sent to live with an aunt, who brought her to the Big Sisters agency. Two years behind in school, Amy was distrustful of all adults because of her traumatic background. Shy and stressful, she found it extremely difficult to express her feelings.

231

She was matched with Jane, a thirty-four-year-old mother of three minor children. For the first six months of the match, Jane spent considerably more time with Amy than the three hours per week required by the agency. Much of their time together was spent in Jane's home, just doing the things that a loving, well-adjusted family did. Amy accompanied Jane's family on shopping trips, to the movies, and to church. They even went camping together.

Gradually, over the next fifteen months, Amy became more trusting and responsive. Because someone loved her, she realized that she must be a worthy person worth loving. Her self-image and self-confidence increased, as her negative attitude receded. Her grades improved. Jane is concerned about what may happen to Amy when their match is ended, since her aunt has only limited financial resources. As their match continues, Jane hopes to help Amy become increasingly self-reliant. Regardless of what the future brings, Amy faces a life filled with hope, when only despair existed before.

Art and Hugh

The right Big Brother is not always on an agency waiting list when a particular Little Brother needs help. Sometimes, when a specialized need is indicated, the caseworker must seek just the right person in the community, then convince him to volunteer.

Art, age fifteen, felt that no one really cared what happened to him because of an unstable home life, occasioned by his parent's recent divorce. One way that he reacted to his feelings of despair was by engaging in negative attention-getting behavior at school. He regularly arrived late for classes, frequently interrupted his teachers with needless questions, and engaged in loud, unnecessary talking.

But a near-crisis was precipitated when Art confessed to a friend that he had created a pipe bomb in chemistry lab, had placed it in his locker, and was afraid that it might explode. The concerned friend, evidencing a high degree of emotional maturity and responsibility, promptly notified school authorities. Needless to say, Art received more attention than he wanted, as police, firemen, and a special bomb squad rushed to the school, evacuated the building, and gingerly removed the door from his locker. Although they found only a worn pair of sneakers and a sweatshirt, no one — especially the police — took the hoax lightly.

After a thorough review of the matter, juvenile authorities decided that Art needed a Big Brother. The Big Brothers/Big Sisters caseworker, learning from Art's school counselor that he had high grades in chemistry and math, but only average marks in other subjects, decided to build on those strengths. But there were no Big Brothers whose work or other interests involved scientific fields. He turned to the personnel manager of a nearby ethical drug manufacturer, who found just the right person—Hugh, a thirty-three-year-old Ph.D. in the firm's quality control department.

After being briefed on both the BB/BS program, as well as on Art and his difficulties, Hugh somewhat cautiously agreed to become Art's Big Brother. The two met each Saturday morning in Hugh's lab. Art was briefed on current projects. He was allowed to work on a computer. He attended a pharmaceutical convention with Hugh, where he was introduced to other scientists. Now, at age sixteen, he thinks that he might want to go into medicine. He realizes that if he is to achieve his goal he must have a strong academic record in all areas, and he is exceedingly proud of the fact that he has been able to raise his grade average significantly. But most of all, he is proud of his friendship with Hugh and, incidentally, the feeling is mutual.

Mike and Bob

Bob, a black lawyer, with a successful practice in a large Ohio city, went to a Big Brothers orientation session at the local agency at the urging of a friend, who had been successfully matched for several years. Bob had been raised in a home without a father. He knew what it meant not to have an older man to talk with when important decisions had to be made. But Bob had been lucky. He had not been a Little Brother, but a high school teacher had taken an interest in him and had helped him to obtain a full six-year scholarship to college and law school.

When Bob learned that there were more black Little Brothers on the agency's waiting list than all other Little Brothers combined, and that some of them had been waiting more than two years for a Big Brother, he volunteered immediately. After the required investigation, he was matched with Mike, a shy, gangling youth of fifteen, who was extremely introverted. Mike had never known his father. He constantly drew attention to deep-seated feelings of rejection by rebellious behavior. His teachers reported that his attitude was affecting his grades.

Bob attempted to build Mike's self-esteem by pointing out his good attributes. Mike lived in a neighborhood where there were many Hispanics, from whom he had picked up a fair knowledge of Spanish. Bob, too, spoke Spanish, and he sought to capitalize on this coincidence by helping Mike improve this skill through further study. They even visited a Spanish art exhibit. Mike was also encouraged to participate in organized sports. His pride knew no bounds when he won a bowling trophy. Mike learned to ice-skate at a local sports arena. These physical

activities provided an excellent, socially acceptable outlet for his former, negatively-channeled aggression, and his new language skills gave
a wondrous boost to his self-esteem. These gains were reflected in his
relations with others. His grades improved. As he was once helped,
Bob now hopes to obtain scholarship aid for Mike.

Nancy and Barbara

When little is expected of a child, he or she is likely to live up to
that expectation. No one expected much from ten-year-old Nancy; not
her divorced mother who had recently remarried and moved to another
state, nor her elderly grandmother, with whom Nancy's mother had
left her, nor her father, who was an alcoholic. So Nancy hung around
the corner delicatessen with other children in her neighborhood, where
she became highly proficient in the use of profanity, which she often
used to shock her teachers. One afternoon, she and several friends stole
a carton of beer from a parked car and drank it behind the deli. An
increasingly severe discipline problem, Nancy was suspended from school
about a month before the end of the term.

That was when her fifth-grade teacher called Big Brothers/Big Sisters.
A caseworker from the agency visited Nancy's home and talked with
her grandmother. He explained that a Big Sister could be of assistance
in helping Nancy resume her academic career. Nancy, herself, exhibited
a contentious, belligerent attitude, possibly to hide her feeling of insecurity. She said that she did not need a Big Sister. However, her
grandmother brought her to the agency where she was soon matched
with Barbara, who was a secretary at a local manufacturing plant.

The first few visits left Barbara wondering if she really wanted to be
a Big Sister. She was dismayed at Nancy's profanity and her claims of
drug and alcohol use (there was no indication that she had ever exper-
imented with drugs). The caseworker told Barbara that Nancy was
deliberately trying to provoke her, possibly to determine if she was
sincerely interested in her welfare. She urged Barbara to be patient.

With the caseworker's support and counsel, Barbara ignored Nancy's
profane outbursts, and other antisocial traits. Instead she made it a
point to compliment, and thus reinforce, all positive actions. After
Nancy returned to school, Barbara helped her with homework almost
every night. Nancy learned that Barbara really cared for her; she worked
hard to achieve the goals that she had set for herself with Barbara's
help. During the first quarter of the following school year, her grades
rose from Ds and Fs to all Cs, and after-school soccer practice left no
time to hang around the corner deli.

Harry and Ed

Harry, age twelve, had been physically and emotionally abused by his father who had a severe drug problem. After his parents were divorced when Harry was seven, he never saw his father again. For several years, Harry was a quiet, restrained child. Then, at around age ten, his mother asked a neighbor, a Little League coach, to try to find a place for Harry on his team. The neighbor did the best he could with Harry—gave him a lot of individual attention—but, even so, the boy spent a lot of time on the bench. Harry became acutely aware of the relations of other boys with their fathers; he became increasingly bitter because he did not have a loving father.

Suddenly, Harry was no longer a quiet, mannerly child. He became rebellious and untrustworthy at home. He fought with peers, was accused of stealing candy at a supermarket, and once even attempted to run away from home. Clearly, Harry needed a man to identify with and to talk with about things that he did not feel comfortable in discussing with his mother.

Harry was referred to Big Brothers/Big Sisters by his school counselor. The BB/BS caseworker encouraged him to participate in group activities that were sponsored by the agency for unmatched children while he was waiting for a Big Brother. However, during this period, Harry did not mix easily with others. Finally, Harry was matched with Ed, a forty-one-year-old salesman, who had a fourteen-year-old son of his own.

For the first few weeks, Ed did not involve his son in his relationship with Harry. He wanted his Little Brother to know that he was his special friend alone. Gradually, Ed brought his son along when he met with Harry, and the three of them participated in sports events, visited museums, attended concerts, and worked on do-it-yourself projects.

Ed served as a strong, much admired role model for Harry, who still had unpleasant memories of his own father's actions. He no longer provoked fights with friends. His relations with his mother improved. His social skills showed marked improvement; he joined several school clubs and took part in activities at the local YMCA. Harry's mother credits Ed for the positive changes in her son's life, but Ed says that Harry had the most to do with effecting the improvements. As Ed put it, "He merely needed someone to point the way now and then."

Tom and Dave

Overprotection of a child can sometimes be as bad as having no concern at all. Tom, an eleven-year-old West Coast Little Brother, had been "babied" by his mother to an extent that had left him with absolutely no confidence to do anything. His father had been killed when Tom was three. He was an only child, and his mother lived in constant fear that something would happen to him, too. She would hardly let him cross the street unsupervised; he was not allowed to participate in organized sports for fear of injury.

Not believing himself worthy of accomplishment, Tom did poorly at school, and his peer relations suffered. He was referred to the BB/BS agency by a school counselor. After considering Tom's needs, the caseworker matched him with Big Brother Dave, a thirty-one-year-old businessman, who had also lost his father at an early age. Extremely outgoing and friendly, Dave was currently president of a local service club, active in politics, a licensed pilot, and an accomplished skier.

He encouraged Tom to develop a participating interest in sports. It was not easy for Dave to help Tom overcome his deep-seated feelings of inadequacy. It was more than a year before Tom became relaxed, outgoing, and confident, and his negative feelings were replaced with a positive outlook. Dave imbued Tom with the idea that he could do almost anything if he really wanted to, and if he was willing to work hard. Today, Tom is motivated by challenge. He eagerly welcomes the opportunity to gain new knowledge and skills. He knows he will not be successful in everything he does, but he also knows that no one gets anywhere without trying.

Anita and Kathy

When you are a nine-year-old girl, living with a single mother and three brothers, each of whom has a different father, when your home is in the poorest section of the city, and the staff of the local parochial school you attend is so overburdened that individual guidance and assistance are impossible — you cannot expect to have the brightest outlook. Anita, the girl who found herself in this situation, had learned not to expect too much from life. She was painfully shy, had poor grooming habits, and extremely poor manners.

She was referred to Big Brothers/Big Sisters by a social worker from a church-sponsored welfare agency in the southeastern city where she lived. Fortunately, Kathy, a young attorney, had recently contacted the BB/BS agency and offered her services as a Big Sister. In fact, Kathy had indicated that she would especially like to have a difficult case. She was assigned to Anita.

During their regular weekend visits, they mostly did chores around Kathy's apartment. This was an intentional approach. Kathy wanted to expose Anita to an environment that was quite different from the only one she had known. Kathy showed Anita how to wash and style her hair and care for her skin. Together, they worked on a new dress for Anita. Kathy chose the pattern, and Anita selected the material—

possibly the first meaningful decision that she had ever made. After several months, and hours of practicing good table manners at Kathy's, the pair went to a nice restaurant. Anita wore her new dress.

Meanwhile, her newly-gained self-esteem became manifest in her schoolwork, in acquiring new skills (swimming and roller skating), and in a happier disposition. Anita is beginning to understand that she need not accept what fate hands her. She has choices, and she is learning that desired goals can be attained through planning and self-discipline.

Bill and Alan

Bill was twelve years old when he was referred to a Midwest Big Brothers/Big Sisters agency, shortly after his parents' divorce. He was not an economically deprived child, nor had he been in trouble. But his mother felt that Bill was reaching an age when a male influence was vitally important and his own father had moved to another state.

The agency caseworker found that Bill had a great need for encouragement and support. He had been very close to his dad, and the divorce had created a painful void in his young life. As is common in such situations, he wondered if he had been the cause in any way for the breakup of his parents.

Fortunately, Bill did not have to wait long for a Big Brother. Alan, vice-president of a local metal fabrication company, as well as a Vietnam veteran and father of two children of his own, had volunteered a short time before. He felt that society had been good to him; he wanted to give something back. The two were matched — becoming good friends almost at once. Alan encouraged Bill to become involved in neighborhood group activities, such as Little League. Bill became a great outfielder. Along with the fathers of the other boys, Alan was always present at his games. Although Bill, as a Little Brother, was being aided by a social-service agency, Alan taught him to become aware of the needs of others by inviting him to participate in a March of Dimes walkathon. Bill also worked with Alan at various BB/BS agency fund-raising events.

By becoming involved in group activities, becoming cognizant of the needs of others who were less fortunate, and by knowing that someone cared what happened to him, Bill forgot his own troubles, developed self-confidence, and became a friendly, helpful, outgoing person.

Henry and Frank

The extent to which many Big Brothers and Big Sisters go to help their matches is often truly inspiring. Consider the case of Henry and

Frank. Twelve-year-old Henry was born totally deaf. His parents and two brothers had normal hearing. For the past six years, Henry had attended a community-supported school for the deaf in the rather heavily populated mid-Atlantic city where he lived. The school had notified his mother, now divorced and dependent on welfare for support, that Henry was increasingly becoming a discipline problem in ways that seemed aimed at attracting the attention of his teachers and peers.

The school guidance counselor observed that Henry seemed to want approval, but did not know how to seek it in positive ways. He indicated that the school did not have the resources to work extensively with individual children, and suggested that Henry's mother might want to contact Big Brothers/Big Sisters.

A few weeks before, Frank, a well-known dentist in the community, had contacted the BB/BS agency and volunteered to become a Big Brother. Frank's two boys were in college. He missed the times he had spent with them in various outdoor activities. Frank had indicated that he might be interested in a handicapped child. Because of his kind, patient, and understanding manner, coupled with his medical background, the caseworker thought he would be perfect for Henry.

The match was made and a not unanticipated barrier immediately surfaced. Frank did not feel that he could make much headway with Henry when all of their communications had to be in writing. He immediately enrolled in a sign language and lip reading course being offered in the evening by a local university. During the three-month course, Frank continued to see Henry, who helped him refine his sign language techniques.

They had a great time practicing together every Saturday afternoon. Within several months, they were communicating with each other in an easy relaxed manner. That is when they began to enjoy a lot of other activities, like fishing and hiking. Frank even introduced Henry to cross-country skiing. Henry was overwhelmed that anyone would take so much interest in him. His teachers were nearly overwhelmed at the change in Henry's personality and the improvement in his grades. But it was all quite simple. His Big Brother really cared what happened to him, and Henry was not about to let him down.

Amelia and Ellen

Five children, ranging from two to fourteen, were simply too many for Amelia's mother to care for, so Amelia, the oldest, as well as the only girl, was sent to live with her grandmother. Besides, mother and daughter did not get along too well, with the former often voicing the opinion that she simply could not handle Amelia anymore. Amelia attended school only intermittently, had been sexually active for some time, and was presently involved with a boy of eighteen. She suffered from an acute case of acne, was considerably overweight for her age, and her overall appearance attested to poor personal hygiene. She was extremely insecure and had a poor self-image. She had no girl friends.

A short time after her fifteenth birthday, Amelia reluctantly accompanied her grandmother to the Big Brothers/Big Sisters agency in the Midwest city where they lived. At about this time, Ellen, head nurse at a local hospital, had just concluded a successful match and had asked for another Little Sister. As is the case in a number of BB/BS agencies, Big Sister applicants outnumber clients. But even though several other women who had never been matched were on the waiting list, it was felt that Ellen could provide the most help for Amelia.

The match was made and over the next few months the pair became good friends. Ellen began by helping Amelia obtain medical care for her complexion and weight problems. They discussed Amelia's sexual encounters and the dangers involved, both physical and emotional. Ellen never criticized Amelia or made value judgments. With the help of the agency caseworker, Ellen began a program of helping Amelia resume her education and improve her grades, while at the same time helping her to improve her personal appearance. One weekend, they attended a personal grooming clinic sponsored by a local department store.

Ellen's objectives were to build Amelia's self-esteem as well as to help her to begin making personal decisions regarding her lifestyle and future. She wanted her to realize that there were other ways to gain personal recognition besides being sexually promiscuous. As Amelia became more pleasant, attractive, and self-assured, her peer relations improved and she became involved in group social activities at school. Amelia now wants to become a beauty operator when she graduates from high school, and Ellen is already helping her to obtain career information related to that occupation.

Mary and Carol

Fourteen-year-old Mary had attempted suicide when she was only eleven. Little wonder. At the time, she was living with a chronically ill mother, and a father who had been arrested several times for physically abusing various members of the family, which included three younger children. It was after one of these violent episodes, involving Mary's mother, that Mary tried to take her own life by swallowing an overdose of aspirin. The father finally left the home and Mary and her brother and two sisters did what they could to help their mother.

Mary was referred to Big Brothers/Big Sisters in the northwestern city where the family lived by the pastor of the family's church. A psychological appraisal revealed that she had not suffered extensive emotional damage, but that her background had deprived her of the opportunity to gain many of the social skills that most girls her age possessed. She was matched with Carol, a suburban housewife with two preschool children of her own. Carol had achieved excellent results in a similar case.

The BB/BS caseworker, Carol, and Mary's mother formulated a list of goals which they felt Mary could achieve during the coming year. These included an improvement in personal appearance, improvement in grades, and increased self-esteem. Although they went to an occasional fashion show or movie, Mary and Carol spent a great deal of time just talking about whatever was on Mary's mind. When visiting in Carol's home, Mary was able to observe the everyday events in the life of a well-adjusted family. Almost all of the goals previously set for Mary were attained within the period indicated, largely because of Carol's influence as a role model.

Eddie and Lou

Eddie's father was in prison. His family was on welfare. Eddie had been placed on probation for shoplifting; he needed all the help he could get. He was thirteen when he was referred to Big Brothers by his school counselor. The school official reported that Eddie was absent frequently from his classes, that he was indifferent, hostile, and disruptive. He provoked fights with other students and had even fought with teachers. He was an extremely insecure kid who lacked direction and who had, thus far, rejected the attempts of teachers, his probation officer, and a priest to provide guidance and assistance.

Lou, age thirty-five, was a manufacturer's representative, who had recently volunteered to be a Big Brother. He was an avid outdoorsman who loved fishing, hunting, and white-water rafting. He believed strongly in the character-building role of participative sports, and had served as a Little League coach. He told the caseworker that he would like a Little Brother who could share his interests. Eddie had not shown much interest in anything, but Lou appeared to be a kind, loving, and patient person who would not be too quick to make value judgments. The caseworker felt that these attributes would be helpful in assisting Eddie to overcome his feelings of insecurity, increase his self-confidence, and redirect his efforts into purposeful pursuits.

Eddie and Lou were matched. Fishing, backpacking, and other outdoor activities occupied their weekends. As Eddie realized that someone cared about him, he no longer felt the need to engage in hostile, negatively directed behavior. His grades improved. He became interested in school sports and was elected captain of the junior varsity basketball team. The pair remained matched until Eddie graduated from high school and entered the service, but both agree that they will always remain friends. Of their relationship, Eddie later said, "He didn't criticize me when I made mistakes. He was always there when I needed someone to talk with. He believed in me. I couldn't let him down."

Fred and Robert

Handicapped children do not need sympathy. They need sincere concern, understanding, and increased self-confidence. Fred, age eight, and an only child, suffered from a crippling disease in early childhood which left him with a partial limp. Because of his disability, his divorced mother had always been overly protective. Fred never learned to assume responsibilities that he was quite capable of handling. Instead, he had developed a whining, complaining personality, often using his handicap as an excuse for lack of accomplishment.

His mother referred him to Big Brothers/Big Sisters. He was matched with Robert, who was disabled as a result of infantile paralysis and had to wear leg braces. Needless to say, Robert gave Fred little sympathy, and the latter quickly learned not to expect any. Instead, Robert focused attention on the many things that Fred could do. Fred learned responsibility and concern for others when he and Robert participated in a fund-raising campaign for the BB/BS agency, as well as for another social-service organization.

Fred took pride in accomplishment; he knew that his Big Brother expected him to do his very best in everything he tried. His grades went from Fs to As during a one-year period. Robert was a member of the local YMCA, where he taught Fred how to swim — a skill his mother was afraid to let him attempt before. A highlight of his young life was winning a local swimming tournament in the freestyle category. Fred no longer views himself as handicapped—simply as someone who, through a little extra effort, can do as well as anyone else.

George and Adolph

All of the participants in the final three cases are, with the permission of the principals, fully identified. George P. Burke was thirteen when his mother and father separated and, several months later, were divorced. This was in 1957. The family, originally from Lexington, Kentucky, had been living in Florida. After the divorce, George and his mother returned to Lexington, where they lived with George's grandmother. An older brother was in the armed forces, serving in Korea at the time.

Missing his father and lacking a male role model or any male influence, George became increasingly dejected and dispirited. Formerly an extremely active sports-minded boy, he now appeared to lack motivation for almost any activity, including his schoolwork. George's mother and grandmother were warm, caring persons, and the family was not economically deprived. George had a comfortable home life. It was just that he was almost fourteen now and he needed a man with whom to share male-oriented experiences, someone to talk with, and especially someone who shared his interest in sports.

George's Little League coach, who was also a Big Brother, knew what George needed. He asked him if he would like to have a Big Brother, and referred him to the Lexington Big Brothers/Big Sisters agency. George showed little enthusiasm until he learned who his new Big Brother was to be. He was Adolph Rupp, coach of the University of Kentucky Wildcats championship basketball team, and known worldwide as the "Baron of the Bluegrass," and "the Winningest Coach in the History of Basketball." During his phenomenal forty-two-year tenure as coach of the Wildcats, Coach Rupp was credited with 879 victories, against only 190 losses. His teams won 27 Southeastern Conference championships, and became NCAA champions an incredible and unsurpassed four times — in 1948, 1949, 1951, and 1958. His players earned seven Olympic gold medals. Rupp died in 1977.

George was overwhelmed that anyone as famous as Coach Rupp could be interested in him and his welfare. But it was true. After the match by the Lexington agency, Coach Rupp immediately made George an "assistant coach." His duties included being responsible for towels and jackets during games, keeping equipment together, and serving as water boy. He traveled with the team.

George spent time with Rupp's family, where he was welcomed by Rupp's wife and son, who also took an interest in his welfare. Rupp was a well-known breeder of fine cattle, and he often took George along when he visited his nearby farms. During the winter, Coach Rupp provided George with "sideline" passes to University of Kentucky football games. No teen-age boy's ego or sense of self-esteem received greater reinforcement. George's grades improved, and he again became a happy, well-adjusted boy. His friendship with Adolph Rupp continued for many years after the match was dissolved. After graduation from high school, George attended the University of Kentucky for two years. His education was interrupted by a severe accident. Although he later resumed his college career, complications from the accident again forced him to withdraw and prevented him from graduating. He then entered sales work. Today, George is branch manager for a Lexington building supply company. He recently contacted the Lexington BB/BS agency and indicated his interest in becoming a Big Brother. He will never forget what a one-to-one friendship once did for him.

Tracy and Kathy

Tracy Sutton was six and in the first grade when she was matched with Big Sister Katherine "Kathy" Young in 1977. Kathy became a caseworker for BB/BS of Vigo County, Terre Haute, Indiana, and later became director of that agency. It is not unusual for caseworkers and agency executives themselves to become Big Brothers and Big Sisters. Tracy and Kathy recently observed the seventh anniversary of their friendship — a record at that agency for a single match. When Tracy first came to Kathy's attention, she was a shy, reticent child, from a single-parent home, who was having trouble with her schoolwork and experiencing interpersonal difficulties, involving her teachers and peers.

Tracy Sutton (*left*) and Kathy Young

Kathy's immediate objective was to gain Tracy's trust and confidence. She did this by letting her know that she was sincerely interested in her welfare. Only real emergencies interfered with their regular visits. In fact, during the first five years of their match, Kathy missed seeing Tracy on a weekly basis only five times. The pair quickly developed a deep love and respect for one another. Tracy learned that no matter what happened to her, she could turn to Kathy for guidance and assistance.

Having helped Tracy to gain more self-confidence, improve her interpersonal relationships, and increase her self-esteem, Kathy sought to help her improve her academic record. Tracy had trouble with reading and reading comprehension. Kathy used a practical approach to remedy these difficulties. When they were out driving, she asked Tracy to read and interpret billboards and other signs. When they did Kathy's weekly shopping at the supermarket, Tracy was encouraged to notice labels on boxes and cans.

Kathy also sought to teach her about prices, values, and budgeting during these trips. These efforts, coupled with Kathy's assistance with homework assignments, resulted in a marked improvement in Tracy's grades. Tracy is thirteen now. She loves school and gets along well with her teachers. An "A" on a report or test merits a dinner at a restaurant of her choice, courtesy of Big Sister Kathy.

Tracy is looking forward to high school and, perhaps, college. Two years ago, she wrote a letter to the editor of the Weekend Messenger, a Terre Haute newspaper, telling what her Big Sister means to her. It is a beautiful letter, and permission has been obtained from both Tracy and the publisher to reproduce it here:

> Dear Editor:
>
> My name is Tracy Sutton. And I would like very much to share with you something that means and is very special to me. I have a Big Sister named Kathy Young. On Jan. 25 we have been together five whole years as a little and big sister. I love her just as if she was my real sister. I have a brother, 13, a sister, 14, and Kathy acts like a big sister to them too. My whole family loves her. Yeah, you get a birthday, and Easter, and Christmas once a year, but you only get a good friend and a for real big sister or brother once in a lifetime. Santa didn't give me her, God did. If you have a little spare time on hand you would be surprised how happy you could make someone. Also, if you haven't joined the Big Brother/Big Sister, do so. I know a lot of children are still waiting. Please don't keep them waiting long. I thank God for mine, and everybody who helps keep her going day by day. Thanks for listening to me.
>
> Tracy Sutton, 11
> Terre Haute, Ind.

Paul, Howard and Robert

Paul C. Winn was only two in 1939 when his father died. His mother remarried but shortly before Paul completed junior high school his mother and stepfather were divorced. Young Paul began manifesting his feelings of aggression and frustration by becoming involved in fights

244

at school. After being suspended, he came to the attention of the Flint (Mich.) Youth Bureau, a BBA affiliate. now known as Big Brothers of Greater Flint.

The agency's director, the late Joseph T. Ryder, matched Paul with Big Brother Howard Sprague, the owner of the local 7-UP bottling plant. Howard, a hearty, outgoing man, got Paul reinstated in school. Discovering that Paul's mother was having financial problems, he gave Paul a job in his plant. Howard and Paul became great pals. They spent a lot of time together. When Paul turned sixteen, Howard taught him to drive.

When Paul's mother was forced to give up her apartment and move in with her sister, there was no room for Paul. He asked his Big Brother if he could sleep in a truck at the 7-UP plant. Howard would have none of that. He invited Paul to move in with him and his wife. That was in 1954. For the first time in his life, Paul was exposed to a warm, loving home atmosphere.

Before school was out that year, Paul's mother found another apartment and Paul moved back with her. During the summer of 1954, Paul's mother learned that she had cancer. She died the following February, when Paul was a junior in high school.

In 1960, former Little Brother Paul C. Winn, then a midshipman at the U.S. Naval Academy, visited with President Eisenhower at the White House.

Paul moved to the YMCA and enrolled as a senior that fall, but all did not go smoothly. Howard Sprague moved to another town late in the year, and Paul got a new Big Brother, Robert Layfield, the manager of the 7-UP plant. Paul and Robert got along very well, but the pressures of having no parents, living alone, having to earn part of his expenses and still maintain his grades, all became too much for Paul. He began hanging around a local pool hall. Then one day, near the end of his senior year, he foolishly tossed a package of firecrackers through the door of a barber shop. Suspended from school again, he was allowed to return only if he agreed to do his classroom work and spend his free periods in the assistant principal's office for the remainder of the year.

Shortly before graduation, Joe Ryder called Paul to his office and asked him how he would like to attend the U.S. Naval Academy at Annapolis. If Paul could pass a competitive examination, a Michigan congressman had agreed to appoint him. Paul was not confident of passing the examination, but because of Ryder's efforts on his behalf, he agreed to give it a try. He took the exam, but did not know how he did. After several weeks passed and he did not hear, he assumed that he had failed and enlisted in the Marines. But in mid-October, word reached him at the Marine Corps Recruit Depot in San Diego that he had indeed passed. He subsequently applied for a transfer to the Naval Academy, which was granted.

Midshipman training is not easy. In fact, it was more difficult than anything Paul had ever come up against. He decided to resign, and notified his Big Brother of his plans. Robert Layfield and Joe Ryder held an "emergency session" to discuss strategy. They decided to be frank with Paul, express their disappointment in his decision, and tell him that nobody likes a quitter. That was enough for Paul. He could not let them down. He stayed at Annapolis, completed all four years, and received a commission as a lieutenant in the Marine Corps in June 1961. In 1960, when President Dwight D. Eisenhower was named Big Brother of the Year by Big Brothers of America, Paul participated in the presentation ceremony at the White House. Noting Paul's insignia as chief petty officer of midshipmen, the President remarked, "The highest I ever got as a cadet was color sergeant."

Paul attained the rank of major in the Marine Corps. He served with the Joint Chiefs of Staff, receiving the joint services Commendation Medal for his work, and in Vietnam, where he received the Naval Commendation Medal. He retired from the Marines after completing twenty years of service. Today, he is an assistant vice-president and director of data processing systems development for a large, nationwide insurance company. He and his wife, Diane, have two sons and a daughter. Getting started in the right direction made the big difference in Paul Winn's life and for that he credits Big Brothers of Greater Flint, Joe Ryder, agency director, and his two Big Brothers.

* * * *

Forest Wells

Wendol Jarvis

10

Big Brothers/Big Sisters of America Today

A national organization is formed and supported by local groups to help them develop and maintain nationally accepted, uniform standards, methods, and practices; gain national recognition for their cause; gain a national forum and the effectiveness of national advocacy; benefit from the exchange of ideas and information; and, through group participation, perform certain tasks and functions more efficiently and economically than each group could do so alone. As a product of its member bodies, the national organization is never stronger or more effective than its constituents make it. In other words, the degree to which the parent body aids its members is dependent on the latter's level of support.

Today's national Big Brothers/Big Sisters organization has been demonstrating its effectiveness for more than forty years, first as Big Brothers of America (BBA) and, after the merger with Big Sisters International (BSI), as Big Brothers/Big Sisters of America (chapter 6).

Headquartered in Philadelphia, the national organization is governed by the board of directors, administered by the national staff, and consists of an honorary board, a development council (fund raising), a professional group concerned with the maintenance of casework standards, and a national membership. The functions of each of the groups are discussed briefly.

The National Staff

The staff, headed by the national president and chief operating officer (COO), who is elected by and responsible to the board of directors, consists of approximately thirty-five persons, who serve in five major areas: the President's Office, Corporate Planning and Administration,

Resource (funds) Development, Communications, and Agency and Program Services. For the most part, these departments are headed by staff vice-presidents. The national organization functions through twelve contiguous, geographically designated regions.

Agency and Program Services

An early projection called for placing national field representatives in each region under the jurisdiction of Agency and Program Services (A&PS). Because of high staffing costs, this was not feasible. Instead A&PS created four administrative districts, each encompassing three regions. Each district is headed by a director, who is assisted (depending upon number of agencies served) by one or two field representatives. These staff employees represent the first echelon of the national organization, facilitate the administration of national services at local levels, aid in local-national communication, and provide agency evaluative services. This structure has proved to be exceedingly effective. In addition to providing periodic agency appraisals to insure compliance with Minimum Operating Standards (chapter 8), the field staff consults with agency executive directors and their staffs on a wide range of activities and problems, which relate to the four major national staff functions. The directors of field services and national field representatives, all of whom are required to have casework backgrounds, report directly to the national vice-president of Agency and Program Services.

This department is also responsible for the administration of specialized services, especially those relating exclusively to either boys or girls; for the administration of special research projects, generally carried out under restricted grants from private foundations or federal and state agencies; for coordination of the BB/BSA annual meeting; and for the administration of the BB/BSA Education Institute, the federation's training arm, which conducts seminars and conferences in the various regions throughout the year. The Institute is also responsible for creating and distributing all educational materials.

Communications

The national Communications Department is responsible for all publications, including a general newsletter which is circulated throughout the Movement and two specialized newsletters, produced respectively for local board presidents and agency executive directors. This department produces the BB/BSA Annual Report. It handles the production of recruiting and fund-raising materials, including films, public service announcements for radio and television, pamphlets, brochures, and promotional materials, such as bumper stickers, banners, T-shirts, lapel emblems, and scores of similar materials, which are made available to agencies on a nonprofit basis.

The Communications Department handles celebrity relations, including the scheduling of celebrity appearances at agency functions. Other functions include the coordination of four annual competitions: an essay contest for Little Brothers and Sisters; a photo contest open to all agency personnel, volunteers, and Little Brothers and Sisters; a competition to select a Big Sister and Big Brother of the Year, to be honored at the BB/BSA annual meeting; and a national journalism awards contest (chapter 6). The journalism competition is open to all published writers who have written articles about the problems of single-parent families and how such difficulties were handled. Plaques and cash prizes are awarded. Additional information on this program is available from BB/BSA and is also included in the annual awards edition of *Editor & Publisher* magazine. The department originates all national news releases, and is responsible for arranging press conferences and for media relations in general. It coordinates Big Brothers/Big Sisters week activities at the national level, and is responsible for many BB/BSA annual meeting functions.

Resource Development

The primary function of the Resource Development Department is fund raising for the support of BB/BSA. Only a little over one-third of BB/BSA's needed revenue comes from agency fees. The remainder must be raised through gifts and grants from corporations and foundations, through restricted grants that cover special projects, from gifts by individual national board members, and through promotional events, several of which were discussed in chapter 6.

This department licenses the Bowl For Kids' Sake program, discussed in chapters 6 and 8, to agencies and is also responsible for several fund-raising dinners, discussed in chapter 6. The department spearheads special fund-raising campaigns, including capital funds solicitations.

Corporate Planning and Administration

The Corporate Planning and Administration Department is primarily responsible for handling the federation's financial affairs: agency fees collection, the handling and processing of other income, disbursements, all accounting and bookkeeping functions, including payroll, and the administration of employee benefits for the national organization. This department is also responsible for financial planning, including all costs and income projections, and budget preparation and administration.

Cynthia Klotzbach

A representative of the BB/BSA Agency & Program Services Department, *far right*, provides on-site program assistance at a local agency.

Shull Photo Service

A national field representative, *right*, discusses a forthcoming recruiting campaign with officials of a Big Sisters agency.

252

District directors and field representatives gather at BB/BSA headquarters in Philadelphia to discuss plans for the coming year.

Personnel administration is a function of the Corporate Planning and Administration Department and, in recent years, it has assumed responsibility for the establishment and coordination of all electronic data processing activities (EDP) within BB/BSA.

National Board of Directors

The maximum number of directors permitted by the BB/BSA constitution is seventy-five. The actual number at any particular time is slightly under this number. Two members are elected from each of the twelve regions by the members (agencies) in those regions. The remaining members are elected at large by the members at each annual meeting of BB/BSA.

The chairman of the board and chief executive officer (CEO) is elected by the directors. The directors also elect four vice-presidents who head major operating committees, which represent and work with the four major staff departments (Corporate Planning and Administration, Resource Development, Communications, Agency and Program Services) and the President's Office. Other officers elected by the directors include the national treasurer, and the national board secretary. The president and chief operating officer (COO), and the counsel to the board, are appointed by the directors. The entire board meets three times each year. During interim periods the business of the federation is conducted by an executive committee, consisting of approximately twenty persons and appointed and chaired by the chairman of the board and CEO.

Other national committees, subcommittees, and task forces are concerned with special functions and projects. These include committees or subcommittees dealing with the constitution and bylaws, standards and practices, legal matters, financial audits, professional practices, relations with foundations and other funding sources, and the annual meeting. There is also a nominating committee. The applicable national vice-president appoints the chairpersons of these committees, with the exception of the nominating, audit, and constitution and bylaws subcommittees, whose chairpersons are appointed by the chairman of the board and CEO. Nonstaff membership on all committees is voluntary. Committees include, in addition to staff and board members, national professional staff council (NPSC) representatives.

The two board members from each region are known as the regional president and vice-president and represent the agencies in their regions to the board. Under regional constitutions and bylaws, they may form regional councils and appoint regional committees to deal with agency operations and administration. The regional officers work closely with the national staff field representatives, and may plan conferences and seminars in conjunction with the BB/BSA Education Institute.

Honorary Board

The BB/BSA Honorary Board includes former national board members who rendered distinguished service to the board or staff for many years, as well as other persons who have made a significant impact on the Movement. Several members have been designated Members for Life. Chairman of the Honorary Board is Gerald R. Ford. William H. Webster, director of the Federal Bureau of Investigation (FBI), is a member. Honorary members are appointed by the national Board of Directors and, while living, can only be removed by them. Honorary Board members often volunteer to assist with special projects, and use their influence in fund-raising activities.

National Development Council

The National Development Council includes persons who are actively engaged in fund-raising activities for BB/BSA. Elected by the national board, they may make personal contributions, or acquire contributions through their companies, foundations with which they are associated, or through other sources.

Professional Groups

Since near the beginning of the Movement, professional employees have endeavored to maintain and improve their levels of professionalism. Today, these professionals, who include agency executive directors and caseworkers, belong to a Professional Staff Council (PSC) within each region. Each regional PSC elects officers, including a chairperson who, in turn, belongs to the National Professional Staff Council (NPSC). The twelve members of the NPSC elect officers, including a chairperson, who sits as an ex-officio member of the national board. The chairperson of the NPSC also selects other committee members to sit on the four board operating committees, to help insure that the interests of professional employees are considered in all committee decisions. The activities of the NPSC and its predecessors have also been discussed in earlier chapters.

National Members

National members of BB/BSA include all of its affiliated full-member agencies whose fees are paid in full, and all individuals (known as corporate members) who have made a personal gift to BB/BSA during the past year of a specified amount (during the mid-eighties the amount was $500). All members are entitled to a minimum of one vote on matters that might come before the BB/BSA annual meeting of members, held in conjunction with the BB/BSA national conference. (This combined gathering has been known as the annual meeting throughout most of the federation's history. Recently it has been referred to as the national conference. For consistency, this volume has used the former term throughout.) Eligible full member agencies could be entitled to up to five votes, depending upon the amount of their annual fees to BB/BSA. As indicated in chapter 8, these agencies pay BB/BSA an annual affiliation fee based on their total annual expenditures.

Board Minutes

Minutes of all board meetings, executive committee meetings, board committee meetings, and the annual meeting of members are available for inspection by the public at BB/BSA national headquarters in Philadelphia, as are the federation's annual reports for the past several years. Also available for inspection are copies of agency affiliation agreements and minimum operating standards, as well as a number of comprehensive operations manuals produced for agency guidance.

* * * *

In 1964, an eleven-year-old Little Brother in Bucks County, Pennsylvania, wrote to the President of the United States to tell him about the Big Brother program. In his reply, the President said, "Never forget that you are privileged to have a Big Brother counsellor, a person who is vitally interested in your well-being: spiritual, moral and physical. Strive to attain the highest degree of excellence your abilities and skills will allow. Have confidence in your Big Brother and in his judgments with regard to your personal habits and activities. Respect his decisions and obey his instructions. Discuss your problems with him and cooperate to resolve them. Your Big Brother will ask little more of you — and nothing less!"

Lyndon B. Johnson

CHRONOLOGY

1902 Ernest K. Coulter, founder of the organized Big Brothers Movement in 1904, helps organize the first children's court in New York City.

Ladies of Charity, which later becomes Catholic Big Sisters of New York, begins befriending girls who come before the New York Children's Court.

On December 27, Judge Julius M. Mayer, New York Children's Court, announces that he has recently received the promises of ninety influential men each to befriend one boy who had been before his court. Judge Mayer does not use the term *Big Brother* at this time, although he later becomes associated with the Jewish Big Brothers of New York.

1903 On July 4, Cincinnati businessman Irvin F. Westheimer reportedly befriends a hungry boy he finds scavenging through a garbage can; he later claimes that this experience inspired him to begin Big Brothers work in that City.

1904 On December 3, Ernest K. Coulter, clerk of the New York Children's Court, speaks to the Men's Club of New York's Central Presbyterian Church, and obtains forty volunteers, who each agree to befriend one boy who has been in trouble. Organized Big Brothers Movement begins.

1907 Big Brothers activity begins in Milwaukee, Wisconsin.

1908 Jewish Big Sisters work is underway in New York City. This work could have begun much earlier. Exact date is unknown.

Mrs. Willard Parker begins work that later develops into Protestant Big Sisters of New York.

1909 *Good Housekeeping* magazine reports that influence of the New York Big Brother Movement has spread to hundreds of other cities.

Big Sisters work begins in Milwaukee.

An estimated 1,000 Little Brothers are reported participating in the New York City Big Brothers program.

On November 26, the Big Brother Movement of New York City makes application for a state charter.

1910 Mrs. W. K. Vanderbilt, Sr., joins Mrs. Willard Parker to form a more formal Protestant Big Sisters organization in New York City.

Jewish Big Brothers Agency is in existence in New York City.

Hampton's Magazine reports that there are Big Brothers organizations in twenty cities with juvenile courts.

In December, Irvin F. Westheimer and several other Cincinnati citizens hold a meeting to discuss the formation of a Big Brothers group in that city.

1911 On February 23, the Big Brothers Association of Cincinnati is organized. Irvin F. Westheimer is elected president.

Benevolent and Protective Order of Elks (BPOE) indicates interest in Big Brothers work.

1912 On June 7, Protestant Big Sisters of New York City obtains state charter.

Mrs. W. K. Vanderbilt, Sr., becomes first president of the Protestant Big Sisters of New York City. Mrs. Madeline Evans is first employee.

New York Times reports Big Brothers activity in twenty-six cities.

1913 Big Brothers work is underway in St. Paul.

Renegade Big Brothers leader, Jack Robbins, launches campaign to find the worst boy in each of twelve states.

Big Brothers activity is reported in Denver.

Everybody's Magazine reports that there is Big Brothers activity in forty cities in the United States, Australia, and Canada — first noted reference to foreign activity.

1914 *Chicago Journal* newspaper publishes names of Jack Robbins's twelve worst boys and reports that the boys were sent to the "Last Chance Boys Ranch" near Reno, Nevada, under the supervision of writer Upton Sinclair.

Big Brothers work begins in St. Louis, Missouri.

Elks (BPOE) in 901 lodges reports caring for 5,000 Little Brothers.

Ernest K. Coulter embarks on nationwide lecture tour on behalf of Big Brothers Movement.

Area federation of Big Brothers and Big Sisters agencies is formed in Greater New York City.

Planning begins for a national Big Brothers and Big Sisters organization.

1915 Big Brother Association of Philadelphia begins.

Big Sisters program begins in Kansas City, Missouri.

Catholic Big Brothers work is underway in New York City.

Jewish Big Brothers Association of Los Angeles is formed.

1916 Jewish Big Brother Bureau of Baltimore is organized. Name later changes to Jewish Big Brother League.

Charter is granted to a Big Sisters group in Pittsburgh.

Ernest K. Coulter announces that Big Brothers work has spread to ninety-six cities.

1917 Elks (BPOE) reports that they are caring for 30,000 Little Brothers.

Good Housekeeping magazine reports that a Big Brothers society has been formed in Tokyo.

On May 28 and 29, the first national conference of Big Brothers and Big Sisters organizations is held in Grand Rapids, Michigan. This meeting leads to the later organization of the Big Brother and Big Sister Federation (BB/BSF).

1918 There is an indication of a national conference in St. Louis.

Brooklyn (N.Y.) Catholic Big Sisters is organized.

Big Brothers activity reportedly is engaged in by 1,152 Elk lodges.

Catholic Big Brothers of New York is incorporated.

1919 There is an indication that a national conference is held in Cincinnati.

1920 Rowland C. Sheldon becomes part-time executive secretary of the national organization.

New York Big Brother Movement reportedly is serving 1,300 Little Brothers.

1921 National organization holds annual conference in Toronto.

On October 5, a delegation from the national organization calls on President Warren G. Harding at the White House.

On November 2, 1921, the Big Brother and Big Sister Federation is incorporated in New York State.

1922 In February, *The Ounce*, the first national publication, makes its debut.

Big Brothers work begins in Waterbury, Connecticut, the first in that state.

In May, the first known use of radio to publicize Big Brothers work occurs in St. Louis, when a broadcast is made on station KSD.

On June 6, 7, and 8, the annual conference of the Big Brother and Big Sister Federation is held in Minneapolis.

For the first time standards for agency operations are published by the Big Brother and Big Sister Federation.

Unisex word "Brister" is coined to mean both Big Brother and Big Sister.

Fifty of 106 known Big Brothers and Big Sisters organizations in the United States and Canada are affiliated with the Big Brother and Big Sister Federation.

1923 On May 15 and 16, the national conference of BB/BSF is held in Washington, D.C.

Black Big Sisters work is underway in Louisville, Kentucky.

Black Big Sisters are active in Brooklyn, New York.

Theodore Roosevelt, Jr., becomes treasurer of BB/BSF.

Colored Big Brothers Association is organized in Milwaukee, Wisconsin.

On December 23, the first motion picture based on a Big and Little Brother relationship is released by Paramount Pictures.

1924 Rowland C. Sheldon becomes full-time executive of BB/BSF.

Catholic Big Brothers of Baltimore is organized.

Big Brothers Association of Philadelphia opens dental clinic. A medical clinic opens in 1930.

1925 On January 13, BB/BSF holds its annual meeting in New York City. Humorist Will Rogers addresses delegates.

(Approximate year) BB/BSF prohibits publication of Little Brothers and Little Sisters names and photographs.

On June 8 and 9, BB/BSF holds its first conference for agency executives.

President Calvin Coolidge becomes patron of BB/BSF.

Arthur Seher, executive secretary of Milwaukee Big Brothers, conducts first known survey to determine support of the Movement by the press.

Charles Brandon Booth, of Salvation Army Booths, joins staff of BB/BSF.

1926 On February 4, Catholic Big Brothers of Los Angeles is organized.

Annual meeting of BB/BSF is held at Chicago.

1927 (Approximate year) BB/BSF protests unauthorized use of names *Big Brother* and *Big Sister*.

Annual meeting of BB/BSF is held in Cleveland.

Plan for evaluating agencies is presented to board of BB/BSF.

Big Brothers of Dallas is incorporated.

Dr. Herbert D. Williams joins staff of BB/BSF. He is probably the first person within the Movement to utilize scientific methods in the study of child behavior.

1928 Black Big Brothers and Big Sisters work is underway in Memphis.

Three Big Brothers and three Big Sisters groups are flourishing in Cincinnati.

Annual meeting of BB/BSF is believed to have been held in Memphis.

Black Big Sisters groups are active in Columbus and Toledo, Ohio, and in Jersey City, New Jersey.

1929 Jewish Big Brothers Association of Boston is incorporated.

1930 On March 8, 600 delegates attend a BB/BSF meeting in New York City.

1931 Minneapolis Big Brothers is incorporated.

On November 17, the annual meeting of BB/BSF is held in New York City.

1932 An unsuccessful attempt is made to obtain a federal charter for BB/BSF.

1933 New York Big Brother Movement is serving 1,984 boys.

(Approximate year) Statewide Big Brothers association is formed in Illinois.

1934 President and Mrs. Franklin D. Roosevelt become patrons of BB/BSF.

1935 Annual meeting of BB/BSF is held in New York. Famed criminologist Sheldon Glueck is elected president.

1937 Big Brother and Big Sister Federation is dissolved.

1938 Big Brothers of Denver is incorporated (although formed many years earlier).

1939 Big Brothers of Columbus, Ohio, is incorporated.

Big Brothers representatives explore possibility of forming a new federation.

National Study and Planning Committee is created to conduct study to determine feasibility of forming a new federation.

1940 National Study and Planning Committee reports on one of the most comprehensive studies of the Movement ever conducted.

In May, a National Committee on Big Brother and Big Sister Service is created to continue to pursue the formation of a national group.

1944 In January, the National Committee on Big Brother and Big Sister Service is discontinued.

In May, an informal group meets at the National Conference of Social Work in an effort to revive interest in a national organization.

1945 New study is launched to determine need for a new federation.

On November 19 and 20, Joseph H. McCoy hosts a meeting in New York, attended by Charles G. Berwind of Philadelphia and others, to form the Temporary Big Brother National Committee.

1946 In June, the foundation is laid for a new Big Brothers federation at Camp Wyomissing, Stroudsburg, Pennsylvania.

On December 24, Big Brothers of America (BBA) is incorporated in New York State.

1947 Gilbert H. Gendall becomes temporary BBA executive secretary. Office is opened at Philadelphia Big Brother Association headquarters.

Big Brothers of America receives its first matching grant from John D. Rockefeller III.

On November 8, BBA holds its first meeting of the Council of Delegates at Buffalo, New York.

Technical and Advisory Committee is created (forerunner of today's NPSC).

1948 On January 31, Charles G. Berwind issues the first BBA annual report.

On March 1, Donald Jenks becomes the first permanent executive secretary of BBA.

Folk artist Norman Rockwell produces sketch that becomes the symbol for BBA.

Big Brother Bulletin makes debut.

On December 14, the BBA Council of Delegates adopts minimum standards for BBA.

1949 Regional Director Program is implemented.

Annual meeting of BBA is held in Cleveland.

1950 From January 15 to 21, the first Big Brother Week is observed.

Annual meeting is held in Atlantic City.

General Douglas MacArthur praises Big Brothers Movement.

1951 Benjamin Van Doren Hedges becomes BBA executive vice-president.

Big Brother of the Year Program, naming a prominent person, begins. Associate Justice Tom Clark of the Supreme Court is first person named.

BBA annual meeting is held in Minneapolis.

J. Edgar Hoover is named Big Brother of the Year.

On September 20, the first meeting of the BBA Executive Committee is held, although the committee was created several years earlier.

1952 Felix Gentile becomes executive director of BBA.

BBA annual meeting is held in Chicago.

Ernest K. Coulter, founder of the organized Big Brothers Movement, dies.

1953 BBA annual meeting is held in Dallas.

1954 Nonsectarian Big Brothers group is formed in Baltimore.

BBA annual meeting is held in Cleveland.

BBA approves individual national memberships in an effort to raise funds.

1955 BBA annual meeting is held in New York.

1956 BBA annual meeting is held in St. Louis.

1957 Stanley B. Adams becomes BBA executive vice-president.

Goesta Wollin succeeds Stanley B. Adams, becoming BBA executive director.

BBA annual meeting is held in Hamilton, Ontario.

1958 BBA annual meeting is held in Philadelphia.

On September 2, BBA is chartered by Congress.

1959 On May 19, the first woman is elected to the BBA board.

BBA annual meeting is held in Los Angeles.

1960 (Approximate year) Practice of holding BBA regional meetings begins.

Big Brother Bulletin discontinues because of lack of funds.

Thomas E. O'Brien becomes BBA executive director.

BBA annual meeting is held in Cincinnati.

1961 BBA annual meeting is held in Flint, Michigan.

1962 BBA annual meeting is held in New York City.

1963 BBA annual meeting is held in Columbus, Ohio.

1964 BBA annual meeting is held in Chicago.

Big Brother Bulletin is reactivated.

1965 BBA annual meeting is held in Boston.

Board launches "Era of Growth" Program.

Dick Van Dyke becomes a BBA national vice-president.

1966 BBA annual meeting held in Baltimore.

1967 Kresge Company and Thom McAn Shoe Company agree to promote Movement through their stores.

BBA retains first professional fund-raising firm.

BBA annual meeting is held in Anaheim, California.

Dr. Randolph Taylor, the nation's first black Little Brother, is named Big Brother of the Year.

1968 BBA annual meeting is held in Toronto.

1969 BBA annual meeting is held in Detroit.

BBA has 150 affiliated agencies.

1970 On June 20, Winifred Derry chairs a meeting in Washington, D.C., to investigate the possibility of forming a Big Sisters federation.

Winifred Derry is elected president of the unincorporated Big Sisters group.

On August 3, Big Sisters International (BSI) is incorporated.

Victor Gelb is elected national president of BBA, succeeding Charles G. Berwind; Berwind becomes chairman of the board.

BBA annual meeting is held in Cleveland.

New BBA recruiting film, A *Friend for Joey*, premieres.

1971 After death of BSI founder Winifred Derry on August 26, Mildred Montague becomes BSI president.

BSI headquarters is moved from Washington, D.C., to Chattanooga, Tennessee.

On May 25, 1971, BSI and BBA officials establish a dialogue; possibility of merger is discussed.

BBA annual meeting is held in San Francisco.

BBA observes its twenty-fifth anniversary; reports 208 affiliates.

1972 On June 22-23, BSI holds its first annual meeting in Chattanooga.

Lee Meyer is elected president of BSI.

On April 20, Charles G. Berwind resigns as chairman of the BBA board.

First black woman, Esther Edwards, becomes a member of the BBA board.

BBA annual meeting is held in Richmond, Virginia.

On November 9, Charles G. Berwind dies.

1973 On January 15, Lewis P. Reade is named executive vice-president of BBA.

The first Lilly grant is made for the purpose of investigating the possibility of merger of BBA and BSI.

Name of *Big Brother Bulletin* is changed to *Big Brother Ambassador*.

The BBA annual meeting is held in Atlanta, Georgia.

In July, BSI holds its second annual meeting in Fond du Lac, Wisconsin.

1974 On January 21, 1974, the BBA Executive Committee votes to recognize Irvin F. Westheimer's 1903 act of kindness to a hungry boy as the official beginning of the Movement.

BBA annual meeting is held at Lake of the Ozarks, Missouri.

Maurice Schwarz is elected president of BBA.

BSI annual meeting is held in Scottsdale, Arizona.

Judy A. Weill is elected BSI president.

BBA and BSI appoint merger committees.

Judy A. Weill is elected BSI president.

BSI headquarters is moved from Chattanooga to Philadelphia.

Sharyn Forrest becomes BSI coordinator.

(Approximate year) *Big Brother Ambassador* discontinues and is later replaced with the *Communicator*.

1975 BSI and BBA annual meetings are held concurrently in Denver.

1976 BSI has forty-two affiliated agencies.

BSI and BBA annual meetings are held concurrently in Indianapolis. Both groups vote to endorse in principle the idea of a merger.

Hilda Patricia Curran is elected president of BSI.

1977 BSI is merged into BBA at concurrent annual meetings of two organizations in Orlando, Florida.

Merger creates 357 agencies in all classifications.

Don A. Wolf is elected first president of BB/BSA.

A new symbol and logotype are adopted by BB/BSA.

On November 11, 1977, President Jimmie Carter signs a bill to amend the BBA congressional charter, changing it to BB/BSA.

1978 Grant from the Kellogg Foundation launches Citizen Board Development Program (CBDP).

BB/BSA annual meeting is held in Washington, D.C.

Independent Order of Foresters (IOF) agrees to support BB/BSA as a three-year social-service project.

1979 On September 14, 1979, David W. Bahlmann becomes BB/BSA executive vice-president.

Touche Ross completes an evaluation of BB/BSA effectiveness.

Executive Newsletter and *Presidents Letter* are launched.

BB/BSA annual meeting is held in San Francisco.

1980 BB/BSA annual meeting is held in Louisville, Kentucky.

William Mashaw is elected BB/BSA president.

On December 31, Irvin F. Westheimer dies.

1981 BB/BSA annual meeting is held in Philadelphia.

Yanoff Study of BB/BSA Citizen Board Development Program is completed.

1982 In February, President Ronald Reagan receives a BB/BSA delegation in the Oval Office.

BB/BSA National Journalism Awards Program is launched.

BB/BSA annual meeting is held in St. Louis, Missouri.

Albert L. Brown is elected president.

1983 BB/BSA annual meeting is held in San Diego, California.

Capital funds campaign is launched to finance new headquarters building for BB/BSA.

1984 BB/BSA annual meeting is held in Memphis, Tennessee.

Mark K. Kessler is elected BB/BSA chairman of the board and chief executive officer. David W. Bahlmann becomes president.

BB/BSA notified by postmaster general that it will be honored with a commemorative stamp in 1985.

In October, BB/BSA occupies its new headquarters at 230 North Thirteenth Street in Philadelphia.

1985 BB/BSA annual meeting is scheduled for Cleveland, Ohio.

1986 BB/BSA annual meeting is scheduled for Clearwater, Florida.

1987 BB/BSA annual meeting is scheduled for Spokane, Washington.

1988 BB/BSA annual meeting is scheduled for Milwaukee, Wisconsin.

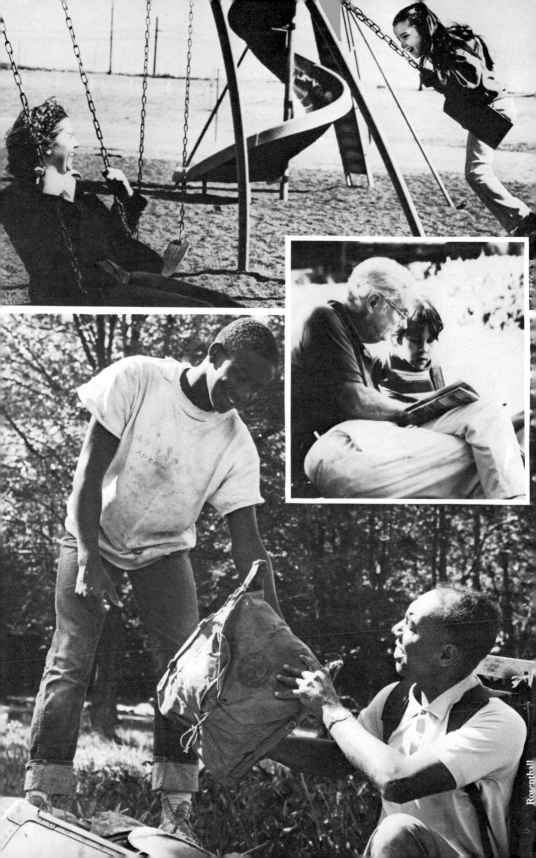

Rosenthal

APPENDIX 1

Agencies Affiliated with the Big Brother and Big Sister
Federation, Inc., in 1925

Arkansas
BB, c/o Boys' Club, Little Rock
California
Jewish BB Association, Los
Angeles
BS League, Los Angeles
BS, Oakland
BS, Sacramento
BS, San Diego
Boy's Work Committee Rotary
Club, San Francisco
Canada
BS, Hamilton
Montreal Association of BB
BB Movement, Toronto
BS Association, Toronto
Colorado
BB Movement, Inc., Denver
BS Movement, Inc., Denver
Connecticut
BB and BS Council, Hartford
BB Committee, BS Committee
Jewish Charities, Hartford
BB, Waterbury
District of Columbia
BS, District of Columbia
BS Committee, District of
Columbia
Catholic BB, District of Columbia
Florida
BB, Jacksonville
Illinois
BS Association, Chicago
Jewish BS Movement, Chicago
Indiana
BB's Association, Evansville
BB and BS Department, Family
Welfare Society, Indianapolis
BB Committee, Terre Haute
Kentucky
BS, C. J. W., Louisville
Maryland
BB Association, c/o Holy Name
Society, Baltimore
BB League, Baltimore
Colored BB and BS League,
Baltimore

Massachusetts
Jewish BB Association, Boston
Michigan
Travelers' Aid and BS, Detroit
BB Organization, Inc., Grand
Rapids
Minnesota
BB, Duluth
BB Committee, Minneapolis
BS, Minneapolis
Catholic BB, St. Paul
Missouri
BS, Council Jewish Women,
Kansas City
BB Organization, Inc., St. Louis
BS of St. Louis, Inc.
Nebraska
Men's Service League, Omaha

New York
Brooklyn Catholic BS, Inc.
Brooklyn Jewish BB and BS
Association
Brooklyn Juvenile Protective
Association
Brooklyn Urban League, BS Club,
Brooklyn
BS of Queens Borough, Flushing
Catholic BS of Queens, Jamaica
BB Movement, Inc., New York
BS, Inc., New York
BS, Ladies of Charity, New York
Catholic BB League, New York
Jewish BB, New York
Jewish BS, New York
BS Council, Inc., Rochester
BS, Schenectady
BB Committee, Inc., Syracuse
BS Co-operating Committee,
Yonkers

Ohio
BB Association, Cincinnati
BB and S Clubs, c/o Federation of
Churches, Cincinnati
Catholic BB League, Cincinnati
Catholic BS, Cincinnati
Jewish BS Association, Cincinnati

BS Council, Cleveland
BS, Federation Women's Club,
  Youngstown
Inter-club Committee on BB Work,
  Youngstown
Pennsylvania
BB Association, Philadelphia
BS Association, Philadelphia
Jewish BB Club, Pittsburgh

BB Organization, Scranton
Philippine Islands
Office of Public Welfare
  Commissioner, Manila
Texas
Big Brother Headquarters, Dallas
Wisconsin
BB and S, Milwaukee Central
  Association of Racine

APPENDIX 2
Unaffiliated Agencies in 1940
(No national federation existed at that time)

California
Catholic BB, Inc., Los Angeles
Catholic BS, Los Angeles
Jewish BB Association, Los Angeles
Protestant BB, Los Angeles
BS of Alameda County, Oakland
BS Organization, San Francisco
Jewish Committee for Personal Service, San Francisco
Catholic BB, San Jose

Colorado
BB Movement, Denver
BS Organization, Inc., Denver
BB, Inc., Pueblo

Connecticut
BS, Girls' Service League, Bridgeport
BS, Inc., Stamford

District of Columbia
BS, District of Columbia

Florida
Boys Home Association of Jacksonville

Georgia
BS, Savannah

Illinois
BB Association, Chicago
BS, Inc., Chicago
Protestant BS, Service Council for Girls, Chicago
BB Association, Danville
BB Association of Evanston
BS Association, Freeport
BB&BS, Peoria
BS Association, Peoria
BB, Rockford
BS Association, Rockford
BB Association, Rock Island
BB Association, Springfield
BB&BS Association, Waukegan

Indiana
BS, Inc., Evansville

Maryland
Associated BB&BS of Maryland, Baltimore
Catholic BB Association, Baltimore
Jewish BB League, Baltimore

Massachusetts
Jewish BB Association, Boston

Michigan
BS Department, Jewish Social Service Bureau, Detroit

Minnesota
BB, Inc., Minneapolis
BS Association, Inc., Minneapolis
Jewish BS, Minneapolis
Catholic BS, St. Paul
Children Service, Inc., St. Paul

Missouri
BB Organization, Inc., St. Louis
BS of St. Louis, Inc.

Nebraska
Catholic BB, Omaha

New Jersey
Jewish Child Guidance Bureau, Newark

New York
Catholic BB League, Bronx
Catholic BB, Brooklyn
Protestant BS Council, Brooklyn
Church & Mission Federation, Brooklyn
BB&BS Service, Jewish Welfare Society, Buffalo
Catholic BS, Buffalo
Catholic BB of Queens, Jamaica
BB Movement, Inc., New York
BS, Ladies of Charity, Inc., New York
The BS, Inc., New York
Harlem BB Association, New York
Jewish BB&BS, New York
Youth Service Bureau, Rochester

Ohio
BB Association, Akron
BS Association, Akron
BB Association of Cincinnati
BB Club, Cincinnati
BS Club, Cincinnati
Catholic BB League, Cincinnati
Catholic BS, Cincinnati
Valley BB Association, Cincinnati
Catholic BS, Cleveland
Jewish BB Association, Cleveland
Jewish BS, Cleveland
BB Association of Columbus

BS Association, Columbus
Colored Big Brothers, Columbus
Colored BS Department, Columbus
Catholic BB&BS, Dayton
BB Movement, Youngstown
BS, Youngstown
Oklahoma
BS Organization, Oklahoma City
Ontario
BB Association, Hamilton
BS Association, Hamilton
BS Association of Ottawa
BB Federation, St. Catharines
BB Movement, Toronto
BS Association, Toronto
Catholic BB, Toronto
Catholic BS, Toronto
Jewish BB Movement, Toronto
Jewish Child Welfare Association,
  BS Department, Toronto
Pennsylvania
BB Association, Philadelphia
Boys Department, Jewish Welfare

Society, Philadelphia
BB, Catholic Boy Welfare Bureau,
  Pittsburgh
Negro BB, Pittsburgh
Thorn Hill BB, Pittsburgh
BB Organization, Scranton
BS Association, Inc., Scranton
Quebec
BB Department, Montreal Boys
  Association
BS Association, Montreal
Catholic Girls Association, Inc.,
  Montreal
Texas
Dallas BB, Inc.
BB Program, Houston YMCA
BS Department, San Antonio
Washington
BS Service, Seattle
Wisconsin
BB&BS, Milwaukee
Wyoming
Wesley Foundation, Laramie

APPENDIX 3
Agencies Affiliated with Big Brothers/Big Sisters
of America in 1984

Alabama
BB/BS of Greater Birmingham
BB/BS of Northeast Alabama,
Gadsden
BB/BS of Huntsville & Madison
Co., Huntsville
BB/BS of Tuscaloosa Co.

Alaska
BB/BS of Anchorage, Inc.
BB/BS of Juneau, Inc.
BB/BS of Sitka

Arizona
BB of Flagstaff
BS of Northern Arizona, Flagstaff
BB/BS of Colorado River, Lake
Havasu City
Valley BB, Phoenix
Valley BS, Phoenix
Yavapai BB/BS, Prescott
BB/BS of Tucson, Inc.

Arkansas
BB of Pulaski Co., Inc., N. Little
Rock

California
BB/BS of Placer Co., Auburn
BB/BS of the Peninsula, Belmont
Mother Lode BB/BS, Diamond
Springs
North Coast BB/BS, Inc., Eureka
BB/BS of Fresno
BB/BS of Nevada Co., Grass Valley
Lake Country Council BB&S,
Lakeport
BB of Greater Los Angeles
BS of Los Angeles
Catholic BB, Inc., Los Angeles
Jewish BB Association of Los
Angeles Co.
BB/BS of Yuba/Sutter Cos., Inc.,
Marysville
BB/BS of Stanislaus Co., Modesto
Calaveras/Amador BB/BS,
Mokelumne Hill
BB/BS of Napa-Solano Cos., Napa
BB of East Bay, Oakland
BS of East Bay, Oakland
BB/BS of Tulare Co., Porterville

BB/BS of Greater Sacramento Area
BB of San Diego Co., Inc.
BB/BS of San Francisco Bay Area
BB/BS of Santa Clara Co., San
Jose
BB of Marin, Inc., San Rafael
BB/BS Santa Cruz/Monterey, Santa
Cruz
BB/BS of Sonoma Co., Santa Rosa
BB/BS of San Joaquin Co.,
Stockton
BB/BS of Orange Co., Inc., Tustin
Mendocino BB&S, Inc., Ukiah
BB/BS of Ventura Co.

Colorado
Pikes Peak Y/BB/BS Program,
Colorado Springs
BB, Inc., Denver
BS of Colorado, Inc., Denver

Connecticut
Shoreline BB/BS Association,
Branford
BB&BS of Fairfield Co., Bridgeport
BB/BS of Enfield, Inc.
BB/BS of Southcentral
Connecticut, Hamden
BB/BS of Greater Hartford, Inc.
BB/BS of Meriden
BB/BS of Northern Middlesex Co.,
Middletown
BB/BS of Central Connecticut,
New Britain
BB/BS of Southern Connecticut,
New London
BB/BS of Wallingford
BB/BS of Greater Waterbury

Delaware
BB/BS of Delaware, Inc.,
Wilmington

District of Columbia
BB of National Capitol Area
BS of Washington Metro Area,
Inc.

Florida
BB/BS of Manatee Co., Bradenton
BB/BS of Pinellas Co., Inc.,
Clearwater

BB/BS of Nassau Co., Fernandina
Beach
BB/BS of Lee Co., Inc., Fort Myers
BB/BS of Broward, Fort Lauderdale
BB/BS of Greater Gainesville
BB/BS of Greater Jacksonville, Inc.
BB/BS Monroe Co., Key West
BB&S of Polk Co., Inc., Lakeland
BB/BS of Brevard, Inc., Melbourne
BB/BS of Greater Miami
BB/BS of New Port Richey
BB/BS of Central Florida, Inc.,
Orlando
BB of Charlotte Co., Punta Gorda
BB/BS of Sarasota, Inc.
BB/BS of St. Johns Co., St.
Augustine
BB/BS of Greater Tallahassee, Inc.
BB/BS of Greater Tampa, Inc.
BB/BS of South Sarasota Co.,
Venice
BB/BS of Palm Beach Co., West
Palm Beach

Georgia
BB/BS of Metro Atlanta, Inc.
BB/BS of Dalton-Whitfield Co.,
Inc., Dalton
BB Association of Macon
Milledgeville Area BB
Coosa Valley BB/BS, Rome
BB/BS of Tiftarea, Tifton
BB/BS of Waycross

Hawaii
BB/BS of Honolulu, Inc.
BB/BS of the Big Island, Inc.,
Kailua-Kona
BB/BS of Maui, Inc., Wailuku

Idaho
BB/BS of Southwest Idaho, Inc.,
Boise

Illinois
Family Counseling Services,
Aurora
BB/BS of Coles Co., Charleston
BB/BS of Metro Chicago
BB/BS of Vermilion Co., Danville
BB/BS of Macon Co., Decatur
Family Service — BB/BS of DeKalb
Co.
BB of the Fox River Valley, Elgin
BS of Kane Co., Elgin
BB/BS of St. Clair Co., Fairview
Heights

BB of Freeport
BB/BS of Lake Co., Gurnee
BB/S of Will Co., Joliet
Heart of Illinois BB/BS, Peoria
BB/BS of Northern Illinois,
Rockford
BB/BS of Marion Co., Salem
BB/BS Organization of Sangamon
Co., Inc., Springfield Family
Service Association of DuPage
Co., Wheaton

Indiana
BB/BS of Madison Co., Anderson
Five-Co. BB/BS, Columbus
BB/BS of Fayette Co., Connersville
BB/BS of Elkhart Co.
BB/BS of Southwestern Indiana,
Evansville
BB/BS of Fort Wayne, Inc.
BB/BS of Clinton Co., Frankfort
BB/BS of Lake Co., Gary
BB of Greater Indianapolis, Inc.
BS of Greater Indianapolis, Inc.
BB/BS of Howard Co., Inc.,
Kokomo
BB/BS of Wabash Valley, Inc.,
Lafayette
BB/BS of Grant Co., Inc., Marion
BB/BS of East Central Indiana,
Inc., Muncie
BB/BS of Henry Co., Inc., New
Castle
BB/BS of Miami Co., Peru
BB/Branch, Richmond
BB/BS of Fulton Co., Rochester
BB/BS of St. Joseph Co., South
Bend
BB/BS of Vigo Co., Inc., Terre
Haute
BB/BS of Wabash Co., Inc.
BB/BS of Cass Co., Walton·

Iowa
BB/BS of Southeast Iowa,
Burlington
BB/BS of Cedar Rapids/East
Central Iowa, Cedar Rapids
BB/BS of Clinton
BB/BS of Greater Des Moines, Inc.
BB/BS of Emmet Co., Estherville
BB/BS of Johnson Co., Iowa City
BB/BS of Siouxland, Sioux City
BB/BS of Black Hawk Co.,
Waterloo

Kansas
BB/BS of Emporia
BB/BS of Southwest Kansas,
  Garden City
BB/BS of Central Kansas, Great
  Bend
BB/BS of Manhattan
BB/BS of Topeka, Inc.
BB/BS of Sedgwick Co., Wichita

Kentucky
BB&S of Bowling Green
BB&S of Corbin, Inc.
BB/BS of Frankfort, Inc.
BB/BS of Lexington
BB/BS of Kentuckiana, Louisville
BB/BS of Owensboro
BB/BS of Shelby Co., Shelbyville
BB/S of Pulaski Co., Inc.,
  Somerset
BB/BS of Winchester

Louisiana
BB/BS Program—Family/Youth
  Counseling, Lake Charles
BB of Greater New Orleans
BS of Greater New Orleans, Inc.

Maine
BB/BS of Kennebec Valley,
  Augusta
Downeast BB/BS, Inc., Bangor
BB/BS of Waldo Co., Inc., Belfast
BB/BS of Boothbay, Boothbay
  Harbor
BB/BS of Greater Portland, Inc.
BB/BS of York Co., Inc., Saco

Maryland
BB&BS of Central Maryland, Inc.,
  Baltimore
Jewish BB&BS League of Baltimore
BB&BS of Upper Eastern Shore,
  Easton
BB/BS of Frederick Co., Inc.
BB of Washington Co., Inc.,
  Hagerstown
Family Service Agency/BS of
  Washington Co., Inc.,
  Hagerstown
BB&BS of Southern Maryland,
  Inc., Leonardtown

Massachusetts
BB/BS of Greater Attleboro Area
BB Association of Boston
BS Association of Greater Boston

Old Colony BS Program, Brockton
BB/BS of Greater Fall River, Inc.
BB/BS of South Middlesex, Inc.,
  Framingham
BB/BS Association of Franklin
  Co., Inc., Greenfield
BB/BS of Cape Cod & The
  Islands, Hyannis
BB/BS Association of Greater
  Lawrence, Inc.
BB/BS of Greater Lowell
BB/BS Program of New Bedford
Jewish BB/BS Association of
  Greater Boston, Newton
BB/BS of Hampden Co.,
  Springfield

Michigan
BB/BS of Allegan Co.
BB/BS of Gratiot Co., Alma
BB/BS of Alpena
BB/BS of Lake Co., Baldwin
BB/BS of Southcentral Michigan,
  Battle Creek
Tuscola Co. BB/BS, Inc., Caro
Michiana BB/BS, Coldwater
BB of Greater Dowagiac/
  Cassopolis, Inc., Dowagiac
BB of Greater Flint
BB/BS of Otsego Co., Gaylord
Mid-Michigan BB/BS, Grand
  Rapids
BB/BS of Mid-Michigan, Harrison
BB/BS of Livingston Co., Howell
BB/BS of Dickinson Co., Iron
  Mountain
BB/BS of Jackson Co., Inc.
BB/BS of Greater Kalamazoo
BB/BS of Greater Lansing, Inc.
BB/BS of Lapeer Co., Inc.
BB of Midland Co.
BB/BS of Monroe Co., Inc.
BB/BS of Muskegon
BB of Ishpeming-Negaunee,
  Negaunee
BB/BS of Niles-Buchanan, Inc.,
  Niles
BB/BS of Petoskey/Emmet Co.,
  Petoskey
BB/BS of Presque Isle Co., Rogers
  City
BB/BS of Saginaw Bay Area, Inc.,
  Saginaw
BB/BS of Clinton Co., St. Johns

BB/BS, Inc. (Detroit Metro Area), Southfield
BB/BS of Montcalm/Ionia Cos., Stanton
BB/BS of Newaygo Co., Inc., White Cloud

Minnesota
BB/BS of Northeast Carlton Co., Cloquet
BB/BS, Minneapolis
BB/BS of St. Cloud, Inc.
BB/BS of Greater St. Paul, Inc.

Mississippi
BB/BS of the Golden Triangle, Columbus

Missouri
Family Service of Columbia, Inc.
BB&S of Greater Kansas City
BB/BS of Rolla
BB/BS of Greater St. Louis
Southeastern Missouri BB/BS, Sikeston
BB/BS of Springfield, Mo. — CODAC, Springfield

Montana
BB/BS of Yellowstone, Inc., Billings
BB/BS of Gallatin Co., Bozeman
BB/BS of Butte
BB&S of Great Falls, Inc.
BB/BS of Northern Montana, Havre
BB/BS of Flathead Co., Kalispell
BB&S of Lake Co., Ronan
North Co. BB/BS, Shelby

Nebraska
BB/BS of Southeast Nebraska Fairbury
BB/BS of Fremont
Grand Island BS
Third City BB, Grand Island
BB/BS of Hastings, Inc.
BB/BS of Northeast Nebraska, Inc., Norfolk

Nevada
BB/BS of Southern Nevada, Inc., Las Vegas

New Hampshire
Seacoast BB/BS of New Hampshire, Exeter
BB/BS of the Monadnock Region, Inc., Keene

BB/BS of Greater Manchester, Inc.
BB/BS of Greater Nashua

New Jersey
BB/BS of Essex Co., Bloomfield
BB/BS Association, Camden
BB/BS of Atlantic Co., Cardiff
BB/BS of Hunterdon Co., Flemington
BB/BS of Monmouth Co., Freehold
BB/BS of Morris Co., Morristown
BB/S of Sussex Co., Newton
BB/BS of Middlesex Co., Old Bridge
BB/BS of Somerset Co., Raritan
BB/BS of Burlington Co., Riverside
Cumberland Co., BB/BS Association, South Vineland
BB&S Association of Mercer Co., Trenton
BB/BS of Warren Co., Washington
BB/BS of Bergen-Passaic, Inc., Wayne

New Mexico
BB/BS of Albuquerque
BB/BS of San Juan Co., Farmington
BB/BS of Las Vegas
BB/BS of Las Cruces
BB/BS of Santa Fe
BB/BS of Sierra Co., Truth or Consequences

New York
BB/BS of Albany Co., Inc.
Montgomery BB/BS, Amsterdam
BB/BS of Auburn & Cayuga Cos., Auburn
BB/BS — Greater Utica Area, Barneveld
Be-a-Friend Program, Inc., Buffalo
BB/BS Suffolk Co., Long Island, Commack
BB/BS of Fulton Co., Inc., Gloversville
BB/BS of Nassau Co., Hampstead
BB/BS of Ulster Co., Kingston
BB/BS of Niagara Co., Lockport
BB/BS of Putnam Co., Mahopac
BB Inc. of New York City
Catholic BB of New York, Inc.
Jewish BB — Jewish Board of Family and Children's Services, New York

BB/BS of Orange Co., Inc., Newburgh
BB/BS of Clinton Co., Plattsburgh
BB/BS of Dutchess Co., Poughkeepsie
Community Partners for Youth, Inc., Rochester
BB/BS of Schenectady Co.
BB/BS of Syracuse
BB/BS — Family Services of Westchester, White Plains
BB/BS of Yonkers

North Carolina
BB/BS — Asheville & Buncombe Cos., Asheville
BB/BS of Charlotte, Inc.
BB/BS of Catawba Valley, Hickory
BB/BS of High Point YMCA
BB/BS — Kinston-Lenor Co., Kinston
BB/BS of Lower Neuse, Inc., New Bern
BB/BS — Iredell Co., Statesville
BB/BS — Forsyth Co., Inc., Winston-Salem
BB/BS — Caswell Co., Inc., Yanceyville

North Dakota
BB of Grand Forks Co.

Ohio
BB&S of Greater Akron, Inc.
BB/BS of Ashtabula Co.
BB&S of Belmont Co., Bellaire
YMCA BB/BS — Canton Area
Southcentral Ohio BB/BS Association, Inc., Chillicothe
BB/BS Association of Cincinnati
BB/BS of Greater Cincinnati, Inc.
Catholic BB of Cincinnati
BB/BS of Greater Cleveland
Jewish BB Association, Cleveland
BB/BS Association of Columbus, Inc.
BB/BS of Coshocton Co.
BB/BS of Greater Dayton
BB/BS of Delaware Co.
BB/BS of Hancock Co., Inc., Findlay
BB&S of Greater Hamilton, Inc.
BB/BS of Warren Co., Lebanon
BB/BS of Allen Co., Lima
BB/BS of Columbiana Co., Lisbon

BB/BS of Marion Co.
BB&S of Greater Massillon
BB&S — Greater Middletown Area, Inc.
BB/BS Association of Knox Co., Inc., Mt. Vernon
BB/BS — Tuscarawas Co., New Philadelphia
The BB/BS of Licking Co., Newark
BB/BS of Lake Co., Plainesville
BB/BS — Meigs/Gallia/Jackson, Pomeroy
BB/BS of Scioto Co., Portsmouth
BB/BS of Portage Co., Ravenna
BB/BS of Shelby Co., Sidney
BB/BS of Springfield
BB/BS of Seneca Co., Tiffin
BB/BS — Northwestern Ohio, Inc., Toledo
BB/BS of Miami Co., Inc., Troy
BB/BS of Wayne Co., Wooster
BB/BS of Mahoning Valley, Inc., Youngstown
BB/BS of Zanesville, Inc.

Oklahoma
BB/BS of Cleveland Co., Norman
BB/BS of Greater Oklahoma City, Inc.
BB/BS of Stillwater
BB/S of Tulsa

Pennsylvania
BB/BS of Lehigh Co., Allentown
BB/BS of Blair Co., Altoona
BB of Bucks Co., Inc., Doylestown
BS of Bucks Co., Inc., Doylestown
BB&BS of Erie Co., Inc.
BB/BS of Westmoreland Co., Inc., Greensburg
BB/BS — Catholic Social Services, Harrisburg
BB/BS of Lancaster Co., Inc.
BB&S of Crawford Co., Meadville
BB&S of Beaver YMCA, New Brighton
Montgomery Co. BB/BS, Norristown
BB/BS Association of Philadelphia
BS of Philadelphia
BB/BS of Greater Pittsburgh
BB&S of Berks Co., Reading
BB/BS of Lackawanna Co.,

Scranton
BB/BS — Southwestern
Pennsylvania, Washington
BB/BS of Chester Co., Inc., West
Chester
BB/BS of Luzerne Co., Wilkes-
Barre
Rhode Island
BS of Rhode Island, Providence
South Carolina
Brothers & Sisters, Inc., Columbia
BB/BS — Phillis Wheatley
Association, Greenville
BB/BS Program, North Charleston
South Dakota
BB&S of the Black Hills, Rapid
City
Tennessee
Chattanooga BB/BS Association
BB/BS of Clarksville
BB/BS of Maury Co., Columbia
Kingsport Area BB/BS Agency
BB/BS of Knoxville
BB/BS of Greater Memphis
Buddies of Nashville
BB/BS of Anderson Co., Oak
Ridge
Texas
BB/BS of Abilene, Inc.
BB/BS of Amarillo
BB/BS of Arlington
BB/BS of Austin, Inc.
BB/BS of Rio Grande Valley,
Brownsville
BB/BS of Coastal Bend, Corpus
Christi
BB/BS of Metro Dallas
BB/BS of Denton Co.
BB/BS of El Paso, Inc.
BB/BS of Tarrant Co., Fort Worth
Gulf Coast BB/BS, Galveston
BB/BS of Hereford, Inc.
BB/BS of Houston
BB/BS of Lubbock, Inc.
BB/BS of Midland
BB/BS of Lamar Co., Paris
BB&S, Alamo Area, Inc., San
Antonio
BB&S of Wichita Co., Wichita
Falls
Utah
BB/BS of Northern Utah, Ogden
BB/BS — Greater Salt Lake, Salt
Lake City

Vermont
BB/BS of Windham Co.,
Brattleboro

Virginia
BB/BS of Danville Area, Inc.
BB/BS of Washington Co., Emory
Rappahannock BB/BS, Inc.,
Fredericksburg
BB/BS of the Peninsula, Inc.,
Hampton
BB/BS — Harrisonburg/
Rockingham Co., Inc.,
Harrisonburg
BB&S of Central Virginia, Inc.
Lynchburg
BB&S of Smyth Co., Inc., Marion
BB — Martinsville/Henry Co.,
Martinsville
BB/BS of New River Valley, Inc.,
Radford
BB/BS Metropolitan Richmond,
Inc.
BB/BS of Roanoke Valley, Inc.
BB/BS of Tidewater, Inc., Virginia
Beach
BB/BS — Waynesboro/Staunton/
Augusta, Waynesboro
BB/BS of Greater Williamsburg
BB/BS — Winchester/Frederick
Co., Winchester

Washington
BB/BS Northwest Washington,
Inc., Bellingham
BB/BS of Northeast Washington,
Colville
Tri-County BB/BS, Moses Lake
BB/BS of Thurston Co., Olympia
BB — Seattle/King Co., Seattle
Puget Sound BS, Seattle
BB&S of Spokane
BB/BS of Tacoma-Pierce Co.,
Tacoma

West Virginia
BB/BS of Clarksburg
BB/BS of the Tri-State, Inc.,
Huntingdon
BB/BS of Berkeley Co.,
Martinsburg
BB/BS of Parkersburg
BB/BS of Weirton, Inc.
BB/BS of Wheeling, Inc.

Wisconsin
BB/BS of Fox Valley Region, Inc.,
  Appleton
BB/BS of Rock Co., Inc., Beloit
BB/S of Ozaukee Co., Cedarburg
BB/BS of Fond du Lac Co., Inc.
BB/BS Northeastern Wisconsin,
  Green Bay
BB/S of Dane Co., Madison
BB/BS of Manitowoc Co., Inc.
BB/BS — Marshfield Area
BB/BS of Taylor Co., Medford
BB/BS of Metro Milwaukee
BB/BS of Price Co., Phillips
BB of Greater Racine, Inc.

BB of Shawano Co.
BB/BS of Sheboygan Co., Inc.
BB/BS of Marathon Co. Area,
  Wausau
Wyoming
BB/BS of Central Wyoming,
  Casper
BB/BS of Northeast Wyoming,
  Gillette
BB/BS of South East Wyoming,
  Laramie
BB/BS of Carbon Co., Inc.,
  Rawlins
Special Friends/Sweetwater Co.,
  Rock Springs

INDEX

Note: Bold type indicates illustrations